The Korean Wave
from a Private Commodity to a Public Good

The Korean Wave
from a Private Commodity to a Public Good

EDITED BY
YEONHEE YOON
KIWOONG YANG

KOREA
UNIVERSITY
PRESS

Korea University Press
145, Anam-ro, Seongbuk-gu, Seoul, 02841 Republic of Korea

 Published January 2020

ISBN: 979-11-90205-22-1 93330

Printed in Republic of Korea

Contents

Foreword ... 7
Michel Hockx (University of Notre Dame)

Preface ... 8
Yeonhee Yoon (University of Notre Dame) and Kiwoong Yang (Hallym University)

About the Contributors ... 15

Part 1: K-Pop as a Gateway to Korea

Chapter1
Exuberant *Hallyu* and Formidable Students:
Two Faces of South Korean Youth Culture 21
Susan D. Blum (University of Notre Dame)

Chapter 2
Korea's Place in the World: Its Effort to Enhance Soft Power 32
Jaewoong Lee (Ministry of Foreign Affairs, Republic of Korea)

Part 2: Identity-dimension of the Korean Wave

Chapter 3
(Re)Imagined Communities: Korean Diaspora, Identity,
and Pop Culture 45
Ji-Yeon Jo (University of North Carolina-Chapel Hill)

Chapter 4
Drama Consumption in Transnational South Korea: Korean American
Women and Intraethnic Othering 69
Adrienne Lo (University of Waterloo), Megan Rim (University of Michigan), Lee Jin Choi (Hongik University), and Nancy Abelmann (University of Illinois at Urbana-Champaign)

Part 3: Interest-dimension of the Korean Wave

Chapter 5
A Hybrid Model of Bridging Nation Branding and Country Image:
A Case of the Korean Wave 89
Jaebeom Suh (Kansas State University)

Chapter 6
Yet to Crest: The Korean Wave and Korean Language Learning 106
Yeonhee Yoon (University of Notre Dame)

Part 4: Power-dimension of the Korean Wave

Chapter 7
The Anti-Korean Wave in Japan: Identity Clash 117
Yeonhee Yoon (University of Notre Dame)

Chapter 8
The Korean Wave as a Soft Power 130
Kiwoong Yang (Hallym University), Maddalena Ciesa (Max Mara)

Part 5: A Rivalry with the Korean Wave

Chapter 9
Between Fans: History and National Identity
in Online Debates on Axis Powers Hetalia 145
Kathryn Hemmann (George Mason University)

Chapter 10
Lost and Found in "Cool Japan" 155
Heather Bowen-Struyk (DePaul University)

Appendix: Trends of the Korean Wave

The Korean Wave in the World Seen through Statistics 167
Kiwoong Yang, Kyungeun Lee and Jeounghwa An (Hallym University)

Index ... 201

Foreword

Back in 2006, the University of Notre Dame embarked on a trajectory to grow and develop its capacity in Asian Studies, as well as its interaction and engagement with Asia. Unlike Asia-related programs at other universities, Notre Dame has not inherited a perspective on Asia that stems from the Cold War. Our approach is not antagonistic but collaborative, not rooted in domestic strategic concerns but inspired by a global view. Working across disciplines, yet emphasizing our traditional strengths in the liberal arts, we offer a model of "rounded education on Asia" that brings together scholarship, teaching, and social concern.

Since 2006, the number of faculty committed to Asian Studies has more than doubled and entire new focus areas have opened up, allowing us to expand our range of interests across Asia, especially East Asia and the South Asian subcontinent. The Liu Institute for Asia and Asian Studies, founded in 2011 with a generous gift from the RM Liu Foundation, co-ordinates and supports these efforts. The Institute is part of the Keough School for Global Affairs, the first new school opened at Notre Dame in a century, whose mission to promote "integral human development" underlies everything that we do.

In this context, we are proud to have supported the work that has led to this publication. We congratulate the editors on promoting a unique interdisciplinary perspective on popular culture and international relations, featuring contributions by both humanists and social scientists, and focusing on a hugely significant transcultural phenomenon – the Korean Wave – that originated in Asia yet spread across the globe. The questions of identity, interest, and power raised by this publication, based on a series of conferences held on our campus, are as significant as they are innovative. I hope you, the reader, will be inspired by this collection to pursue your own inquiries and further develop the study of Korean culture in global context.

Michel Hockx
Professor of Chinese Literature
Director, Liu Institute for Asia and Asian Studies
University of Notre Dame

Preface

As East Asia has emerged as a center of gravity in contemporary international relations, partly owing to the region's fast-growing economy and democratic consolidation over the past two decades, now seems to be the perfect time to publish a book on East Asian popular culture -and specifically, the Korean Wave-with regard to identity, interest, and power.

The main chapters of this book consist of papers presented at the 2014 and 2016 Korean Studies Conferences at the University of Notre Dame.

The primary objective of this book is to explore the extent to which we can challenge or extend current debates around ideas of popular culture and the ways in which we might situate research on East Asian popular culture and the Korean Wave within its rapidly transforming political, economic, and cultural contexts. This book also seeks to outline a new research agenda that explores the various processes that determine the sociocultural consequences of these phenomena.

Among the authors who are currently engaged with these issues, this book and the conferences from which it stems present an opportunity to exchange innovative frameworks through which to analyze these issues.

The main theme of the 2016 ND Korean Studies conference was "Identity, Interest, and Power in East Asian Popular Culture." In recent years, there has been an explosion of global interest in the popular culture of East Asia. Although incredibly fascinating, it remains an underdeveloped area in interdisciplinary research. The purpose of the conference was to exchange and enhance our understandings of East Asian popular culture in an innovative and interdisciplinary framework. The conference sought to undertake an inventory of diverse discourses on East Asian pop culture with an eye to issues of social identity, interest, and power.

The conference delved into three dimensions of East Asian pop culture: (national) identity, (social/cultural) interest, and (political) power. The participants attempted to reach a conceptual understanding of interdisciplinary discourses regarding issues of identity, interest, and power in the transnationalization of East Asian pop culture and to shed new light on the linkages between pop culture and international relations in East Asia.

First, conference participants discussed the identity dimension of pop culture such as in the formation of transnational identities, as well as in the clash between national identities in the context of pop cultural productions in East Asia. Second, participants examined the interest dimension of East Asian pop culture such as the phenomena of the Korean Wave or Cool Japan and their corollary effects on global and local culture. Third, participants explored the power dimension of East Asian pop culture in terms of Joseph Nye's notion of 'soft power', which denotes the ability to shape the preferences of others and exert a positive influence by means of attraction instead of aggression.

The theme of the 2014 Notre Dame Korean Studies Conference was "Korean Wave beyond Nationality." Although there are ever more increasing transactions of Korean popular culture among East Asian countries, friction over the globalization of Korean popular culture also seems to be an uncomfortable prospect in light of the effort to create a regional cultural community among the receiving countries. Our premise is that this friction is not merely an issue of accepting and consuming Korean popular culture but that it is related to underlying political processes and the legitimation of cultural identities between various actors both at the domestic and international levels. National governments, as well as different groups such as civil organizations, media, and individuals, are deeply engaged in this process of the politicizing of the Korean Wave.

Focusing on these conflicts over the globalization of Korean popular culture, conference participants were asked to engage with the following questions as deeply as possible: what can be done at the grass-root national and international levels to mitigate conflicts pertaining to the globalization of the Korean Wave in Asia? What is the role of hybridity and translocality in the Asianization of the Korean Wave? What is the role of popular culture in constructing the Asian region as a whole?

As Kiwoong Yang articulates in chapter 8, "The Korean Wave As a Soft Power": The national "brand" of Korea was a private commodity born of the entertainment industry's entrepreneurial spirit. In the form of the Korean Wave, this competitive advantage surpassed commercial utility and eventually became a "public good" that could benefit the entire nation.

The title of this book, The Korean Wave: from a Private Commodity to a Public Good, refers to the idea that the Korean Wave has now crossed its nation's borders and become an international public good. Because the Korean Wave has so far surpassed its national borders to become a subject of global attention, we consider the Korean Wave through the lenses of power, interest, identity, politicization, and the "anti-Korean wave".

This book consists of six parts in eleven chapters.

Part I, K-Pop as a Gateway to Korea, is composed of two chapters as follows. In chapter 1, "Exuberant Hallyu and Formidable Students: Two Faces of South Korean Youth Culture," Susan Blum explores two images of South Korean youth culture: first, that of uniformed students preparing for their university entrance examinations after having surpassed most of their international competitors on high-school comparative tests, and secondly, the image of exuberant, sexy but wholesome K-Pop stars dancing in perfect harmony. This chapter considers the role of national support for what in some settings would be considered inconsequential popular culture and situates it within the national desire to brand South Korea as youthful and vibrant. Governmental and societal support for Hallyu as a form of soft power has to be understood as stemming in part from a recognition of its East Asian and other regional audiences. The role of youth, and images of youth, must be kept in mind.

In chapter 2, Jaewoong Lee discusses Korea's place in the world and its efforts to enhance its soft power in the global arena. In recent decades, Korea has achieved a remarkably high level of economic growth, which has allowed the country to rise from the rubble of the Korean War into the ranks of the Organization for Cooperation and Development (OECD). Having achieved rapid economic development, the Korean government promotes soft power to enhance the country's status on the international stage. To this end, Korea strives to enhance its cultural exchanges with countries and promote the Korean wave. Examples of this effort include the implementation of cultural programming such as performances, exhibitions and film festivals aimed towards improving intercultural understanding between Korea and many other countries.

Part II, Identity-dimension of the Korean Wave, comprises chapters 3 and 4.

In chapter 3, Ji-Yeon Jo analyzes how Korean popular culture influences the ways in which later-generation diaspora Koreans form affective connections to their ethnic identity and to their ancestral homeland. Between 2009 and 2014, during the course of two research projects, Jo conducted interviews with over seventy later-generation Korean Americans, Korean Chinese, and Koreans from the Commonwealth Independent States (CIS). These interviews suggest that the popularity of Korean wave among non-Koreans worldwide and the growing economic strength of South Korea have imbued Korean culture with global symbolic value, which has in turn encouraged diaspora Koreans to embrace their ethnic Korean identity. For Korean Chinese and CIS Koreans, Korean popular culture offers images of modernity and generates a longing to learn about and visit their ancestral homeland. For Korean Americans, Korean popular culture serves as a primary vehicle for learning the Korean language, maintaining family bonds, and establishing coethnic friendships. Jo contends that the ways in which each diaspora receives and appropriates Korean popular culture reflect their respective diasporic specificities.

In chapter 4, Adrienne Lo et al. have sketched the ways that Korean American women undergraduates in Illinois drew upon Korean dramas to make sense of their relations with their South Korean peers. While consumption of South Korean media is often depicted by the South Korean press as a practice that brings people across the globe together, Lo et al. found that watching K-dramas sharpened the sense of division felt by Korean Americans from their fellow South Korean undergraduates on campus. Korean American women undergraduates marveled at the seemingly effortless transnational life of the figure of the South Korean student, someone who could be at home anywhere.

They located themselves as subjects who were "out of place" no matter where they were - or, as Lo et al. put articulates, targets of scorn by White Americans, South Koreans, and Korean Americans alike. Rather than seeking common cause with their South Korean undergraduates, these Korean American women set them apart as possessing a degree of privilege and cosmopolitan belonging that Korean Americans could only dream of.

Part III, Interest-dimension of the Korean Wave, consists of chapter 5 and 6.

In chapter 5, "The Korean Wave and Nation Branding," Jaebeom Suh argues that national branding goes beyond a simple concept of country-of-origin and/or country image. Several studies in the field of business have viewed a country's image as potentially having a "halo effect"—meaning that the product quality of a foreign brand is often contingent on the consumer's image of the its country of origin. In other words, the definition of a country's image is often limited to consumers' general perceptions of the quality of products made in a given country, which implies product category-specific perceptions. One of the main benefits of nation-branding is that its effect goes beyond a specific product category; more importantly, the effect of a nation's brand significantly influences not only its economic value, but also perceptions of its political and cultural identity. Suh's study examines the effect of the Korean Wave on the national branding of Korea and how the Korean Wave plays a significant role in global business and relates to the formation of national identity.

In chapter 6, Yeonhee Yoon finds that the proliferation of a culture abroad begets positive regard for the culture's society of origin, and moreover that as an audience's desire to enjoy that culture intensifies, this affinity can engage them as potential language learners. However, what remains is the question of the authenticity and persistence of motivation in the transition from audience members to students language. Yoon explores the possibilities and means of turning potential learners — those who are enthusiastic about the Korean Wave, but not totally committed to engaged in full-scale Korean language learning — into "true learners". For instance, while the number of Korean learners and sales of Korean textbooks increased significantly as the Korean wave spread though Japan and Europe, the number of students who took formal Korean classes at high schools or universities did not increase significantly. Yoon argues that policy development and scholarly research should be undertaken with the aim of helping potential Korean learners become true Korean learners and speakers. To this end, she suggests developing a communication-oriented Korean textbook that utilizes Korean popular culture as a teaching aid; she further proposes building digital learning environments centered on 'cultural education' for potential learners to compliment the textbook such that the global fans of the Korean Wave who have become interested in the Korean language can persist in learning Korean.

Part IV, Power-dimension of the Korean Wave, consists of chapter 7 and 8.

In chapter 7, Yeonhee Yoon discusses the intercultural conflicts accompanying the process of deterritorialization of a particular culture and the process of the universalization of particularism as articulated by Roland Robertson. This chapter explains the causes and characteristics of the wave of anti-Korean sentiment among Japanese that followed the introduction of the Korean Wave phenomenon to Japan. The difference between the anti-Korean wave in Japan and the same phenomenon in China can be explained in terms of a national identity clash. Yoon argues that the anti-Korean wave in China is less a friction between national identities than a result of cultural and economic competition; however, the anti-Korean wave in Japan is related to a conflict of national identities that has been fomented and deteriorated by reactionary cultural politics promoted by the Japanese popular culture industry. This controversy exemplifies why the anti-Korean wave in Japan has accumulated toward a general anti-Korean sentiment and shows how readily historical and diplomatic conflicts can influence the transmission and reception of popular culture.

In chapter 8, Kiwoong Yang discusses Korean Pop Culture as a "soft power." Originally coined in 1990 by American political scientist Joseph Nye, the term soft power describes the capacity to change the behavior of others by means of attraction and persuasion. Nye points to three primary sources of soft power: culture, political values, and foreign policy. Yang argues that South Korea has impressive potential for soft power. He points out that, in addition to its economic success, Korea has developed a truly democratic political system, characterized by human rights, free elections, and the fair transfer of power between different political parties. He argues that South Korean culture serves as an attractive force that extends beyond these material and political successes. In this chapter, Yang analyzes how the Korean wave has multiplied the effects of soft power. He investigates the concept of soft power, then develops a model for understanding the process by which a particular country can use cultural, social, economic, and political interactions in a global framework to increase its soft power. Finally, moving from theoretical to practical terms, he discusses the specific form of soft power that is manifest in South Korea.

Part V, A Rivalry with the Korean Wave, consists of chapter 9 and 10.

In chapter 9, Kathryn Hemmann discusses history and national identity in light of online debates regarding the Japanese manga series Axis Powers Hetalia. In Axis Powers Hetalia, World War II is a game played between two teams of handsome men. The Hetalia franchise, which began as an amateur webcomic written by Japanese author Himaruya Hidekazu, anthropomorphizes the world powers of the early twentieth century as attractive young men. Although the original comic plays with national stereotypes and caricatured reenactments of historical events-America sports a bomber jacket and guzzles hamburgers, Germany enjoys making cuckoo clocks and is serious to a fault, and Italy, the namesake of the series, is a pasta-loving coward who depends on Germany to protect him-other incarnations of the franchise focus less on historical jokes and references and more on the homoerotic tensions that arise between these masculine representations of countries, pitted in heated competition with each other. Because of its humor and female-oriented fanbase, the Hetalia franchise became a major site of internet-based fandom activity between 2011 and 2012. During the height of Hetalia's popularity, the interaction between international fandom communities led to major online disputes concerning national identity and the erasure and marginalization of the role of certain nations and viewpoints in mainstream histories as represented in the manga. Hemmann focuses her discussion on the online activities of young South Koreans who were able to articulate a pointed critique of Japanese historiographical attitudes regarding the military and political conflicts in East Asia during the twentieth century. Kathryn argues that online debates concerning Hetalia demonstrate a sophisticated reworking of the Eurocentric and masculinist constructions of modern history among transnational communities of contemporary media fans.

In chapter 10, " Lost and Found in "Cool Japan," Heather Bowen-Struyk analyzes "Cool Japan". In 2002, Douglas McGray famously declared that "post-industrial Japan may not make anything anymore, but it does make cool," referring to growing international interest in Japanese popular culture like anime, manga, video games, television dramas and pop music. While it has not been as economically successful as initially hoped, "Cool Japan" has been much celebrated as an example of successful national rebranding. But "Cool Japan" embodies the central contradiction associated with youth: while it celebrates the rich entertainment industry of youth culture, at the same time, young people are bearing the brunt of the country's now quarter-century-long economic recession. To explore this contradiction, Bowen-Struyk presents and analyzes the work of activist and writer Amamiya Karin (1974-), whose writing uses the vernacular of "Cool Japan" to advocate for youth in poverty.

In the Appendix, Kiwoong Yang and Kyungeun Lee present recent trends in the Korean Wave by introducing important statistical data that will be useful to researchers interested in the material effects of the Korean Wave found in '2015 Korean Wave White Paper' published by the Korean government. This paper introduces the trends of the global cultural content industry as well as Korea in particular and presents major trend statistics by category as follows: trends in the World content industry, trends of the Korean content industry, export trends of the Korean content industry, consumer trends, and the economic and political effects of the Korean Wave. Finally, Yang and Lee examine the economic and soft power effects of the Korean Wave.

We sincerely appreciate the interest and contributions of this book's co-authors and their participation in the 2014 and 2016 Korean Studies Conferences at the University of Notre Dame, and we gratefully acknowledge the support of the Liu Institute of Asia and Asian Studies, the Institute for Scholarship in the

Liberal Arts, and Office of Undergraduate Studies at the University of Notre Dame. We also would like to thank the Korea University Press for their support.

Yeonhee Yoon & Kiwoong Yang

About the Contributors

Chapter1 Exuberant *Hallyu* and Formidable Students: Two Faces of South Korean Youth Culture

Susan D. Blum, Ph.D., University of Michigan-Ann Arbor, is Professor of Anthropology at the University of Notre Dame. She has been Director of the Center for Asian Studies and Chair of the Department of Anthropology at Notre Dame, where she has taught since 2000. Her writings have included Portraits of "Primitives": Ordering Human Kinds in the Chinese Nation (2001), Lies that Bind: Chinese Truth, Other Truths (2007), My Word! Plagiarism and College Culture (2009), and edited volumes China Off Center: Mapping the Margins of the Middle Kingdom (with Lionel M. Jensen, 2002) and Making Sense of Language: Readings in Culture and Communication (2009, 2013, 2017). She recently published "I Love Learning; I Hate School": An Anthropology of College, which includes comparative material about East Asia.

Chapter2 Korea's place in the world: its effort to enhance soft power

Jae-woong Lee is former Deputy Consul General of Korean Consulate General in Chicago. He Joined Foreign Ministry in 1993, studied international relations from 1999 to 2001 at the University of Chicago, worked as Director for Global Green Growth in the Foreign Ministry from 2012 to 2013, and posted at embassies in the Netherlands, Ghana and Korean Mission to UN in New York.

Chapter 3 (Re)Imagined Communities: Korean Diaspora, Identity, and Pop Culture

Ji-Yeon O. Jo, Associate professor of Korean Language and Culture, Department of Asian Studies at the University of North Carolina at Chapel Hill, received her doctorate in Culture, Curriculum, and Change from the School of Education at the University of North Carolina at Chapel Hill. Her research and teaching interests include the Korean diaspora, ethnic return migration, and Asian American Studies and she has published several book chapters and articles in peer-reviewed academic journals. Her book, "Homing: An Affective Topography of Ethnic Korean Return Migration (University of Hawai'i Press, 2017)" addresses some of the most vexing and pressing issues of contemporary transnational migration—citizenship, cultural belonging, language, and family relationships—and highlights their affective dimensions. She is currently working on a second book project, "Documenting Diasporas: Explorations of Diasporic Affect in the Films and Documentaries of Korean Diasporas." This project explores Korean diaspora films and documentaries produced by diaspora

Korean filmmakers around the world and critically investigates how their films and documentaries question, (re)imagine, and articulate diaspora Korean subjectivities in different spaces. joj@email.unc.edu

Chapter 4 Drama Consumption in Transnational South Korea: Korean American Women and Intraethnic Othering

Adrienne Lo is Associate Professor in the Department of Anthropology at the University of Waterloo. Her work has appeared in the Routledge Handbook of Linguistic Anthropology, the Handbook of Language Socialization, Language in Society, and the Journal of Sociolinguistics. She is the co-editor of Beyond Yellow English: Toward a Linguistic Anthropology of Asian Pacific America (Oxford University Press, 2009) and South Korea's Education Exodus: The Life and Times of Study Abroad (University of Washington Press, 2015).

Megan Rim is a Ph.D. student specializing in Digital Studies in the Department of American Culture at the University of Michigan. She is interested in race, digital spaces and technologies, and social movements. More specifically, her work examines discourses of digital play and labor about people of color and how people of color navigate off and online spaces of protest.

Lee Jin Choi is Assistant Professor in Department of English Education at Hongik University, South Korea. Her research focuses on second language acquisition and practice with emphasis on sociolinguistic competence in language learning and use in South Korea. Her work has been appeared in Language in Society, Language & Education, Multilingua: Journal of Cross-Cultural & Interlanguage Communication, International Journal of Bilingualism and Gender & Language.

Nancy Abelmann was the Harry E. Preble Professor of Anthropology, Asian American Studies, and East Asian Languages and Cultures and Associate Vice Chancellor of Research at the University of Illinois at Urbana-Champaign. Her works include The Intimate University: Korean American Students and the Problems of Segregation (Duke University Press, 2009); No Alternative? Experiments in South Korean Education (University of California Press, 2012); South Korea's Education Exodus: The Life and Times of Early Study Abroad (University of Washington Press, 2015); and Making Family Work: How Korean American Teens and Parents Navigate Immigrant America (New York University Press, forthcoming).

Chapter 5 A Hybrid Model of Bridging Nation Branding and Country Image: A case study of the Korean Wave

Jaebeom Suh is an associate professor of Marketing at Kansas State University. He earned his Ph. D. in Marketing from the University of Alabama. He published numerous books and journals in the International Journal of Service Industry Management, Journal of Business Research, Journal of Brand Management, International Journal of Management Science, and more. His research area includes consumer protection, customer satisfaction and loyalty, internet of things, financial service products, and brand equity.

Chapter 6 Yet to Crest: The Korean Wave and Korean Language Learning
Chapter 7 Anti-Korean Wave in Japan: Identity Clash?

Yeonhee Yoon is a professor of the practice of the Korean Language and Culture at the Department of East Asian Languages and Cultures and faculty fellow at the Liu Institute of Asia and Asian Studies at the University of Notre Dame. She received her Ph.D. in Korean Linguistics from the University of Hawai'i at Manoa. Her research interests include Intercultural Pragmatics, Second Language Acquisition, and Korean popular culture. Her current project focuses on Korean History and Culture through Film, Korean Popular Culture and migration, Korean Language and Culture for International Negotiations and Diplomacy, and Korean language for academic purpose. Her recent publication include "Korean Hedges in Spoken Discourse" (2016) and "Korean Society" in Essentials of Korean Culture (2013).

Chapter 8 The Korean Wave as a Soft Power

Kiwoong Yang received his Ph.D. from the University of Tokyo in Japan. He is a 2015-16 academic year visiting fellow at Notre Dame's Liu Institute for Asia and Asian Studies, is a tenured professor in the department of politics and public administration and a dean of the Graduate School of Global Cooperation at Hallym University, South Korea where he specializes in international relations among China, Japan, Korea, and the United States. He also serves a guest scholar for the academic year at Notre Dame's Kellogg Institute for International Studies as well as taught a course titled Conflict and Cooperation in International Relations of East Asia for the fall 2015 semester and is currently teaching China, Japan, and Korea- The Impossible, Indispensible for the Spring 2016 semester. He is the author of numerous articles and books, including "South Korea and Japan's frictions over history" Asian Perspective (2008) (written in English), Diplomacy and Negotiations in East Asia (2013) (written in Korean). While in residence at the Liu Institute, his research examines the escalation and negotiation of conflict in international relations of East Asia including such issues as the North Korea problem, historical conflicts and maritime territorial disputes among South Korea, China, and Japan.
Maddalena Ciesa is now working as Content Coordinator for Max Mara Fashion Group, after over three years spent in the Communication and Marketing field with Calzedonia Group. Both Italian Groups are key players in the worldwide fashion system. She received her M.A. in Marketing and Communications from the University of Verona, Italy, and her B.D. in International Economics and Management from the University of Padua, Italy. Maddalena is also keen on music, art, design and how they relate and reflect in society. Her educational background in marketing has given her a broad base to approach to her passions from different point of views.

Chapter 9 Between Fans: History and National Identity in Online Debates on Axis Powers Hetalia

Kathryn Hemmann, Associate Professor of Japanese Literature and Popular Culture, received her Ph.D. in 2013 from the University of Pennsylvania, where her graduate research centered around Japanese fiction and graphic novels written during the past three decades. Her book project, Writing Women Readers: Manga Cultures and the Female Gaze, focuses on fannish interpretations of popular manga series, specifically those of the bestselling four-woman artistic team CLAMP. She examines how these writers and artists negotiate highly gendered realms of narrative discourse, arguing for the application of a female gaze to genres that have generally been understood as taking a male audience for granted. Kathryn is currently studying Japanese console-based role playing games, including those in the Final Fantasy, Legend of Zelda, and Pokémon series. She is especially interested in readings that focus on environmental issues, such as attitudes toward the natural world, the politics of geography, and the ontological formation of the human, the inhuman, and the posthuman. khemmann@gmu.edu

Chapter 10 Lost and Found in "Cool Japan"

Heather Bowen-Struyk (bowen-struyk.com) is a visiting assistant professor at the DePaul University. She has also taught at the University of Chicago, the University of Notre Dame, the University of Michigan, Lake Forest College, and Loyola University Chicago. With Norma Field, she is co-editor of For Dignity, Justice, and Revolution: An Anthology of Japanese Proletarian Literature (University of Chicago Press 2016). She co-edited a volume of essays, Red Love Across the Pacific, with Ruth Barraclough and Paula Rabinowitz (Palgrave 2015). Bowen-Struyk is the guest editor of the Fall 2006 positions: east asia cultures critique special issue on "Proletarian Arts in East Asia: Quests for National, Gender, and Class Justice."

Part 1

K-Pop as a Gateway to Korea

Chapter 1

Exuberant *Hallyu* and Formidable Students: Two Faces of South Korean Youth Culture[1]

Susan D. Blum

I have studied China for more than thirty years, but in the last seven years or so I have added a fascination with Korea—perhaps unconsciously riding the *Hallyu* wave. The family dramas that compelled many people in China in the 1990s were not really what drew me in.

My first genuine foray into the Korean Wave began in part because I had an undergraduate research assistant from South Korea, who at my request described her experiences in Korea's intense education system. Ever since, I have been comparing it to that of other East Asian countries and to that of the US.

Pursuing that curiosity, I have had two occasions to visit South Korea, in 2011 and in 2013, and I have developed a deep interest in Korea's educational zeal—which is both embraced and deplored by its citizens and leaders. I've visited two of the SKY universities, especially Yonsei, and spent time at an alternative secondary school, The Haja School in Seoul, and I've worried about the single-minded focus on examinations and the strict sorting that results, as well as worrying—I'm a worrier!—about the expense and exhaustion created by *hagwon*, supplementary schools. I've wondered about South Korea's consistent appearance at the top of international PISA tests (OECD 2012a, 2012b). I've been dismayed about the suicide rate among South Korean teenagers (Kim 2014). I've followed the international rankings of South Korean universities (QS World University Rankings 2016, Times Higher Education 2016) and have participated in a panel reviewing grant applications for World

1 Slightly modified from a keynote address given on April 25, 2014 at a conference at the University of Notre Dame, Korean Wave Beyond Nationality: Conflicts Over the Globalization of Korean Popular Culture

Class University projects. I've admired Korea's technological leadership. I've even got a Samsung phone.

But when in 2014 I was invited to give a talk on K-Pop, for the first time I spent some time immersed in the pleasing and catchy and soft-focus world of K-Pop. It reminded me a bit of the Taiwan music of the 1980s, and of the Japanese music (that I missed, mostly) of the 1990s. It was reminiscent of the so-called girl bands and boy bands that my daughters recall with bemusement from their elementary-school years in the US but that I did not really come to know so well. I have since learned that this similarity was deliberate; when Lee Soo-man, founder of SM Entertainment, and the person most responsible for the specific creation of K-Pop, encountered the Backstreet Boys in the middle 1990s, he was impressed. He studied their techniques and deliberately imported many of them—later modified—into the Korean pop music scene (Seabrook 2015: 152-155).

In South Korea's embrace of "soft power," something mentioned by every analyst of K-Pop, I'm struck with comparisons with China. China has been busily attempting to support Confucius Institutes and to promote its romanticized version of traditional, timeless Chinese culture, with performances of ballets and celebrations of supposedly ancient aspects of that Chinese culture (Lahtinen 2015, Paradise 2009). The opening ceremony of the Beijing Olympic Games in 2008 invoked the claimed "five-thousand-year history of China" and its embrace of "Confucianism" with its archaic dress and formations (Williams 2008, Yardley 2008). The focus is on continuity with the past and pushes a story of Chinese essentialism.

In contrast, South Korea—which also, as you may see in other chapters of this book, uses political and commercial support for such activities—embraces the apparently frivolous pop culture that people actually seek (Korea Tourism Organization n.d., Korea.net 2016). Official tourism sites promote K-Performance, K-Pop, K-Dramas. As Evan Osnos puts it in the *New Yorker* (2012), we can almost hear the Chinese thinking, "Why didn't we think of that?"

Every country is now trying to "brand" itself and to "export" as many things as possible, whether cell phones and refrigerators (I also have a Samsung refrigerator) or movies, patents, and pop icons.

Since, as I've learned, K-Pop is enormously expensive to produce and is supported by huge companies as well as state funding, it is worth inquiring into why.

So I will think with you a little about the role of *Hallyu* and its embrace by the Korean government, and why this might be so enthusiastically done. And I speculate—try out a theory—that some of it has to do with youth, and how

South Korea hopes to be perceived.

Education

South Korea has been discussed as a country with "education fever" (Seth 2002). South Korean students consistently perform extremely well on the international PISA tests given every three years to an assortment of fifteen-year-olds in OECD countries. The OECD, the Organisation for Economic Co-operation and Development, is a creation of developed countries—a club that a few scant decades ago would not have included South Korea. As in economics, in education South Korea has come a long way in seemingly no time.

An organization called the "Center on International Education Benchmarking" tries to explain how, in lightning speed, the South Korean population has become one of the most educated in the world: "No doubt South Korea's brand of Confucianism, with its values of hard work, reverence for education, frugality and strong family structure helped, but those values had been part of the culture for a couple of millennia and cannot by themselves explain what happened." They quote expert Clark Sorensen, who regards the construction of the education system as part of Korea's "'national project,' by which he appears to mean that it was successful less because of the particular features of the system than because of the sheer determination of the Koreans to build a world class country, and the commitment of every citizen to do his or her part in the grand design. Education was, in the minds of the Korean people, a central part of that grand design from the start" (NCEE n.d.).

According to the CIA World Factbook, South Koreans are 97.9% literate and average 17 years of education. (It could be relevant that the youth (15-24) unemployment rate is 9%.) And while South Korea spends only 5% of its GDP on education (CIA World Factbook 2016), families spend far more on the notorious supplementary education, cram schools or hagwon, that keep students working until deep into the night. In *The Birth of Korean Cool*, her account of encountering Korea as a child initially brought up in the United States, Euny Hong (2016: 40-45) discusses the attempt to prohibit private tutoring. Students were encouraged to reveal which classmates were violating this prohibition. By the late 1990s, the government realized that the ban was violated, and capitulated. Currently (2016) there are instead curfews—currently ten p.m.—on cram schools; police raid schools that violate the curfew on teaching. Some schools engage in subterfuges to make it appear they are doing something other than teaching.

This has been seen as necessary because students are uniformly exhausted. The typical daily routine of a high school student, according to Jisoon Lee (2002), is something like this:

Table 1 The typical daily routine of a high school student

Time	Daily routine
05:30~06:30	Gets up and studies for an hour or so
06:30~07:30	Has a quick bite and goes to school
07:30~17:30	Daily school life. Takes about 7 different subjects every day. Takes about 18 different subjects altogether in a year.
17:30~19:00	Comes home and has dinner. Or, stays in school and has dinner there.
19:00~22:00	Studies alone or with visiting private tutors at home. Or, participates in the study programs held at school. Or, attends private preparatory schools to take extra lessons in at least two subjects. Or, goes to tutor's place to get private lessons. The tutor(s) may or may not be the student's school teacher(s). Typically a student combines some of each component.
22:00~01:00	Those who come home directly after school continue with home study. Those who remain at school return home and study more. Those who go to preparatory schools or private tutors come home and continue with home study. All go to bed at about 1 a.m. Some portion of the home study may be done in commercially run reading rooms.

Source: Lee 2002: 7.

You can see the endless day, with activities plotted from five-thirty wakeup to one a.m. bedtime. Most of the day is devoted to studying, whether in school or in the many activities connected to it. Yes, the results are impressive. Yet the country is consumed with anxiety about the unhappiness and mental illness, even suicide, of youth. In 2015 two young girls, just sixteen years old, left a suicide note that said "We hate school" (Hu 2015). The connection between suicide and school—academic pressure, examination anxiety—is widely understood (Carney 2015, Yoon 2015).

And despite the celebrated accomplishments of South Korea's youth, youthful Korea is in part only a wish.

Aging Society

In 2013 NPR reported that South Korea is the fasted-aging country in the world (Kuhn 2013). What that means is that people are living longer—a good thing for them and their families, but a challenge for healthcare and the economy (Pew 2014). And people are having fewer children—an environmental benefit, but an economic and social burden.

There are different ways to measure this: One way is to look at the birthrate per 1000 population. The CIA World Factbook puts the South Korean birthrate at 8.26 children per 1000 population, fifth lowest in the world (China's is 12.17) (CIA World Factbook n.d., East-West Center n.d.).

Table 2 Key Demographic Statistics for South Korea

Birth rate	8.3 births / 1,000 population (2017 estimate) [China: 12.30]
Total fertility rate	1.25 children born/woman (2017 estimate) [OECD average: 1.71]
School life expectancy	17 years
Literacy	97.9%
Life expectancy at birth	82.5 years (2017 estimate)

Sources: CIA World Factbook n.d., East-West Center n.d., AFP 2013.

Another is the fertility rate. In 2011 in South Korea the average number of children born to a woman over a lifetime was 1.01; the OECD average is 1.71 (AFP 2013). Clearly the South Korean society, like that of almost all developed countries, is aging. Youth are shrinking as a proportion of the population. According to Bruce Stokes (Stokes 2014), in a list titled "The countries that will be most impacted by aging population," Japan is first and South Korea is second, followed by China, Germany, Spain. And Asians tend to be worried about this (Pew 2014).

So in this context of an aging society filled with serious students, intent on testing well and lingering over their studies, anxious and filled with stress, a playful and youthful wave of attraction, K-Pop and its variants, seems helpful.

K-Pop and *Hallyu*

The Korean Wave is said to have started with the one-way dissemination of Korean TV dramas and films from the 1990s, in what Dal Yong Jin calls "Hallyu 1.0" (Jin 2012). But the Hallyu that has really taken off in the last five years or so, Hallyu 2.0, is different (Lee and Nornes 2015). Hallyu 2.0—like "Web 2.0," where interaction is key—interacts with its fans, which you may explore by searching for "Hallyu" or "K-Pop" or "Korean Drama" and "reaction," and includes the popular world of games. Like "fan fiction" and other forms of what Henry Jenkins calls "convergence culture," participation in these interactive phenomena is made possible by technological innovations and the penetration of smart phones and Internet access throughout the world. It is relevant that Internet speeds and ubiquity place South Korea at the top of every list. The government's Cultural Content Office, with an annual budget of half a billion dollars, supports Korea's popular culture as its "soft power" initiative. Another fund, estimated at $1 billion in 2014, invests in pop culture (Hong 2014: 101-102), including K-Pop, and expects to make a profit.

K-Pop, the overproduced, artistically derivative globally popular form of group bands, with lengthy contracts regulating very young people's every move, and focused on formulaic songs and surgically enhanced physical appearance, has taken the world by storm. Euny Hong writes of this deliberate construction: "The bands are prefabricated and treated like a consumer product right from the beginning" (2014: 132). K-Pop may have a different reception in different societies (see, e.g., Chung 2015, Lyan and Levkowitz 2015), but there is something for everyone. It is brilliant in its appeal to various audiences in varying ways.

K-Pop portrays South Korea as it wishes to be seen in many domains, both educational and pop-cultural—and ultimately commercial and political:

- It is multilingual. Though the Korean language is considered difficult for many speakers, the use of World English, or Chinese, alongside Korean in many songs provides a way in. Performers are recruited from beyond Korea, and bilingual performers are especially sought-after (Seabrook 2015: 153). Apparently all over the world, young people are learning Korean because of K-Pop (Chow 2015).
- K-Pop is connected to world pop culture, and is filled with allusion—Super Junior clearly alludes to the early Beatles (Generasia 2016).
- Musically it is not especially challenging. The tunes are catchy. They do not use the pentatonic scale so common throughout Asia, and typical of traditional Korean high culture. Filtered through Japan's rule over Korea, Western popular music and its diatonic scale are the underlying resources; US popular culture alone is not the dominant factor (Lie 2012: 343). The global influence of the Western diatonic scale makes K-Pop accessible to audiences throughout the world (Lie 2012: 346).
- The performers are irresistibly appealing; the form is familiar; even the hiphop songs are not violent or threatening. John Lie calls them "clean, well-crafted performers" (2012: 355); Euny Hong on meeting Kim Heonjun, the head of the successful break-dancing troupe Jinjo Crew, notes that "as with most young Korean celebrities, his rebellious exterior belies

an exceptional politeness" (2014: 103). John Seabrook emphasizes that "good looks are a K-pop artist's stock-in-trade...K-pop artists rarely play instruments onstage. Where K-pop stars excel is in sheer physical beauty" (2015: 158). They are often trained for as long as seven years before they perform a single time. The group synchronization developed over years of shared training makes the whole thing appear seamless.

- While it is cosmopolitan, some is also notably and recognizably Korean. There are very clear traces of South Korean life. For Westerners, it piques curiosity and provides a peek into this foreign country, both as specifically Korean, evident in the appearance of *hangul*, and as East Asian more generally, visible for example in the origami and cherry blossoms that appear in some videos.
- In some sense the Korean Wave has also provided an aspirational future for Chinese, in its modernity, with cell phones, Seoul with its modern features, urban, tall buildings, subways, and happy, carefree, free youth. The youthful and carefree face is especially appealing in East Asia and the Middle East.
- The lives hinted at invoke student life, such as videos featuring high school football—US football demonstrated in a field and in the context of school locker rooms (Girls' Generation n.d.). Given the dominance of school in teens' lives, and the increasingly uniform look of schools internationally, this will resonate transnationally as well as with Korean youth.
- It is exuberant; wholesome; filled with attractive youth—faces not creased with anxiety but smooth and lovely. Many are teens; most have had some sort of plastic surgery. Gender roles are conventional and thus unchallenging: the young women of Girls' Generation addressing slightly older men as *oppa* 'elder brother of a female' (Epstein and Turnbull 2014: 38-319).

Support

And this success, the creative industry that is such an attractive investment for governments and companies, has led not only to crass commercial embrace of these products. Government and public support also indicates support for self-presentation, a version of itself as youthful, healthy, happy, polished, disciplined, accessible, and fully integrated into the world. Sometimes it is fanciful and other-worldly. But it is different from the fierce competitive industrial or educational actor that is South Korea. This one is friendly and welcoming.

If education is serious, with adult and future goals, then K-Pop and *Hallyu* products are the other face, the fanciful, youthful, playful, cuddly teen culture face of a country busily branding itself.

And as South Korea, like its East Asian neighbors, is an aging population, the portrayal of youth is critical. The world market must always cater to youth, entering the peak of their purchasing power and maintaining loyalties developed in youth as they enter adulthood.

K-Pop as a Gateway to K

K-Pop is an easy entrance point for appreciating Korean culture in general, appealing to many people outside South Korea. Korean youth, with the smooth surface of orderly performances, are appealing. Unlike, say, Chinese attempts to isolate what is Chinese, Korean popular culture demonstrates familiarity with and welcoming of global cultural phenomena. It is as if the door is being held open and the world is invited in—the whole world, through the Internet, through circulation of semiotic (symbolic) resources that are familiar. Despite the challenge of the Korean language, people are picking up its flavor, like its foods, to add a set of resources to those wishing to make the globe their territory. Despite the serious adult involvement in shaping, marketing, and profiting from the young performers, the appearance of spontaneity and easy health are easy and have an approachable surface.

How long this phenomenon will last is anyone's guess. The dramas that preceded K-Pop's popularity, in Hallyu 1.0, seemed poised to sweep the world, with their family emotion and memorable characters. As Japan's Hello Kitty and anime wane, along with the Japanese economy, and as fickle international tastes seize the next thing, it is possible that K-Pop's day in the sun will also end quickly, superseded by some creative product from somewhere new. Meanwhile, Korea's brilliance at studying international trends and riding them may serve it well, as support for popular images of youth circulate domestically and abroad. K-Pop is competing as a plausible career goal alongside the more familiar one of working in companies. When a call for potential K-Pop artists was issued, 4 percent of the population auditioned (compared with .03 percent of the US population auditioning for *American Idol*) (Hong 2014: 126). Just as acting was regarded as licentious and sinful in the Renaissance but has become respectable in the contemporary world, K-Pop stardom is regarded as a worthy childhood aspiration.

For now, Korea's discovery of a successful formula for capitalizing on a combination of youth, marketing, beauty, technology, and the circulation of aesthetic resources has led the world to Korea's door, which is wide open. Many people—including me—have enjoyed walking right through it.

References

AAFP. 2013. "Low Birthrate Could Slash South Korea's Youth Population in Half by 2060: Report." *The Japan Times*. Accessed January 8. http://www.japantimes.co.jp/news/2013/01/08/asia-pacific/low-birthrate-could-slash-south-koreas-youth-population-in-half-by-2060-report/#.V3wErpMrKIZ

Carney, Matthew. 2015. "South Korean Education Success Has Its Costs in Unhappiness and Suicide Rates. AM with Michael Brissenden." Accessed June 16. ABC News (Australia). http://www.abc.net.au/am/content/2015/s4255647.htm

Chow, Kat. 2015. "Way More College Students Are Studying Korean. Is 'Hallyu' The Reason?" NPR Code Switch. April 3. Accessed November 8, 2017. https://www.npr.org/sections/codeswitch/2015/04/03/397263103/way-more-college-students-are-studying-korean-is-hallyu-why

Chung, Hye Seung. 2015. "Hating the Korean Wave in Japan: The Exclusivist Inclusion of Zainichi Koreans in Nerima Daikon Brothers." In *Hallyu 2.0: The Korean Wave in the Age of Social Media*, edited by Sangjoon Lee and Abé Markus Nornes. Ann Arbor: University of Michigan Press, 195-211.

CIA World Factbook. 2017. Korea, South. https://www.cia.gov/library/publications/the-world-factbook/geos/ks.html

CIA World Factbook. N.d. Birth Rate. https://www.cia.gov/library/publications/the-world-factbook/rankorder/2054rank.html

East-West Center. N.d. Declining Birth Rates Raising Concerns in Asia. http://www.eastwestcenter.org/news-center/east-west-wire/declining-birth-rates-raising-concerns-in-asia

Epstein, Stephen, and James Turnbull. 2014. "Girls' Generation? Gender, (Dis) Empowerment, and K-pop." In *The Korean Popular Culture Reader*, edited by Kyung Hyun Kim and Youngmin Choe. Durham and London: Duke University Press, 314-336.

Generasia. 2016. Super Junior. http://www.generasia.com/wiki/Super_Junior

Girls' Generation. N.d. http://www.girlsgenerationusa.com/

Hong, Euny. 2014. *The Birth of Korean Cool: How One Nation is Conquering the World Through Pop Culture*. New York: Picador.

Hu, Elise. 2015. The All-Work, No-Play Culture of South Korean Education. Morning Edition, NPR. Accessed April 15. http://www.npr.org/sections/parallels/2015/04/15/393939759/the-all-work-no-play-culture-of-south-korean-education

Jin, Dal Yong. 2012. "Hallyu 2.0: The New Korean Wave in the Creative Industry." *International Institute Journal* 2(1). http://hdl.handle.net/2027/spo.11645653.0002.102

Jin, Dal Yong. 2015. "New Perspectives on the Creative Industries in the Hallyu 2.0 Era: Global-Local Dialectics in Intellectual Properties." In *Hallyu 2.0: The Korean Wave in the Age of Social Media*, edited by Sangjoon Lee and Abé Markus Nornes. Ann Arbor: University of Michigan Press, 2015. 53-70.

Kim, Young-Ha. 2014. "South Korea's Struggle With Suicide." *The New York Times*. April 2. Accessed November 8, 2017. https://www.nytimes.com/2014/04/03/opinion/south-koreas-struggle-with-suicide.html

Korea Tourism Organization.N.d. "Imagine Your Korea." http://english.visitkorea.or.kr/enu/index.kto

Korea.net. 2016. "Gateway to Korea." http://www.korea.net/index.jsp

Kuhn, Anthony. 2013. "South Korea Prepares The Young For A Rapidly Aging Population." NPR. January 4. http://www.npr.org/2013/01/04/168615553/south-korea-prepares-the-young-for-a-rapidly-aging-population

Lahtinen, Anja. 2015. "China's Soft Power: Challenges of Confucianism and Confucius Institutes." *Journal of Comparative Asian Development* 14, 2 : 200-226. doi:10.1080/15339114.2015.1059055

Lee, Jisoon. 2002. *Education Policy in the Republic of Korea: Building Block or Stumbling Block?* Washington, DC: The International Bank for Reconstruction and Development/The World Bank.

Lee, Sangjoon. 2015. "Introduction: A Decade of Hallyu Scholarship: Toward a New Direction in Hallyu 2.0." In *Hallyu 2.0: The Korean Wave in the Age of Social Media*, edited by Sangjoon Lee and Abé Markus Nornes. Ann Arbor: University of Michigan Press, 1-28.

Lee, Sangjoon and Abé Markus Nornes, eds. 2015. *Hallyu 2.0: The Korean Wave in the Age of Social Media*. Ann Arbor: University of Michigan Press.

Lie, John. 2012. "What Is the K in K-pop? South Korean Popular Music, the Culture Industry, and National Identity." *Korea Observer* 43, 3 : 339-363.

Lyan, Irina, and Alon Levkowitz. 2015. "Consuming the Other: Israeli Hallyu Case Study." In *Hallyu 2.0: The Korean Wave in the Age of Social Media*, edited by Sangjoon Lee and Abé Markus Nornes. Ann Arbor: University of Michigan Press, 212-228.

NCEE. N.d. "South Korea." Center on International Education Benchmarking: Learning from the World's High Performing Education Systems. http://www.ncee.org/programs-affiliates/center-on-international-education-benchmarking/top-performing-countries/south-korea-overview/

OECD. 2012a. "Korea-PISA." Accessed November 8, 2017. https://www.oecd.org/pisa/aboutpisa/korea-pisa.htm

OECD. 2012b. "PISA 2012 Results." Accessed November 8, 2017. https://www.oecd.org/pisa/keyfindings/pisa-2012-results.htm

Osnos, Evan. 2012. "Why China Lacks Gangnam Style." *The New Yorker*. October 3.

Paradise, James F. 2009. "China and International Harmony: The Rise of Confucius Institutes in Bolstering Beijing's Soft Power." *Asian Survey* 49, 4 : 647-669.

Pew Research. 2014. "Attitudes about Aging: A Global Perspective." Accessed January 30. http://www.pewglobal.org/2014/01/30/attitudes-about-aging-a-global-perspective/

QS World University Rankings. 2015/16. Top Universities. http://www.topuniversities.com/university-rankings/world-university-rankings/2015#sorting=rank+region=+country=+faculty=+stars=false+search=

Seabrook, John. 2015. *The Song Machine: Inside the Hit Factory*. New York: W W Norton.

Seth, Michael J. 2002. *Education Fever: Society, Politics, and the Pursuit of Schooling in South Korea*. Honolulu: University of Hawaiʻi Press.

Stokes, Bruce. 2014. "The Countries That Will Be Most Impacted by Aging Population." FactTank: News In The Numbers. Pew Research Center. February 4. Accessed November 8, 2017. http://www.pewresearch.org/fact-tank/2014/02/04/the-countries-that-will-be-most-impacted-by-aging-population/

Times Higher Education. 2016. "World University Rankings 2015-2016." https://www.timeshighereducation.com/world-university-rankings/2016/world-ranking#!/page/0/length/25/sort_by/rank_label/sort_order/asc/cols/rank_only

Walton, Brenna. 2012. "K-Pop Has American Fans Learning Korean." *Collide*. Accessed December 5. http://culturecollision.journalism.cuny.edu/2012/12/05/k-pop-has-american-fans-learning-korean/

Williams, Richard. 2008. "Patriot Games: China Makes Its Point with Greatest Show." *The Guardian*. Accessed August 8. https://www.theguardian.com/sport/2008/aug/09/olympics2008.openingceremony

Yardley, Jim. 2008. "China's Leaders Try to Impress and Reassure World." *The New York Times*. Accessed August 8. http://www.nytimes.com/2008/08/09/sports/olympics/09china.html?_r=0

Yoon, Min-sik. 2015. "South Korea Still has Top OECD Suicide Rate." The Korea Herald. Accessed August 31. http://www.koreaherald.com/view.php?ud=20150830000310

Chapter 2

Korea's Place in the World: Its Effort to Enhance Soft Power[1]

Jaewoong Lee

Even though Korea boasts its long history of more than five thousand years, it is relatively new that Korea has become known to the world. Located at the far east of Asia and surrounded by powerful neighbors like China and Japan, Korea only emerged in the international stage as emerging economy in the late twentieth century. Due to Korea's relatively short history in the international arena Korea was not very well recognized among foreigners and its image has been stalled in the old picture of poor and war-torn country. However, in the wake of the twenty first century, the image of and knowledge about Korea has been improved quite drastically with the advent of Korean Wave (K-Wave).

K-Wave is all the rage. These days you can easily notice the very popularity of Korean culture in the world. K-pop fans in North and South America, Asia and even in Africa get together and sing and dance just like the idol groups. When I was in Ghana in 2011, I was amazed to find out the popularity of Korea drama in Ghana. Ghanaians were still remembering "Dae Jang Geum" one of the most successful Korean drama in the world, even though it had been broadcast more than five years before. One of my Ghanaian assistants working at the Korean Embassy would bring Korean drama dvds back home from the Embassy and stay up all night watching them. Korean idol groups – male or female - are so popular worldwide that nowadays their fan bases include Asia, Europe, America and even Africa. The popularity and interests in Korea that started with the K-Wave have been mostly about modern culture like Korean pop songs, new wave dramas, and other TV programs. However, foreigners are

1 This paper is a developed version of presentations that Deputy Consul General Lee presented at Notre Dame University in April 2014 and April 2016. This article explains soft power policy of the Korean Government. However, all the opinions listed here are his own ideas, and they are not reflecting the Government's official position.

expanding their interests about Korea to Korean language, traditional dances, calligraphies and Korean cuisine these days. More and more tourists are visiting Korea, and when they visit, they not only enjoy historic sites, artifacts and traditional architecture, but also actively participate in the Korean culture by joining temple stay, taking ceramic classes and so on.

Thanks to these developments, Korea is more widely and better known to outside world than it was ten, twenty years ago. I want to share three episodes that I have experienced to show how widely and deeply Korea has become known to the world. In 1994 immediately after I joined the Ministry of Foreign Affairs, I took a business trip to Geneva, Switzerland. During my trip, I met an elderly couple from France in the train and had brief dialogue with them. When I told them that I was from Korea, they told me that they had not heard about Korea. I was a bit shocked to realize how little known my country was to foreigners. Sixteen year later in 2011, while working for the Embassy in Ghana, I bumped into very similar situation in the plane on my way to attend a meeting in Dubai. A Ghanaian sitting beside me asked where I was from and I replied accordingly, not sure he would recognize Korea. However, he did know Korea and asked me if I am from South or North. I was pleasantly surprised to find out that Korea had become known to foreigners even in Ghana. Last episode is from May 2016 at Costco in the suburb of Chicago, US. While checking out, the cashier asked my id card for verification and, returning my card, said to me "Gomapseumnida" meaning "Thank you." I was really surprised to meet a cashier who not only knew Korea but also spoke greetings in Korean! She explained that she was crazy about Korean dramas, so she had learned very basic Korean by only watching TV. It was the moment I realized K-Wave has expanded such that even young lady in suburban Chicago knows Korea and Korean culture. Those episodes demonstrate how widely Korea has become known to the world in twenty years. Korea has come so far as it is now, but Korean people and the Korean Government believe that we still have way more to go to make global community to learn more about Korea. That is why the Korean Government is now striving to promote the public diplomacy.

Usually Koreans place high importance on perception about themselves by foreigners. They judge themselves by envisaging the way foreigners will judge them. In addition, Koreans are very keen on earning good marks in the first impressions from foreigners during their visit to Korea. They also want to give lasting good memories to foreigners after they leave. Koreans also want to raise their status in the world in every field including sports, economics, competitiveness index, happiness index, etc. In this respect, I believe, it is worthwhile to see how we Koreans see our stance in international community and how we seek to improve it. In the following, I am going to review Korea's unique geographical location and its history, and how Korea has developed politically, economically and culturally. I will then seek my own answers why the Korean culture has become more popular recently. Lastly, I will discuss the efforts that the Korean Government is investing in order to enhance Korea's soft power.

Geographical and historical place

First of all, I would like to start with Korea's geographical and historical place. As you know, the geographical location of Korea is very unique. As commonly commented, Korea is at the far end of the Eurasian continent. It neighbors one of the biggest and strongest countries, China. Inevitably, Korea has been under great influences of China politically, economically and culturally since the start of the history. Conversely, it could be said that Korea's ambition has been stretched to the continent through China even to Europe. If we look the other side, Korea is directly neighboring with Japan. Even though it is very small in size, Korea has been able to dream big to look ahead into China and Japan for its survival and growth. From the very olden times, Korea has played a bridging role between China and Japan. Chinese civilizations found their way to Korea, and Korean dynasties and people openly adopted them as their own. However, Korea did not just adopt those advanced civilization without any reservations. Koreans adjusted those new cultures into their own by creatively transforming them to meet the needs and tastes. In turn, Korea sometimes exported their own version of culture back to China resulting in the popular trend among the Chinese leaders of Korean tastes. Korea also worked as conveyer of higher civilization to Japan. From the time of Three Kingdoms in the fifth century, many Korean scholars, monks, and artists visited Japan and contributed to building Japanese civilization.

The geographical uniqueness of the Korean Peninsula, however, has unfortunately put Korea under enormous sufferings instigated by foreign aggressions. During its five thousand year history, Korea has been invaded by neighboring countries continuously. Those aggressions were mostly from the northern part bordering with current China, but Japan also caused turmoil throughout the history. Especially since mid-sixteenth century, during Chosun Dynasty, the newly forceful Japan invaded Korea causing transformative geo-political balance shift from then on. In early twentieth century, the imperial Japan annexed Korea and put it under colonial rule for thirty five year, making the era an abomination for all Koreans. In order to redeem the independence, Koreans fought defiantly against Japanese colonial rule. They established a tentative government in China, and operated a consistent resistance until liberation. Even though Korea finally got liberated with the end of the World War II, situation was not getting better. The ideology forced Korea to be divided in two and separate occupation by the Soviet Union and the US. The tragedy culminated in Korea when, in 1950, the Korean War broke out. The Korean War was the most tragic in the history of Korea with more than 1.2 million casualties and has left a deep scar to all Koreans still painful until today. The War also made Korea totally destroyed with no basis for development left. General McArthur who directed successfully the Incheon Landing reversing the course of the war to the advantage of the South once said, "It will take one hundred years for South Korea to recover from the war." Despite all these sufferings for its whole span of history, Korea has survived with resilience and perseverance. It has kept its national identity and territorial integrity. It has not just survived but also preserved its tradition and cultural heritages which have started to flourish in international stage.

Korea's political place in the world

Politically, Korea is a country with full-pledged democracy. When I say that Korea is a democratic country, I only mean South Korea, whereas North Korea is under the communist dictatorship. Like other newly-independent countries, Korea has also undergone some turbulent times for democracy. South Korea has consistently moved ahead in the path toward the democratization, and now we can confidently say that the Korean political system and its operation are, both institutionally and in practice, fully democratic.

Despite the political advancement that Korea has accomplished, Korea is still suffering from the legacy of the Cold War as the only remaining divided country in the world. For this reason, peaceful unification is always our government's highest priority. In March 2014, on the occasion of President Park Geun-hye's visit to Germany, President presented three proposals to the North Korean authorities in the hope of laying the groundwork for peaceful unification during her speech at Dresden University of Technology. These proposals will not only lay the groundwork for the unification but transform the perception of Korean public and foreigners. President Park even mentioned the unification is an economic breakthrough not only for Korea but also for the international community. The presentation of 'Dresden Initiative' is a strong evidence that my government is confident about our status vis-à-vis the North and we should be ready to be unified again in a peaceful way. Still, the incessant provocations of the North are hampering our efforts for conciliation and cooperation. In January 2016, we witnessed North Korea conducted the fourth nuclear test. North Korea has also continuously threatened the peace and security of in Northeast Asia and the world by firing intermediate range test missiles. In order to counter the threat by North Korea, the United Nations Security Council adopted Resolution 2270 in March 2016, containing the most comprehensive and robust sanctions. Together with the international community, the Korean Government is going to spare no efforts in fully implementing the sanctions so that North Korea will feel the pressure and make the right strategic choice to dismantle the nuclear and missile programs, and bringing back the peace and stability in the Korean Peninsula and beyond.

In the international arena, Korea is also trying to play more important roles which are deemed commensurable to its power in order to resolve various problems that the world is facing today such as extreme terrorism, economic slowdown, spread of epidemics and climate change. In 2013, five middle powers – Mexico, Indonesia, Korea, Turkey, and Australia – launched a partnership called MIKTA to work together to fulfill their obligations as major actors in the world in dealing with challenges that the world is facing now. Together with other like-minded countries as well as the U.S., the strong ally of Korea, Korea is going to enhance its efforts to contribute to the peace, stability and prosperity of the world.

Korea's remarkable economic growth

Now I turn to the economic status and the remarkably rapid economic growth of Korea. Korea is the only country in the world to transform from an aid recipient country to a donor country within a span of one's life time. Compared to the year 1960, in 2014 the GNI (Gross National Income) per capita has grown more than three hundred times from 79 US dollars to 28,180 US dollars. During the same period, the GDP (Gross Domestic Product) has grown more than seven hundred times from 2 billion US dollars to 1.4 trillion US dollars, and trade volume growth reaches almost three thousand times from 370 million to 1.09 trillion US dollars. Referring to this economic growth, even Koreans themselves call it 'Miracle of Han River.' In trying to explain this economic growth, most scholars agree that there are several common denominators that are crucial to such development and those are mostly related to the strong will and resilience of Korean people such as strong work ethic, huge emphasis on education for especially younger generation, and commitment for better tomorrow. Those factors contributed greatly in overcoming difficulties Korea faced immediately after the Korean War and other challenges such as lack of capital and limited natural resources. Paralleling with those factors, the government initiative of several five-year economic development plans and entrepreneurship of business sector drove the country into the path toward successful growth.

Korea's path to the economic development has been not without difficulties. In 1997, Korea was severely hit by the Asian economic crisis. The Asian economic crisis, with its severity and expansiveness, caused huge economic downturn and massive lay-offs bringing about lots of melt-down of companies and banks affecting lives of ordinary people deeply. However, Korea confronted those challenges vigorously and transformed the crisis into new opportunity for another economic leapfrogging. Reimbursing the bail-out money of the International Monetary Fund well ahead of the schedule and boldly undertaking the structural and regulation reforms, Korea bounced back from the crisis and moved ahead to the one of the most advanced economies in the world. The resilience and strong foundation of economic structure created after the Asian financial crisis helped Korea endure another challenge called the 'Great Recession' in 2008 which is regarded as the most serious international financial crisis since the Great Depression in 1930s.

Having achieved so far the unprecedented economic success, Korea also strives to take responsibility as befits to its political and economic status in international community. After the crisis in 2008, Korea hosted the G20 Summit in 2010 and the Developmental Aid Summit in 2011. Those are examples that Korea is now trying to contribute to the common cause of the globe and proactively play its role as a mediator between the developed and developing countries. As a way of helping developing countries achieve the growth as Korea did, the Korean Government has launched a developmental aid program to share the experiences of Korea. Through its developmental agencies and relevant ministries, Korea is actively spreading its 'Saemaeul undong', new village movement initiative to countries in Asia, Africa and South America. In addition, as export-driven economy Korea is very much in favor of the world with open economy. Korea has signed the free trade agreements with major economies such as the US, EU, China, and ASEAN. It will always advocate the free and rule-based economic system with the aim of achieving economically prosperous, environmentally sustainable, and socially equitable world.

Korea's soft power

These whole advancements of Korea's place in the geographical, political and economic world lead me to the question of the soft power. Up until recently, Korea has focused on the economic development and democratization, which was quite successful. Korea has also been keen on acquiring the military predominance over North Korea to prevent the North from even devising any false attempt to fall back on another military conflict. Building upon these achievements so far, Korea is now seeking the global recognition as a nation with rich history and cultural resources, i.e. enhancing the soft power. In its effort to get more rightful and better recognition, the strong perception by other countries as a nation of marvelous economic growth with world-leading companies like Samsung, Hyundai, and LG certainly helped boost the image of Korea positively. In addition, the image of Korea as a nation with well-established institutional bases such as human rights, rule of law, good governance has rendered foreigners with good first impression about Korea, having them quite receptive to Korean culture in their first encounter. However, unlike hard power such as military and economic, the soft power cannot be easily strengthened with constant ratio of input and outcome. No matter how hard we try and no matter how much we invest in enhancing soft power, we cannot manipulate general perceptions of ordinary people at our discretion about certain country and/or culture to our advantage. Instead, the consistent and enduring efforts are needed to gradually and incrementally develop a certain image. It is, in this respect, essential to maintain a long-term perspective in devising and implementing plans and policies to enhance the soft power of a country.

Fortunately Korea boasts of its richness of outstanding cultural heritages that provide the abundant resources for soft power. For example, Koreans have been using their own language and unique script – Hangul. Invented by King Sejong the Great, the fourth King of the Joseon Dynasty in the fifteenth century, Hangul is a very unique writing system based on scientific and logical analysis on pronunciation system of Korean. Another popular culture that is gathering much attention is Korean food. Korean foods such as kimchi and bibimbap are already very popular worldwide and there is growing interest in learning more about Korean cuisine. Besides Korean language and script and food, there are many other resources for soft power such as Taekwondo, Korean martial art, cultural artifacts, performing arts, and traditional houses and palaces. The growing popularity of Korean pop culture these days in many countries adds to the already rich resources as powerful source to enhance the soft power. Recent survey by the Ministry of Foreign Affairs of Korea shows that the heat of the K-Wave continues to spread across the world with nearly one thousand Korean pop Culture Societies, voluntarily established in 78 countries with more than 9 million members.

This growing popularity of Korean culture as generally deemed as K-Wave is, I believe, the natural outcome of the continuing advancement of Korea's place in the world. Having sought to reemerge as one of the major countries in the Northeast Asian region and beyond, Korea's political and economic development provided valuable stepping stones upon which the cultural enrichment and prosperity becomes possible. The globalization also contributed to the advancement of the K-Wave. These days, contents of K-Wave such as K-Pop, K-Drama and movies are easily accessible to foreign audiences almost at the same time they are introduced in Korea. The increasing exchanges of people like students between Korea and other countries have accelerated the spread of K-Wave too. Foreign students, especially Chinese studying in Korea are increasing rapidly, and many Korean students are studying abroad. Korea is ranked in the third place next to China and India in its number of students studying in the US. Those students are, intentionally or not, working as civic ambassadors for Korean culture at the frontier. Korea's advanced IT technology and netizen culture have also been helpful to attract more people toward Korean culture. One major success of K-pop song would be 'Gangnam Style' from 2012 which was first introduced in YouTube and went viral with the speed of light to the world becoming a social phenomenon. Last but not least, I want to highlight the attitude and character of Korean people who are open to the new culture from abroad. As I explained above, historically Korea has been continuously influenced by the influx of alien civilizations mostly from China. Korea has eagerly adopted those new cultural and civilization influences and adapted them as their own. In doing so, Koreans creatively revised or transformed them into more advanced culture. At a seminar regarding K-Wave I attended in May 2016, I listened to a criticism by an American scholar that Korean rock music bands are mere followers of western culture and do not truly reflect the Koreanness. I could not disagree enough. Even though the style of music is borrowed from the western culture, there certainly exist emotional echoes that are truly 'Korean' in those rock songs. It is not just about Korean rock music but other genres and different types of art and performances too. If Korean pop culture were only about imitating foreign one, it would not appeal to many audiences worldwide nor arouse empathy among them. In this respect, I believe that the K-Wave is truly Korean as well as cosmopolitan.

Government's effort to raise Korea's place with soft power

Finally, I want to briefly touch upon the government's efforts to increase the awareness about Korea and at the same time raise Korea's place with soft power. As the soft power in devising and implementing foreign policies is becoming more important, the Korean Government has recently been investing quite a lot of efforts to promote its soft power. Mindful of that the soft power can be enhanced most effectively by directly appealing to peoples' mind, the Korean Government is actively engaging with public audiences with so called public diplomacy programs. Previously, diplomacy was mostly the work between diplomats representing respective nations in the platform of bilateral and multilateral meetings and conferences. As the importance of having contacts with ordinary people is getting momentum, governments are investing more heavily into the public diplomacy. The development of new ways of media such as social media services and user created contents also forced governments to put more focuses on public diplomacy. The Korean Government is not an exception. Rather, the Korean Government is exerting itself to become the trailblazer in public diplomacy by aggressively enhancing its personnel and financial resources allocated for public diplomacy programs. In February 2016, the National Assembly of Korea passed the Public Diplomacy Act, and it has been enacted on the fourth of August. By enacting the Act, the Korean Government will be in a better position to coordinate policies among relevant ministries and to implement its policies more effectively.

In devising and implementing its public diplomacy policies, the Korean Government is taking an integrated approach. Korean Day Celebration in a certain country will be composed of various programs including cultural events such as exhibitions, performance and film festivals, seminars or forums on current issues related to Korea, and hands-on experience opportunities like cooking and painting. By taking this kind of integrated approach, we can maximize the effects of the programs and comprehensively increase the awareness about Korea to foreign audiences. The Korean Government is also implementing cultural exchange programs with many partner countries and dispatching artists and performers to countries with relatively little knowledge about Korea as an introductory measure. Korea is striving to expand the Korean proficiency in the world too. Relevant ministries like Ministry of Foreign Affairs, Ministry of Education, and Ministry of Culture and Tourism are working together to provide eager students abroad with more opportunities to learn Korean. The institutions sponsored by the Government to teach Korean are named Sejong Hakdang, meaning Sejong Academy to honor the inventor of Korean script Hangul. Another goal of public diplomacy is increasing the number of Korean friends and pro-Korean opinion leaders. In a democratic society, not only domestic policies but also foreign policies are made through the transparent and legal process to reflect the general opinion of citizens. By attracting more people in other countries to love Korea, the Korean Government is seeking to increase its friends and supporters in international arena on pressing issues like North Korean nuclear problem. Overseas missions like Embassies and Consulates General are at the frontlines of public diplomacy activities. They are tasked to listen to the voices of foreign audiences, then recommend and implement appropriate programs to the government which are tailored to mirror the cultural sentiments and preferences of the posted country or region. Diplomats working at missions build network with politicians, business people, scholars and journalists and, through that network, they spread messages to the international community about Korea.

Through these efforts, the Korean Government ultimately wants to gain deep-rooted trust of people of the world. While the art of negotiation is one of the most important qualities of diplomats, I believe it is equally important to build trust among friends through diplomacy. Trust building would be the best policy measure any country needs to take for the long term benefit. President Park Geun-hye even termed the government's foreign policy in one word: Trustpolitik. Trust cannot be built by one side alone. 'It takes two to tango.' Korea has a similar proverb that "Applause can only made by two hands." As Korea is building up mutual trust with other countries, it will promote its place in the world and strengthen its ties with the world, thus better positioning itself to contribute to the noble cause of world peace, stability and prosperity.

Part 2

Identity-dimension of the Korean Wave

Chapter 3

(Re)Imagined Communities: Korean Diaspora, Identity, and Pop Culture

Ji-Yeon Jo

The history of diaspora traces back to millennia, to the emergence of the Jewish diaspora around A.D. 70,[1] but the word diaspora was not in common use and was absent from the social-science lexicon until the 1960s (Dufoix 2008). Since then, use of the term diaspora has expanded to encompass diverse groups of exiles, expatriates, ethnic minorities, refugees, sojourners, migrants, and overseas communities (Cunningham and Sinclair 2000; Tölölyan 1996). The more encompassing use of the term has generated scholarly debate and exploration around its meaning (Clifford 1997; Cohen 2008; Safran 1991), with some scholars going so far as to argue that the term diaspora may be "theoretically lifeless" (Dufoix 2008) or "'diaspora' [of] diaspora" (Brubaker 2005).

Despite the diversity or diffusion of diaspora's meaning, two major diasporic characteristics stand out: dispersion and connection. Diaspora fundamentally denotes a group of people who are dispersed from their "origin," whether it be national, religious, ethnic, cultural, or geographical, but who are at the same time socially, politically, or emotionally connected to that "origin," either by themselves or by others outside of their group. Esman's (2009) definition of diaspora usefully brings these two characteristics together: "Diaspora covers any transnational migrant community that maintains material or sentimental attachments to its country of origin, while adapting to the limitations and opportunities in its country of settlement" (ibid. 14). However, the ways in which and degrees to which a diaspora "maintains material or sentimental attachment to its country of origin" are shaped by specific geopolitical relationships be-

1 Dufoix (2008) notes that the destruction of the Second Temple in A.D. 70 is considered the start of the Jewish diaspora, but many Jews remained in Israel until the fourth century, when many Jews left Israel to escape persecution under Byzantine rule.

tween the home country and host country, as well as by the passing of time, as material and sentimental attachment to the homeland may diminish over time for long-term or later-generation diasporans. Furthermore, the advancement of technology, telecommunication, and transportation have changes the kinds, modes, and frequency of material connection, which together have created a "compression of time-space" between homeland and hostland (Harvey 1990). The changed ways in which we imagine and experience space and time restructure "geographical imagination" (Cunningham and Sinclair 2000) and inevitably influence how diaspora subjects perceive themselves and the communities where they belong.

This essay investigates the identities of diaspora Koreans, especially later-generation diaspora Koreans, which are mediated by the new mode of distribution and consumption of Korean popular culture. Benedict Anderson (1991) credited the invention and distribution of print technology and printed materials to the "imagination" of modern nation. Diasporans also develop "long-distance nationalism" through the process of imagination (Anderson 1992). It is therefore not farfetched to think that today's instantaneous and spontaneous flow of media and information around the world could open up possibilities for reimagining communities (Morley and Robins 1995). As Stuart Hall (1991) noted, identity is always in "production" and is "never complete, always in process, and always constituted within, not outside, representation." This essay sets out to highlight "processes" in which later-generation diaspora Koreans (re)construct their identities and (re)imagine their communities through their interaction with Korean popular culture.

More specifically, this essay investigates how Korean popular culture currently influences the ways in which later-generation diaspora Koreans form affective connections to their ethnic identity and to their ancestral homeland. Korean popular culture's rapid ascent to global standing, which has taken less than two decades, has spawned extensive academic study of its economic and cultural impact both in South Korea and worldwide. The overwhelming majority of these studies have explored the degree of its popularity around the world, its cultural influences, especially with regard to foreigners, or its economic value to South Korea. Analyses of Korean popular-culture media, such as film, drama, and songs, have been conducted as well (Jung 2009; Kim 2011; Kuwahara 2014; Lee and Nornes 2015). How Korean popular culture affects diaspora Koreans, however, has received little critical attention. The few, but important, scholarly investigations along these lines have focused largely on the Korean diaspora in Japan (Lie 2013; Chua and Iwabuchi 2008).

I intend to fill the void in studying Korean diaspora identities and Korean popular culture by highlighting how Korean popular culture influences the ways in which and the degrees to which diaspora Koreans think of themselves as ethnic Koreans. I also look at how it shapes their perceptions of South Korea itself (hereafter Korea). My investigation and discussion in this essay is enriched by ethnographic interviews from two research projects that I conducted between 2009 and 2014. Although I was not at that time specifically investigating the influence of popular culture, my interlocutors frequently referred to their experiences with Korean popular culture and how it shaped their affective connection to Korea and Koreans. In the first study, from 2009 to 2012, I explored the remigration experiences of diaspora Koreans from China, the Commonwealth of Independent States (CIS), and the United States. I interviewed 65 later-generation diaspora Koreans living in South Korea and over 30 secondary informants who were part of ethnic return migration communities in South Korea and China. The second study, in 2014, focused on second-generation Korean Americans, and involved in-depth, one-on-one interviews with 9 second-generation Korean Americans age between 18 and 29. I concentrate primarily on interview data from both studies to illuminate how Korean popular culture interacts with reshaping diaspora identities and the ways they reimagine communities that lie across diaspora and ancestral homeland.

Korean Diasporas and Their Homeland

The history of modern Korean diaspora traces back to the mid-nineteenth century when ethnic Koreans crossed borders to the Russian Far East and to the Chinese side of the Tumen River[2] to engage in seasonal farming or to settle. Ethnic Koreans migrated, at times forcibly, to other parts of East and Southeast Asia during the Japanese colonial era (1910–1945). After Korea was divided into two Koreas, North and South, in 1948, and after the Korean War (1950–1953), the migration trajectories of ethnic Koreans diverged: a limited number of North Koreans relocated to Second World countries, and South Koreans migrated en masse to the First World countries. According to the Overseas Koreans Foundation, the global Korean diaspora currently encompasses approximately 7 million people in 175 countries. The size of the diaspora Korean population is almost equivalent to 14 percent of the South Korean population or to 9.3 percent of the combined population of the two

2 The Tumen River lies in the northern border region of what is now North Korea.

Koreas. Even if one excludes Korean citizens who temporarily reside overseas and includes only diaspora Koreans with foreign citizenships, the diaspora Korean population remains substantial, at around 5.6 million.[3]

The three diaspora Korean communities presented in this essay exemplify the historically important diasporic trajectories of ethnic Koreans. Thus, the history of modern Korean diaspora is inexorably related to the modern history of Korea, which is intertwined with the history of modernization, Japanese colonialism, Second World War geopolitics, the division of Korea, the Korean War, Cold War geopolitics, and industrialization and democratization in South Korea.[4] This essay focuses on major Korean diasporas in three regions: China, the Commonwealth of Independent States (CIS, the former Soviet bloc), and the United States.

China hosts the largest number of diaspora Koreans, 2.7 million, the majority of whom are descendants of Koreans who migrated to Manchuria between 1885 and 1945.[5] After the liberation of Korea from Japanese colonial rule, in August 1945, 700,000 Koreans returned to the homeland, but many others remained in China due to political and economic instability in the Korean Peninsula. Those who stayed were granted rights equal to those of the dominant Han Chinese, with the establishment of the People's Republic of China, in 1949, and of Yanbian Korean Autonomous Prefecture, in 1952. The majority of Korean Chinese have congregated in the prefecture, which is located in the northeastern part of China. With Koreans forming the thirteenth largest ethnic minority group in China, Chinese ethnic policy has allowed Korean Chinese in Yanbian Autonomous Prefecture to receive primary and secondary education with Korean as the main instructional language while learning Chinese language as a subject of study in the formal curriculum. As a group, the Korean Chinese are high academic achievers and thus pride themselves as Usuminjok (superior ethnics). Korean Chinese can hold high government offices in the autonomous prefecture, but there is no strong evidence that they have been successfully integrated into mainstream Chinese society.

Koreans in Yanbian Prefecture mostly engaged in rice farming and enjoyed relative prosperity and stability until the late 1980s. However, the socioeconomic situation of the Korean Chinese began to deteriorate in post-reform

---

3 The number of Overseas Korean posted on the main page of the Overseas Korean Foundation website is 7,010,000 as of November 2, 2014, which shows some decrease from the 2011 data provided by the foundation (http://www.okf.or.kr/portal/OkfMainView.do)

4 For more detailed discussion of the history of Korean diaspora, see Jo In Press; Lee 2000; Yoon 2004, 2010.

5 Manchuria corresponds to Northeast China, specifically Heilongjiang, Jilin, and Liaoning Provinces.

China, in main part due to the unbalanced development of rural and urban areas. The economic plight of the Korean Chinese coincided with the increased international visibility South Korea experienced after the 1988 Seoul Olympics. As Korean Chinese learned about South Korea's economic prosperity, they quickly developed a transnational ethnic affinity with South Koreans (Song 2009). Prior to the mid-1980s, the Korean Chinese relationship with homeland was largely limited to North Korea; meaningful information exchange and communication between China and South Korea were not feasible under Cold War geopolitics.

Korean migration to Russia—more specifically, to the maritime regions of the Russian Far East—started around the 1860s, due to the dire circumstances they were facing in the Korean Peninsula: severe exploitation by the feudal Korean monarchy; abuse and exploitation at the hands of Korean landlords; and famine and poverty caused by multiple natural disasters that devastated the country during the last few decades of the nineteenth century (Pak 2010; Kim and King 2008).[6] Before and during the Japanese colonial era, Koreans crossed the Tumen River in ever larger numbers, with the total number of registered Koreans in the Russian border region increasing from 34,399 in 1906 to 106,000 in 1923 (Kimura 1987, 87).[7] These Korean Russian communities were tragically uprooted in 1937, when Stalin forcibly deported 36,442 Korean families (171,781 individuals) to Central Asian republics such as Kazakhstan and Uzbekistan; the harsh conditions of the deportation process and the extreme poverty and hardship of resettlement resulted in the deaths of many Korean Russians, especially children and the elderly.[8] Nevertheless, CIS Koreans eventually managed to succeed politically and economically as an ethnic group, especially during the Soviet era. Due to their extended diaspora history and lack of interaction with the homeland, however, the majority of CIS Koreans, especially those of the younger generations, have experienced a profound loss of Korean language and culture.

According to data released by the Korean Ministry of Foreign Affairs (2013), the majority of CIS Koreans live in three countries: 176,411 in Russia, 173,832 in Uzbekistan, and 105,483 in Kazakhstan.[9] On the whole, CIS

6 The Korean government strictly controlled its borders with China and Russia. Those who attempted illegal border-crossings risked confiscation of their property and even death (Pak 2010).

7 If illegal migrants had been included, the actual population number might have been up to 30 percent higher (Kim 2008).

8 Wada (1987, 51) reports that 180,000 Koreans were deported to Central Asia.

9 Data on each country is available at http://www.mofa.go.kr/ENG/countries/europe/index.jsp?menu=m_30_40_10. The original report, which contains more detailed information, is available only on the Korean version of the website http://www.mofa.go.kr/travel/overseascitizen/index.jsp?mofat=001&menu=m_10_40&sp=/webmodule/htsboard/template/read/korboardread.jsp%3Fty-

Koreans have been more detached from their homeland than Korean Chinese and Korean Americans have been, due not only to their geographical distance from the Korean Peninsula, but also to the Soviet Union's distanced political relationships with both North Korea and South Korea. Only after South Korea established diplomatic ties with the Soviet Union/Russia, in 1990, and with republics in Central Asia, in the early 1990s, were diaspora Koreans in the region able to learn about South Korea in a meaningful way.

Although the Korean American diaspora technically originated in 1903, when the first Koreans were brought in to augment the labor force and also to destabilize the Japanese workers union in Hawaii, the majority of today's Korean Americans migrated after 1965, when U.S. immigration policy formally opened the doors (Takaki 1998; Yu and Choe 2003). Like Korean Chinese and CIS Koreans, Korean Americans, as a subset of Asian Americans, have come to be considered a model minority due to their high academic achievement, but they have also been subjected to stereotypes that position them as "forever foreigners" in the United States (Tuan 1998). Korean Americans have been able to maintain closer ties to the homeland than have Korean Chinese or CIS Koreans. Korean Americans have been able to travel between the States and South Korea with relative ease and thus to better maintain transnational family relationships.

Compared to other diasporas, such as the Jewish, Armenian, and Chinese diasporas, the Korean diaspora has a relatively short history. However, its history still long enough to have a sizable population of later-generation diasporans born in diaspora. Diaspora Koreans in China, Japan, and the Commonwealth of Independent States are mostly second, third, or fourth generation. Second- and third-generation diaspora Koreans in the United States, Canada, Germany, and other Western countries are coming of age. Although a wealth of research attends to diasporic/migrant lives, only a small portion of the studies have investigated the lives and experiences of later-generation diasporans. Studies of later-generation Asian/Korean diasporans are even more scarce. Understanding later-generation diasporans is not only important for understanding the changing characteristics of the current diaspora phenomenon, but also necessary to understand intradiversity within each diaspora. Diasporas are integral part of contemporary societies in ever more diversifying and transnationalizing world.

According to existing studies,[10] later-generation diaspora Koreans face par-

peID=6%26boardid=232%26tableName=TYPE_DATABOARD%26seqno=347383).

10 These studies mostly focus on second-generation diasporans (Portes and Hao 1998; Portes and Rumbaut 2001; Rumbaut 2002). There is an even greater dearth of research on third- and later-gener-

ticular challenges, ones that are different from those faced by their parents and grandparents. The first challenge concerns issues and relationships around language, both mainstream and heritage. In most cases, later-generation diaspora Koreans are fluent in the mainstream languages of their countries of diaspora. However, few of them retain meaningful knowledge of the Korean language. For example, the heritage-language retention rate among later-generation diaspora Koreans in major Korean diasporas in the United States, Kazakhstan, and Uzbekistan is under 10 percent. The Korean Chinese are an exception, as the preservation and the practice of Korean have been institutionalized by ethnic minority policy, at least within China's Yanbian Korean Autonomous Prefecture. Scholars have estimated that higher than 80 percent of later-generation Korean Chinese have retained Korean-language proficiency, even though their degrees of proficiency may vary. Lack of balanced bilingualism among later-generation diaspora Koreans has multiple implications. Those who are fluent only in the mainstream language often experience intergenerational conflict, differences with the immigrant generation, and sense of loss surrounding their heritage and ethnic identity (Tse 1998; Tuan 1998). For the later generations who haven't managed to acquire an advanced/professional level of mainstream language proficiency, as in the case of Korean Chinese, social and occupational upward mobility is constrained, which thus delays their integration into mainstream society and places them in a socially and culturally ambivalent, and even precarious, status.

A second challenge faced by later-generation diasporans, one also related to language acquisition, is the issue of belonging. Scholars have noted that later-generation diasporans' status as native-born or as citizens of their states of residence does not guarantee belonging in mainstream culture and society. Diasporans must negotiate between their ethnic identity and national identity, home and host, and insider and outsider. Despite their legal or native-born status, later-generation diasporans are not immune from the kind of social discrimination exerted upon their parents' generation. Scholars have noticed among post-immigrant generations a weakening or diminishing of ethnic identity and of affective attachment to the ancestral/putative homeland.

How later-generation diaspora Koreans imagine and experience the ancestral/putative homeland presents the third major challenge. The native homeland of those born outside Korea is the land of diaspora. However, the presence of the ancestral homeland, whether North Korea, South Korea, or unified Korea, permeates their family and social lives. In contrast to their immigrant-genera-

ation diaspora generations.

tion parents or grandparents, and with the exception of those who have visited Korea, later-generation diaspora Koreans construct their impressions of the ancestral homeland mostly through the limited knowledge and experience available vicariously, through the media and through stories, merchandise, and cultural artifacts shared by family, friends, community.

The images of Korea held by later-generation diaspora Koreans have been variously informed by the milieux of their diaspora countries. Korean Chinese (Choseonjok), CIS Koreans (Koryo saram), and Korean Americans (Chemi Kyopo) have faced distinctive challenges and advantages according to their country of birth. In each country, Koreans occupy different positions relative to the ethnic, racial, cultural, social, political, and economic webs of power, and have thus formed unique diaspora subjectivities that inflect how they imagine Korea.

Korean Popular Culture and Diaspora Identities

Technological advances in telecommunications and in media production and distribution in the last two decades has changed the mediascape of Korean diasporans, making available to them new images and information about the ancestral homeland. Diasporic lives have in the past been characterized as geographic spaces that are distant from (ancestral) homeland or as spaces where they are positioned as ethnic minorities with limited political and social power. Spatial distance limited or delayed the information they received about their ancestral homeland. Thus, diasporans have historically constructed identities that are in between immigrants and natives, as well as in between their two (or multiple) homelands, which encompass the ancestral homeland, previous residence, and place of birth. With technology and globalized media flow, however, diaspora Koreans have become increasingly connected to Korea and issues of identity have become more complex and contested.

The "Korean wave," or hallyu, refers to the global popularity and influence of Korean popular culture, which has been disseminated primarily through the mass media. It encompasses Korean-identified television dramas, movies, Internet games, fashion, and popular music.[11] Hallyu first spread to Asian countries such as Japan, China, and Vietnam, then continued to move outward to the United States, Russia, Europe, Central Asia, and even the Middle East, where it has been enthusiastically consumed (Lie 2013). In this way, Korean

11 Hallyu (Korean Wave), *Korea Herald*, http://www.koreaherald.com/view.php?ud=20170814000686

popular culture has reached diaspora Koreans as well. The memories of home for later-generation diaspora Koreans, in this case mostly imagined and vicarious, are usually shaped by the stories their parents or grandparents tell, by community practices, and by representations of their ancestral homeland in the mainstream society in diaspora. Although diaspora Koreans may be reminded of their ethnic minority status in their everyday lives, their ethnic practices, such as using Korean language or following Korean customs, are often reserved for special occasions. However, the globalized flow of media and the emergence of the Internet have exposed later-generation diaspora Koreans to unprecedented amount of information and images from their ancestral homeland that are both contemporaneous and instantaneous.

According to Morley and Robins (1995, 91), "Film and television media play a powerful role in the construction of collective memories and identities." Individual and collective identities are constructed by difference, that is, by recognition of aspects that one does not possess. Diaspora Koreans are mostly invisible in the mainstream media of their hostlands. It is extremely hard to find diaspora Korean actors, singers, or performers in leading roles or as leading characters. When diasporans are made visible, the mainstream media tend to hypervisualize them (as "foreign" or "alien"), portraying male characters as villains and objectifying female characters as exotic, which can cause diaspora Koreans or other Asian diasporans to distance themselves from their ethnic heritage. In this context, images constructed in Korean popular culture may counterbalance the mainstream images constructed in their countries of diaspora.

In recent years, Korea has deliberately modeled itself as an economically competitive, technologically advanced, and culturally savvy nation—an updated national image that has likely influenced diaspora Korean identities. I therefore focus on Korean dramas (K-dramas), movies (K-movies), and music (K-pop) to investigate how Korean popular culture has shaped diaspora Koreans' images and imagined "memories" of Korea, their ancestral "home." To do so, I trace the paths of how Korean popular culture was introduced in each of the three diaspora regions and how it was received and consumed. I also incorporated my interlocutors' stories, their narratives of how they have encountered and engaged with Korean popular culture. Although Korean popular culture has gained global recognition, its distribution, reception, and consumption differ by diaspora regions, generations, and relations with South Korea.

Korean Chinese

The influence of Korean popular culture in China predates the rise of hallyu, which originated in the late 1990s and early 2000s. Until the early 1990s, Korean Chinese had little exposure to South Korean media; not only was access limited, but possession of such media was also illegal, as the two countries did not have a formal diplomatic relationship. Myeonghui, a second-generation Korean Chinese, recalls how she was able to consume Korean media during her youth.

I was in my teens in the 1980s and used to secretly listened to Korean radio dramas. The stories and the ways they spoke Korean language was very interesting to listen to. I was afraid of getting caught while listening to South Korean radio broadcasting, so I would hide under a thick blanket in my room and turn the sound of radio down while listening. It was very thrilling, but fun. I could have access to South Korean radio broadcasting because we lived well enough to afford a radio transmitter.

Due to ethnic minority policy in China, Korean Chinese in the Yanbian region were able to learn Korean via textbooks supplied by North Korea or produced by Korean educators in Yanbian. As a result, even later-generation Korean Chinese could maintain the ancestral language. The almost instantaneous reception of Korean media among later-generation Korean Chinese, including Myeonghui, is partly due to their language proficiency. At the same time, Yanbian's regional Korean dialect of Korean is primarily influenced by the North Korean dialect. Thus, as Myeonghui reflected, listening to South Korean accents can be "interesting" to Korean Chinese, exposing them to new ways of speaking and communicating in Korean.

During the mid-1980s, Korea popular culture reached the Korean Chinese via another route as well. Due to the humanitarian efforts of the Red Cross, families who been separated for more than forty years following the division of Korea (1948) and the Korean War (1950–1953) were finally able to reunite. The Korean Chinese who visited the homeland under this initiative brought back cassettes of Korean pop songs and other Korean merchandise, which sparked a market for Korean pop culture not only among Korean Chinese, but also among the general Chinese public. In this case, not just personal memories, but material artifacts from the homeland generated imaginings of and yearnings for the homeland.

In August 1988, even before the two countries normalized diplomatic relationships, two prominent Korean singers, Ju Hyun-mi and Cho Yong-phil, performed in China (Yanbian Tonshin 2006).[12] My interlocutors who were young adults in the 1980s recalled their encounters with enthusiasm for Korean popular culture and how they themselves actively consumed it. Yumin, a second-generation Korean Chinese in her forties, remembers an incident involving a popular Korean singer's concert in Yanji, the capital city of Yanbian Autonomous Prefecture. Yumin had enjoyed listening to the singer's music since high school and was eager to attend the show. However, though the concert was initially planned as a public event, it was restricted to a select few at the last minute, and Yumin was therefore unable to attend. Undeterred, she later managed to purchase a videotape of the concert. During my fieldwork, I coincidently met a woman who claimed that she had brokered the pop singer's concert in Yanji. Since the concert had not been approved by the Chinese government, it had been held at midnight to avoid the watchful eyes of Chinese Gongan (public-safety policemen). The woman also told me that she operated a trading company between South Korea and China, and had transported Korean cassette tapes to China (most likely illegally) starting in 1986, six years prior to the normalization of diplomatic relations between China and South Korea. Despite the risks of "traffickers" getting caught by officers of the law under the communist regime, Korean popular culture spread like wildfire among Korean Chinese.

The flow of Korean pop culture and goods inspired in the Korean Chinese a powerful "Korean dream." Myeonghui was among those who nurtured this dream. She was profoundly envious of homeland visitors who managed to visit their relatives in South Korea and to return with Korean media and merchandise. Eventually, she and her family had located her father's long-lost sister in South Korea, but Myeonghui still couldn't legally work in or migrate to South Korea, so she found an illegal route. Though she and her husband weren't poor in China (contrary to popular stereotypes about Korean Chinese illegal migrants), they had learned that South Korea's economic standing was far more advanced than China's, and they imagined they could make a better living in their ancestral homeland. Myeonghui's migration experience did not turn out as she expected, and I elaborate on it extensively elsewhere (Jo In Press), but what I want to emphasize here is her affective connection to South Korea and her desire to seek prosperity and modernity there, both of which were generated by her engagement with Korean media.

12 See the official websites of Cho, Yong-phil (http://www.choyongpil.com/hello/hs?story=timeline) and Ju, Hyun Mi (http://www.juhyunmi.com/bbs/board.php?bo_table=community_03&wr_id=114&page=17)

The popularity of South Korean popular culture has intensified in China over the last two decades, especially among younger-generation diasporans. Korean fashion, cosmetics, and cuisine have become hot commodities as well. As a growing number of Korean Chinese have migrated to South Korea—as marriage migrants, labor migrants, or study abroad students—the flow of popular culture and consumer products to China have increased correspondingly. Whereas Korean popular culture may generate feelings of nostalgia among older-generation diasporans, it represents for the younger generations a rare form of connection to the ancestral homeland. Unlike middle-aged or elder diaspora Koreans, who described hearing stories and songs of Korea from their parents and grandparents, later-generation diaspora Koreans—especially those in their twenties—frequently mentioned that they had not learned much about Korea or even about their family histories from their relatives, so Korean popular culture was often the only connection they could make with their putative homeland.

Lan, a third-generation Korean Chinese, grew up in southeastern China, where ethnic Korean schools were not available. She attended only Han Chinese schools and therefore had not learned the Korean language. Her father had strong ethnic pride and wanted her to study Korean as an extracurricular pursuit, but she refused. Then, when Lan reached high school, she found that her Han Chinese friends were enthusiastic about Korean popular culture, so she started to watch Korean dramas and listen to K-pop. Over time, she watched almost all available K-dramas with her friends. In college, Lan studied abroad in South Korea, where she continued to watch Korean dramas and entertainment television shows. Due to the influence of Korean pop culture, many of Lan's Han Chinese friends also wanted to attend college in Korea. Even Lan's middle-school friend who had migrated to the United States was preparing to study in Korea as an exchange student, inspired by her passion for Korean popular culture. For Lan, Korean popular culture strengthened her ethnic identity, which she had once tried to negate or distance herself from. The affirmation of Korean popular culture by her non-Korean friends and the shared experiences of consuming popular culture undeniably influenced Lan's sense of identity.

CIS Koreans

Korean popular culture reached CIS Koreans later than it reached Korean Chinese and Korean Americans, and resources for delineating its influence in the region are extremely limited. To illuminate the interaction of Korean popular culture and diaspora identities for CIS Koreans, I therefore rely on news articles and the stories of my interlocutors. From what I have been able to gather, CIS Koreans knew little about Korean popular culture in the 1990s, but after Korean popular culture gained worldwide popularity in the late 1990s and early 2000s, it quickly gained traction. According to Lie (2012), Korean Uzbekistanis (Koryoin) consume Korean popular culture through three major sources: Korean dramas broadcast by Uzbekistan's national broadcasting service; K-pop as taught in Korean-language classes and programs; and broadcasts by the Koryoin-managed media service. In a survey of 500 Koryoins, Lee determined that they have widely embraced Korean popular culture and that it has increased their desire to learn Korean. If they can afford to do so, they watch K-dramas via satellite dish, which offers Russian translations; otherwise, they must turn to Uzbekistan national television, though very few of them speak fluent Uzbek. Thus, sales of Korean DVDs and CDs are also increasing among Korean Uzbekistanis who are not fluent in Uzbek (Lie 2012; Park 2004).[13] The embrace of Korean popular culture and the diverse venues that enable cultural consumption in the country are puzzling phenomena, given that, since independence, Uzbekistan has implemented harsher ethnic policies than have other CIS republics.[14] Indeed, many of the Korean Uzbekistanis I interviewed described experiences of social, legal, and linguistic discrimination.

For CIS Koreans, increased exposure to Korean media provided more opportunity to learn about Korea. The newlyweds Mikhail and Sofia were third-generation Korean Uzbekistanis who had recently migrated to South Korea. When they were children, they did not know much about Korea, but they watched Korean dramas as adults, when those media became available in Uzbekistan. They did not know Korean, so they relied on subtitles at first. Eventually, they were able to watch without the subtitles. (They admitted that the storylines of Korean dramas are rather predictable.) They were enticed by the images of Korea and Koreans in the dramas and imagined their ancestral homeland as clean, rich, sophisticated, and cosmopolitan (Jo In Press). Like many later-generation diaspora Koreans whose vision of Korea is primarily informed by popular media, Mikhail and Sofia's images of homeland were constructed by the K-dramas they watched in Uzbekistan. "Korean dramas are the best," they said. "Korean dramas are the most famous and popular." Through popular media, they developed affective connections to South Korea

13 Unlike in Uzbekistan, Korean popular culture did not garner much attention in Kazakhstan even through the mid-2000s, but it gained popularity afterward (Park 2004).

14 The discrimination faced by Korean Uzbekistanis warrants further investigation.

and began to dream of visiting or moving there.

However, Mikhail and Sofia's affective connection did not arise just through consumption of Korean popular culture, but was also influenced by the social and political circumstances in Uzbekistan. During the interview, they both commented about the worsening interethnic relationships between Uzbeks and Korean Uzbekistanis and the increasingly discriminatory ethnic policies that prevented non-Uzbeks, regardless of their residential status, from having access to social mobility. For Mikhail and Sofia, and other Korean Uzbekistanis, the images of Korea(n) portrayed in K-dramas provided alternative ways of relating to their ethnicity and enabled them to form diaspora identities that positively embraced their Korean heritage.

My CIS Korean interlocutors also commented that the rising visibility of Korean popular culture led to the implementation of Korean-language programs at local primary schools and colleges, and sometimes motivated later-generation diasporans to learn Korean. Nina was born in Kazakhstan raised in Sakhalin by her father, a third-generation Koryo Saram, and her mother, who was not ethnic Korean. During her childhood, Nina spoke no Korean, nor was she particularly interested in Korea itself. However, she acquired an interest in both when she began watching Korean dramas, which portrayed Korea as a highly developed country. Nina's image of Korea as an advanced nation influenced her decision to study abroad there.

Korean Americans

Korean-pop-culture media have always been more available in the United States than in other diaspora regions. Even before the Internet was widely used, the majority of Korean Americans living in metropolitan areas consumed Korean popular culture through videotapes and DVDs. Though consumption of K-dramas and K-pop was originally a leisure practice primarily among first-generation diasporans, the emergence of hallyu expanded consumer demographics to include post-immigration (later-generation) diaspora Koreans and non-ethnic Koreans in the United States (Chung et. al 2013; Park 2004). K-dramas and K-pop have been popular there since the 1990s, but the first Korean-pop-culture celebrity to perform on major stages was the singer and actor Rain (Bi), who in 2006 held concerts in Madison Square Garden and in Las Vegas. One of the most globalized stars of the Korean wave, Rain also starred in the American movies Speed Racer and Ninja Assassin. Rain's U.S. success opened the gates to other Korean celebrities—Wonder Girls, Girls'

Generation, JYJ, Psy, and Big Bang, to name a few.

The young Korean American interlocutors in my studies almost unanimously stated that, during their childhood years, few in their communities had meaningful knowledge of Korea and that what they were taught about Korea in school was limited to a blurb about the Korean War. Then, as hallyu gained momentum and Korean electronics and automobiles gained U.S. market share, they noticed that their non-Korean peers increasingly embraced Korean culture, which led them to positively embrace their ethnic Korean identities. Some of these younger-generation Korean Americans took to regularly watching K-dramas and to listening to K-pop on a daily basis. One of them, Yumee, a second-generation Korean American in her early twenties, commented:

The whole [Korean] entertainment industries really got into a lot of different countries [....] people watching more Korean TV and watch[ing] more Korean dramas. People have come to know more about Korea, and in that sense, it is more important to more people to know about it.

Yumee refrained from watching K-dramas when school was in session because they tended to be addictive—it was impossible to stop in the middle of a series, she said, no matter how ridiculous or nonsensical the storylines. For the same reason, Grace, another second-generation Korean American in college, also abstained from watching K-dramas during academic semesters; even during periods when she was not actively consuming Korean pop culture, however, she retained an intense attachment to it (and to her heritage as a Korean American)—9 out of 10 if she were to assign a score.

Even Korean Americans who did not regularly watch K-dramas or listen to K-pop indicated that the increased popularity of Korean popular culture had led them to at least sample Korean media and to better appreciate Korean culture. Paul was in his late twenties when I interviewed him. He had been raised without much exposure to Korean culture and had therefore reached adulthood with only minimal proficiency in Korean and little appreciation for his Korean ethnic and cultural heritage. After he entered college, however, his perspective on Koreans and Korean Americans changed, as he met many smart people who were proficient in both Korean and English and embraced both cultural heritages. His esteem for Korean culture increased when he studied abroad in Latin America.

There were just random people that watched the stuff [Korean dramas], but they don't look like they are fans, necessarily. I had two different cashiers stop me, saying, "Are you Korean?" and I [was], like, yes, and then they were like, "Wow! Do you know this and this?," and I saw the cashiers were even, she was watching K-drama on her [computer] screen as she was working. I am more interested now knowing that there are so many people who are consuming this [Korean pop culture]. Obviously, if there are these random people consuming, there must be that it is quality production, production quality is rather high, so it may be worth watching. I don't feel that for a lot of Latin American shows, for example.

After multiple encounters with avid consumers of Korean popular culture, Paul watched the action and spy K-drama Iris on his own. When asked his opinion of the series, Paul said:

The only reason I chose it was because it was action and spy. It just appealed to me. I was just looking into Korean culture, but I don't want to do the traditional things or love stories, so this kind of fits, so I liked it.

Although my Korean Americans interlocutors appreciated the popularity of Korean popular culture, only two of them, Yumee and Grace, actually enjoyed watching K-dramas. Others found the stories too predictable and unrealistic, nor could they relate to the content. None of them mentioned feeling distanced by K-pop, but many experienced affective dissociation with regard to the dramas. Yet, for Korean Americans, this distance coexisted with positive affective connections to Korea and to the global standing of its popular culture.

Later-generation Korean Americans also utilized social media to encourage each other's consumption of Korean popular culture. Carey, a second-generation Korean American college student, did not typically watch K-dramas of her own accord, but she tried to watch the ones highly recommended by her friends' social-media posts. Other interlocutors who were not in the habit of consuming Korean popular culture also turned to social media when they wanted to choose a K-drama or K-movie to watch or K-pop to listen to. Another avenue for promoting awareness of Korean popular culture among later-generation Korean Americans has been the emergence of legitimate commercial websites that offer Korean selections. Until recently, Korean popular culture has been disseminated by copied videotapes or DVDs for sale at local grocery stores or by questionable websites that post K-dramas and K-movies without paying copyright fees and are therefore subject to being shut down without notice if discovered. However, lawful websites that offer Korean and other foreign entertainment, including Hulu, Drama Fever, and Netflix, have lent greater credibility Korean pop culture. Paul, who I introduced earlier, described his online viewing experience:

I was watching Iris. I watched some of that. I watched and then some of the websites were not completely legal, and then I don't know what happened to it. So I had to find another one. Those were easy to find. I am actually excited because, you know Hulu? They actually had an advertisement about how much Korean they have. There were advertisements specifically for K-Pop and K-drama fans. But I don't think it was for Koreans necessarily. It was just for anyone. So I went to Hulu website, and they had a big Korean section.

Like Paul, Steve felt that Korean popular culture was gaining social acceptance when a theater in his hometown started to release Korean movies simultaneous with their release in Korea, even if the films were open only for about a week at the local theater.

> S: I tried to go to a movie about Korean general, who defeated [the] Japanese. I tried to go watch the movie, because it was playing at Southpoint [Theater].
> J: Oh, Myeong-ryang?[15]
> S: Yeah, that's right. With my work schedule, I couldn't go. I wanted to, but . . . my parents went.
> J: What did they say?
> S: They say it was good.
> J: I think it was played here at the same time it played in Korea.
> S: That's what I mean. Korean pop culture and movies are slipping through here. They are playing one of the most popular movie theaters here. That's kind of what I am saying. When you see that, you see from that kind of perspective.

Korean popular culture existed before Korean Wave (hallyu). However, the global recognition it has achieved in the last twenty years has changed its symbolic value, and this has led later-generation Korean Americans to more thoroughly embrace their ethnic identity, compelling some of them to engage more with hallyu or even to learn the Korean language (Jo In Press; Park 2004). However, positive reception does not always guarantee consumption. Although both Paul and Steve also recognize the increased visibility of Korean popular culture and consumption venues and shared their desire to consume Korean popular culture, they did not become regular consumers. They felt that Korean dramas are rather predictable, with similar plots, so they seem repetitive. Since increased affective connections have manifested to lesser and greater extents, it cannot be argued that Korean popular culture has intrinsic affective value for

15 The movie's English title is The Admiral. It was directed by Kim, Han-min and released in 2014.

diaspora Koreans. Rather, it is the current global embrace of Korean popular culture that has inspired in diaspora Koreans a sense of personal relationship to their heritage culture and ancestral homeland, from which some of them had previously tried to distance themselves. Korean popular culture in this way confers a "distinction" that has redefined and reformulated the symbolic value of ethnic Korean identity (Bourdieu 1984).

Conclusion

The central focus of this essay has been to explore the ways later-generation diaspora Koreans (re)construct their ethnic identities and develop affective attachment to Korea(n) through their interaction with Korean popular culture. According to Cho (2005), the popularity of "Korean Wave" generated three types of discourse in South Korea. First, the cultural-nationalist perspective considers the rise of hallyu to be a "victory" of the national culture. Second, the neoliberal position views Korean popular culture as a lucrative venue for export, which resonates with the preceding era of "export-oriented" industrialization. Third, the postcolonialists warn of the cultural "shallowness" and lack of self-reflection they feel is embodied by Korean popular culture. They also suggest the importance of understanding the interworkings of secular capitalism in Asia while also paying attention to the complexity and multiplicity of cultural flows and to diverse patterns of consumption based on class, gender, and race (ibid. 166–167).

Similar to the discourses that have been generated around Korean Wave in South Korea, diverse discourses around Korean culture have emerged among the diaspora Koreans in my studies. First, despite hallyu's lack of "Korean" elements as argued by Lie (2012),[16] Korean popular culture generates images of and attachment to diaspora Koreans' home(land), allowing later-generation diaspora Koreans to imagine Korea as a place where they could belong. The perceived Koreanness of Korean popular culture inspires diaspora Koreans to identify with and positively embrace their ethnic heritage. Second, the kaleidoscopic, repetitive imagery characteristic of Korean popular culture projects modernity and cosmopolitanism.[17] Hallyu's imagery is somewhat fragmentary,

16 For an extensive discussion of what makes (or does not make) K-pop an expression of Korean popular culture, see John Lie's essay "What Is the K in K-pop?: South Korean Popular Music, the Culture Industry, and National Identity," Korea Observer 43, no. 3 (2012):339–63. Lie argues that Western popular culture and Japanese popular culture have influenced Korean culture extensively and that it is therefore hard to acknowledge that the "K" in K-pop or K-drama represents "Korean."

17 Among these images are highly synchronized and choreographed dances, enticing lyrics in songs,

fabricated, and fantastical, thereby creating an exotic, romanticized picture of Korea that does not reflect its reality. Nevertheless, those imageries generate longing to visit or learn about Korea, the desire to buy Korean consumer products such as fashion items and cosmetics, and to study abroad in Korea. Third, my interlocutors' stories suggest that Korean wave's influence among non-Koreans worldwide and South Korea's growing economic strength have endowed Korean culture with global symbolic value. The newly recognized value and images of Korea(n) provide alternative or counter-images to traditional depictions of diaspora Koreans created by the mainstream societies in their countries of diaspora. This symbolic value encourages diaspora Koreans to cultivate their transnational identity by consuming Korean popular culture, though the actual degree of consumption may not match the degree of their desire.

Although there are many similarities across diasporas in how later-generation diaspora Koreans' receive and consume Korean popular culture, there also are differences that reflect diasporic specificities. The Korean language proficiency of the Korean Chinese enabled them to readily consume Korean popular culture even before the Korean Wave. Furthermore, the Cold War geopolitics that had obstructed information and media exchange between China and South Korea for over four decades propelled their curiosity and enthusiasm for Korean pop culture, to the degree that many risked crossing legal and illegal boundaries during the 1980s.

Korean popular culture was introduced to the CIS regions later than to China or the United States, but it was received with enthusiasm there as well. However, CIS Koreans primarily embraced K-dramas, while other diaspora Koreans consumed all forms of Korean popular culture, including but not limited to K-dramas, K-pop, and K-cinema. Korean popular culture offered a vision of modernity and cultural "comfort" to CIS Koreans, who had been politically and culturally alienated by the discriminatory ethnic policies that emerged after the republics of Central Asia declared independence from the Soviet Union. Among the three major Korean diasporas, CIS Koreans are considered the most assimilated (i.e., Sovietized), and they have the least flexibility in terms of visiting South Korea, due to geographical distance, the high cost of travel, and a stricter visa process than for diasporans in Western countries. Thus, Korean popular culture offers them one of the few opportunities they might have to see and experience, at least virtually, their ancestral homeland,

romanticized storylines in dramas, wealth and cosmopolitan lifestyles in entertainment, beautiful and handsome but somewhat similar faces created by plastic surgeries, and magnificent female or male bodies sculpted by hours of exercise and extensive dieting.

even though, of course, it is not the same homeland their ancestors left.

Korean Americans consume diverse forms of Korean popular culture through diverse venues. Although Korean popular culture has helped Korean Americans to positively embrace their ethnic identity and has increased their sense of pride and value as ethnic Koreans, Korean Americans are especially critical of hallyu's content, regarding it as predictable, too romanticized, and too (culturally) different. Nevertheless, Korean popular culture still serves as a primary vehicle among Korean Americans for learning the Korean language and maintaining family bonds.

The cultural flow of the Korean wave and its popularity, as I have delineated it, continuously influence Koreans in the diasporas, reshaping how they imagine Korea and how they relate to their ethnic Korean identity. At least among my interlocutors, Korean popular culture and its global presence are undeniable magnetizing factors for the growing interest later-generation diaspora Koreans have in Korea. The findings also suggest that compressed spatiality and temporality influence the affectivity of diaspora Koreans. Thus, new forms of media consumption and interaction propels later-generation diaspora Koreans to reimagine communities and reconstruct identities that are more inclusive of their ethnic heritage.

The ways in which each diaspora receives and appropriates Korean popular culture is further inflected by its own diasporic specificities. Despite the growing global popularity of Korean popular culture, it has yet to be incorporated into mainstream media production and consumption in diaspora. For example, Korean Americans consume Korean pop culture primarily through the Internet, since major broadcasting companies and radio stations in the United States rarely air Korean movies or pop songs, while the presence of British or other European pop culture, artists, and entertainers is not uncommon in the mainstream American media.[18] In contrast, Korean dramas and other pop-culture material appear on national TV in Central Asia, the Middle East, and China. How these differences in venue, whether via mainstream media outlets or Internet sites, influence diaspora Koreans' reception of Korean popular culture would be an interesting topic for future investigation.

Although existing studies of later-generation diasporans point to diminishing ethnic identity and increasing loss of heritage language and culture, this

18 Prime examples are British acts such as the Beatles, Led Zeppelin, and Elton John, as well as British movies such as the James Bond and Harry Potter series. Many British actors and actresses are also familiar to American viewers. In contrast, Korean popular singers or movies are rarely seen in the American media, no matter how popular they are globally. One recent exception is Psy, whose song "Gangnam Style" went viral on YouTube in 2012 and who appeared on popular American talk shows such as *Ellen* and NBC's *TODAY*.

study suggests that transnational media consumption of popular culture, in this case Korean popular culture, can reverse these trends and revive diasporans' affective connections to their ancestral homeland. Furthermore, in order to make sense of contemporary diaspora Koreans, it is essential to understand the influence of the transnational flow of media, as well as how those media are consumed and appropriated by popular culture. Diaspora identities are complex and contested, and are constantly in the process of forming and transforming. However, these identities are transforming within their given milieu and in interaction with other social and political agents. Thus, the contexts of identity transformation must be taken into account in order to fully understand the complex and contradictory nature of diaspora identities.

Popular descriptors for diaspora identities include multiplicity, hybridity, and heterogeneity (Bhabha 1994; Lowe 1996). Although later-generation diaspora Koreans' identities are characterized by hybridity, such that they are positioned in-between the native and the immigrant, and belong to both homeland and hostland even before they encounter and consume Korean popular culture, this study suggests that Korean popular culture has introduced yet more complexity into their hybrid identities.

References

[Articles and Book Chapters]

Anderson, Benedict. 1991. Imagined Communities. London, UK: Verso.
Anderson, Benedict. 1992. Long-Distance Nationalism: World Capitalism and the Rise of Identity Politics. Amsterdam: Center for Asian Studies Amsterdam.
Bhabha, Homi. K. 1994. The Location of Culture. New York, NY: Routledge.
Bourdieu, Pierre. 1984. Distinction: A Social Critique of the Judgement of Taste. Cambridge, MA: Harvard University Press.
Brubaker, Rogers. 2005. "The 'Diaspora' Diaspora." Ethnic and Racial Studies 28, no. 1: 1-19.
Cho, Hae-Joang. 2005. "Reading the "Korean Wave" as a Sign of Global Shift." Korea Journal 45, no. 4: 147-182.
Chung, Jason., Darryl Choy., and Grace Yoo. 2013. "The Growing Popularity of Korean Soap Operas among Asian Americans." In Koreans in America: History, Identity, and Community, edited by Grade J. Yoo, 233-245. San Diego, CA: Cognella.

Chua, Beng Huat and Koichi Iwabuchi (Eds.). 2008. East Asian Pop Culture: Analyzing the Korean Wave. Hong Kong: Hong Kong University Press.
Clifford, James. 1997. Routes: Travel and Translation in the Late Twentieth Century. Cambridge, MA: Harvard University Press.
Cohen, Robin. 2008. Global Diasporas: An Introduction. New York, NY: Routledge.
Cunningham, Stuart., and John Sinclair (Eds.).2000. Floating Lives: The Media and Asian Diasporas. Queensland, Australia: University of Queensland Press.
Dufoix, Stephane. 2008. Diasporas. Berkeley, CA: University of California Press.
Esman, Milton J. 2009. Diasporas in the Contemporary World. Malden, MA: Polity Press.
Hall, Stuart. 1991. "Old and New Identities, Old and New Ethnicities." In Culture, Globalization and the World-System: Contemporary Conditions for the Representation of Identity, edited by Anthony D. King, 41-68. London: Macmillan Education Ltd.
Harvey, David. 1990. The Condition of Postmodernity. Malden, MA: Blackwell Publishers.
Jo, Ji-Yeon O. In Press. "Homing Diaspora Koreans: Transborder Belongings and the (Re)Making of Korean Peoplehood." Honolulu, HI: University of Hawai'i Press.
Jung, E.Y. 2009. Transnational Korea: A critical assessment of the Korean Wave in Asia and the United States. Southeast Review of Asian Studies, 31: 69–80.
Kim, German. N. 2008. "The Deportation of 1937 as a Logical Continuation of Tsarist and Soviet Nationality Policy in the Russian Far East." In Korean Diaspora: Central Asia, Northeast Asia and North America, edited by Hesung Chun Koh, 19-44. New Haven: East Rock Institute.
Kim, German. N., and Ross King. 2008. "Introduction." In Korean Diaspora: Central Asia, Northeast Asia and North America, edited by Hesung Chun Koh, 1-18. New Haven: East Rock Institute.
Kim, Youna. 2011. Transnational Migration, Media and identity of Asian Women: Diasporic Daughters. Abingdon, Oxon: Routledge.
Kimura, Hidesuke. 1987. "Korean Minorities in Soviet Central Asia and Kazakhstan," In Koreans in the Soviet Union, edited by Dae-Sook Suh, 85-100. Honolulu: Center for Korean Studies, University of Hawaii.
Kuwahara, Yasue (Ed.). 2014. The Korean Wave: Korean Popular Culture in Global Context. New York, NY: Palgrave Macmillan.
Lee, Kwang-gyu. 2000. Overseas Koreans (Korean Studies Series No. 19), Jimmondang Publishing Company.
Lee, Sangjoon and Nornes, Abé Mark (Eds.). 2015. Hallyu 2.0: The Korean Wave in the Age of Social Media. Ann Arbor, MI: University of Michigan Press.
Lie, John. 2012. "What is the K in K-pop? South Korean Popular Music, the Culture Industry, and National Identity." Korea Observer 43, no. 3:339-363.
Lie, John. 2013. Introduction to "The Globalization of K-pop." Cross-Currents, 9:40-43. Accessed March 17, 2016. https://cross-currents.berkeley.edu/e-journal/issue-9/introduction-k-pop
Lowe, Lisa. 1996. Immigrant Acts: On Asian American Cultural Politics. Durham: Duke University Press.
Morley, David., and Kevin Robins. 1995. Spaces of Identity: Global Media, Electronic

Landscapes and Cultural Boundaries. New York, NY: Routledge.
Pak, Boris, D. 2010. Russia and Korea. Translated by Kyung-Hyun Min. Northeast Asian History Foundation.
Park, Jung-Sun. 2004. "Korean American Youth and Transnational Flows of Popular Culture across the Pacific." Amerasia Journal 30, 1:147-169.
Portes, Alejandro, and Lingxin Hao. 1998. "E pluribus unum: Bilingualism and Loss ofbLanguage in the Second Generation." Sociology of Education, 71: 269–294.
Portes, Alejandro., and Rubén G. Rumbaut. 2001. Legacies: The Story of the Immigrant Second Generation. Berkeley and Los Angeles, CA: University of California Press.
Rumbaut, Rubén G. 2002. "Severed or Sustained Attachments? Language, Identity, and Imagined Communities in the Post-Immigrant Generation." In The Changing Face of Home: The Transnational Lives of the Second Generation, edited by Peggy Levitt and Mary C. Waters, 43-95. New York: Russell Sage Foundation.
Safran, William. 1991. "Diaspora in Modern Societies: Myths of Homeland and Return." Diaspora 1, no. 1:83-99.
Song, Changzoo. 2009. "Brothers Only in Name: The Alienation and Identity Transformation of Korean Chinese Return Migrants in South Korea." In Diasporic Homecomings: Ethnic Return Migration in Comparative Perspective, edited by Takeyuki Tsuda, 281-304. Stanford, CA: Stanford University Press.
Takaki, Ronald. T. 1998. Strangers from a Different Shore (2nd ed.). Boston, MA: Back Bay Books.
Tölölyan, Khachig. 1996. "Rethinking Diaspora: Stateless Power in the Transnational Moment." Diaspora: A Journal of Transnational Studies 5, no. 1:3-36.
Tse, Lucy. 1998. Ethnic Identity Formation and its Implication for Heritage Language Development. In Heritage Language Development, edited by Stephen D. Krashen, Lucy Tse, and Jeff McQuillan, 15–29. Culver City, CA: Language Education Associates.
Tuan, M. 1998. Forever Foreigners or Honorary Whites?: The Asian Ethnic Experience Today. New Brunswick, N.J: Rutgers University Press.
Wada, Haruki. 1987. "Koreans in the Soviet Far East, 1917-1937." In Koreans in the Soviet Union, edited by Dae-Sook Suh, 24–59. Honolulu: Center for Korean Studies, University of Hawaii.
Yoon, In-Jin. 2004. Korean Diaspora. Seoul, Korea: Korea University Press.
Yoon, In-Jin. 2010. "Migration and the Korean Diaspora: A Comparative Description of Five Cases." Journal of Ethnic and Migration Studies 38(3):413-435.
Yu, E., and Choe, P. 2003. Korean Population in the United States as Reflected in the Year 2000 U.S. Census. Amerasia Journal, 29(3): 2-21.

[News Articles]

Lee, Myeong-sook. 2012. "The Influence of Korean Media in the Lives of Koryoin." KOFICE News, July 27, 2012. Accessed March 27, 2016. http://m.kofice.or.kr/c30_correspondent/c30_correspondent_02_view.asp?seq=1211&page=9&search2=%EC%9A%B0%EC%A6%88%EB%B2%A0%ED%82%A4%EC%8A%

A4%ED%83%84
Park, Tatiana. 2004. "Hallyu Fever? Koryoins do not know it well." dongA.com News, September 3, 2004. Accessed March 27, 2016. http://news.donga.com/3/all/20040903/8102904/1#Lowe 1996) ; The Location of Culture. hybrid identity. ded ven before they encoutered plicity and hybridity. Although later-ge
Yanbian Tonshin, 2006. "Biography of South Korea's Top Trot Singer, Ju Hyun-mi." Yanbian Tonshin Blog, September 9, 2006. http://yanbianforum.com/board.html?include=&mode=view&id=24422&lc=1000000&sc=&mc=&gid=nb&

[Web documents]

Cho, Yong-phil Official Website, Timeline, http://www.choyongpil.com/hello/hs?story=timeline.
Ministry of Foreign Affairs, South Korea:
http://www.mofa.go.kr/travel/overseascitizen/index.jsp?mofat=001.

Chapter 4

Drama Consumption in Transnational South Korea: Korean American Women and Intraethnic Othering[1]

Adrienne Lo, Megan Rim, Lee Jin Choi, and Nancy Abelmann

Introduction

In her 2013 inaugural speech, President Park Geun-Hye presented the idea of a "cultural renaissance" in which South Korea would serve as a model for others around the globe:

> 인종과 언어, 이념과 관습을 넘어 세계가 하나되는 문화,
> 인류평화발전에 기여하고 기쁨을 나누는 문화,
> 새 시대의 삶을 바꾸는 '문화융성'의 시대를
> 국민 여러분과 함께 열어가겠습니다.

> Together with the Korean people we will foster a new cultural renaissance or a culture that transcends ethnicity and languages, overcomes ideologies and customs, contributes to the peaceful development of humanity, and is connected by the ability to share happiness (Park, 2013).

This vision of a glorious future in which "culture" serves as a unifying factor, enabling the suturing of ethnic and linguistic divisions, is often heralded as one of the chief accomplishments of hallyu, or "the Korean wave"—the export of Korean popular culture to places outside of South Korea (Ryoo, 2009; Shim 2006). In this utopic vision, which circulates in stories in the lifestyle and business sections of prominent South Korean newspapers, it is

1 This paper was presented at the Korean Wave beyond Nationality: Conflicts over the Globalization of Korean Popular Culture Conference, Notre Dame, IN. We thank Yeonhee Yoon for her kind invitation to the conference and for her patience during the long genesis of this paper. We also thank Michele Koven, Agnes Sohn, and Erica Vogel for their helpful comments on earlier versions.

the consumption of Korean pop music, television, and movies that unites fans from across the world and that also helps stimulate demand for other kinds of Korean products (Ha 2016; J. Lee 2016; W. Lee 2016).

It is not clear, however, how consumers of South Korean popular culture actually take up this media. While research on first generation migrants has illuminated the ways in which such media can open up a space for the constitution of "diasporic nationalism," a "partial yet unending connection with home" (Kim 2011, 108), research on the second generation has been less conclusive. Some have argued that the consumption of such media can link generations across the diaspora. Jung Sun Park, for example, examined how 1.5 and second generation Korean Americans in Los Angeles and Chicago in the early 2000s who consumed Korean dramas "develo[ped] better intergenerational understanding and relations" with parents and grandparents while also "generating new senses of connections…bring[ing] South Korea and its culture closer to the (im)migrant youths, laying the foundation for a sense of community" (Park 2004a, 157). Drama consumption, as Park elegantly demonstrated, can become an experience of commonality among migrants from different backgrounds who find themselves racialized in the US context as "Asian" (Park 2004b).

Other researchers, however, note that some second generation consumers can find the consumption of diasporic media an experience that sharpens their sense of distance from co-ethnics. David Oh's (2015) finely grained research found that consumption of South Korean films served as both "social adhesive" and "social boundary" for second generation Korean American teens from Atlanta and Dallas in the mid-2000s. For some teens, watching films sharpened divisions along intraethnic, interethnic, and gender lines–between "FOBs (Fresh-Off-the-Boats)", "Koreans" and "Twinkies"; Korean Americans vs. White Americans; and boys vs. girls. Similarly, Sun Jung's (2013, 113-115) research has analyzed how Asian Americans on allkpop.com participate in both "Othering" and "identifying with" K pop stars, indicating both their disapproval of K pop stars' "Americanization" while criticizing their accented English. Indeed, while the South Korean press often portrays the consumption of Korean music and television as a stepping stone to the love of all things Korean–language, food, consumer goods, et al—American consumers of foreign media sometimes associated only aspects that they did not approve of with "Japan" or "Korea" (Lukacs 2010; Oh 2015). While love might be one of the emotions generated, the research on second generation consumers of diasporic media testifies to a more ambivalent range of affects—derision, estrangement, and envy, among others.

In this paper, we contribute to this discussion with an examination of how second generation Korean American women understood dramas as a glimpse into the lives of fabulously wealthy South Koreans—lives that felt very distant from their own. An important body of research has examined how second generation Asian Americans position themselves as superior to immigrant peers through disparaging the figure of the "FOB" ('fresh off the boat') " (Chun 2009a, b; Reyes 2007). In locating themselves as cooler, better looking, and socially superior to the figure of the awkward, ill-dressed, and linguistically maladroit fob, second generation youth participate in what Pyke and Dang (2003) have called "intraethnic othering," or the displacement of the stigma of White racism against Asian Americans upon a co-ethnic peer, a process which can involve multiple layers of refraction, othering, and distancing at different scales in transnational encounters (Abelmann 2009, 2012; Park 2009a).

In our data, 2nd generation Korean American women expressed both derision and a keen sense of envy towards lives of South Korean privilege, similar to the ways that South Koreans looked upon Korean Americans in the early 2000s (Kim 2008). Our interviewees, who were undergraduate students at the University of Illinois at Urbana-Champaign, marveled at the lives of leisure and consumption that they saw on screen, which they also associated with South Korean undergraduate peers at the University of Illinois at Urbana-Champaign. As they wondered at this persona's apparent effortless cosmopolitan privilege, Korean American women narrated themselves in the idiom of constraint–hemmed in by the racializing and essentializing gaze of others, including South Koreans who imagined them to have a natural connection to South Korea; White Americans who saw them as uncool geeks; and Korean Americans who replicated White racism on a lower scale in their disdain for drama fans. The landscapes that they populated with figures in audiorecorded interviews illustrate how the consumption of South Korean popular media does not necessarily bind consumers together into a global fan community, but instead can serve to sharpen cleavages between subjects with different experiences of class, race, and gender within transnational South Korea.

Figures and Scales

We ground our understanding of the complexities of intraethnic othering in research on scale (Carr and Lempert 2016). Intraethnic othering, as Pyke and Dang (2003) note, involves the projection of interracial dynamics (e.g. between White Americans and Asian Americans) within intraethnic ones (e.g. between different kinds of Asian Americans). As such, it can be understood as a form of fractal recursivity, or "the projection of an opposition, salient at some level of relationship onto some other level (Irvine and Gal 2000, 38). Gal (2016) explains the ways that this process can be fluid and involve multiple layers of nesting; speakers can switch perspectives and rescale the same opposition multiple times over the course of a single speech event, as they locate figures in relation to one pole of the opposition, and then in relation to the opposite pole. Bringing this framework to bear on the dynamics of transnational South Korea can elucidate how the understanding of oppositions between different kinds of figures is always perspectival, not inherent in participants themselves, but rather a situated view from a specific vantage point (Gal 2016). The fact that participants invert hierarchies, and oscillate between admiration vs. disdain or distance vs. closeness is therefore an expected outcome of the process of fractal recursivity. .

Our analysis also draws upon the notion of "figures" (Agha 2005; Goffman 1974; Irvine 1996). Figures, sometimes referred to as "models of personhood," are "semiotic objectifications that emerge and circulate in discourse" (Wirtz 2014, 15). As Reyes (2016, 312) notes, figures are not the same as "real people", but are instead "ideas about people": "recognizable social personae that circulate among some set of individuals." As interactants invoke figures, they locate themselves and others in envelopes of space-time, crafting transnational selves through layered invocations of multiple worlds (Park 2017). These space-time configurations reach across scales, from the interactional dynamics of an interview, in which one Korean American demonstrates wariness of being judged by her interviewer as an uncool drama fan; to interracial dynamics in the US where White Americans position Asian Americans as uncool; to contrasts between contemporary migration by wealthy South Koreans and earlier waves of migration out of the country. An analysis of the ways that interviewees invoke figures and take stances towards them, pointing to multiple time-space configurations, can reveal how the everyday experiences of transnationalism get produced.

Participants

Our analysis is based on interviews conducted in 2008 at the University of Illinois at Urbana-Champaign, an institution with one of the largest populations of undergraduate international students in the US. International students made up 9% of the undergraduate body, with China, Korea, and India as the three largest sending countries. Students with South Korean citizenship comprised between 2-3% of the total undergraduate population (31,174) and approximately 6% of the graduate populations (10,750), respectively. Asian Americans, in turn, were 13% of the undergraduate population, making Urbana-Champaign (population 118,000) a town with a vibrant Korean community, with Korean churches, markets, hairdressers, karaoke, and 7 Korean restaurants–sites where South Koreans of various migration histories encountered one another. The diasporic South Korean community was itself quite diverse. For many graduate students and visiting scholars, the University of Illinois was their first experience with living in the US. Undergraduates from South Korea, on the other hand, were typically migrants who were well acquainted with American life, having spent several years in high school, and sometimes longer, studying in the US prior to setting foot on campus. The majority of the local businesses which catered to this community were run by local Korean American residents, most of whom emigrated as adults and raised families in the US.

While we recognize that categories of migration are not always neatly dichotomized[2], the South Korean undergraduates generally had South Korean citizenship and families in South Korea, and were expecting to return there after graduation. They had spent their childhoods in South Korea, and usually had several years of pre-college experience living in the US or another English-speaking country (Lo et al., 2015). They were from families that were privileged–able to afford out of state tuition and fees ($26,500/year in 2008), following the expenses of years of pre-college study abroad. For the most part, South Korean undergraduates did not hold down jobs while on campus, or in the summers. They were thus distinct from South Korean graduate students, who usually worked as research assistants and teaching assistants; and from Korean American undergraduates, many of whom worked while attending college and were eligible for scholarships, grants, and student loans to finance their education.[3] Among these three sets of students, undergraduate South Korean students were the most privileged. Admittance to the University of Illinois was for many South Korean undergraduates a sign of success, the culmination of years of hard work.

The Korean Americans were American citizens who had grown up in Illinois with immigrant parents. Most had traveled on a regular basis to South Korea to visit family as they were growing up, and several had spent longer stays during summers while in high school or college. Like the rest of the undergraduate student body, many were from the suburbs of Chicago. For

2 See Abelmann (2012) for a nuanced portrait of the blurry lines between "Korean Koreans" and "Korean Americans."

3 In-state undergraduates paid a tuition rate of $12,100 in 2008

them, attending the University of Illinois was usually not the realization of a long-held dream, but instead the state school that they settled for when their families were not able to afford tuition at a better (and more expensive) private university (Abelmann 2009). They came from a range of class backgrounds, with majors that included accounting, biology, and comparative literature, and were planning to live and work in the US.

Interviews were conducted and audio recorded by Megan, a Korean American undergraduate from Illinois and consumer of Korean dramas at the time of the study. Participants were recruited through announcements at a church with a substantial population of Korean Americans, visits to a Korean American student organization, and personal networks. As active participants in Korean American student networks, interviewees treated the interviewer as someone who was familiar with these settings, but also as someone they were perhaps wary of–a Korean American who might judge them as uncool for watching dramas. Megan told participants that she was doing a class project on Korean Americans and did not identify herself as a drama fan at the start of the interview.

"It was like my weekly Korean lesson just watching that show": Navigating Multilingualism

All of our participants reported that they preferred to watch Korean media with English subtitles. Although they could, for the most part, speak and understand everyday Korean, their comprehension of dramas was impacted by what Sharon called "the language problem—it's hard for me to keep track of everything through just subtitles." Referring to their viewing of Korean media as "my weekly Korean lesson," our interviewees recounted stories about being teased about their proficiency by other Korean speakers, like Hannah, who told us that her dad joked, "You speak like a 7th grader and you write like a 5th grader." Indeed, for most of our interviewees, navigating a Korean website was difficult.

Korean Americans' access to dramas was therefore brokered through English. Although nowadays Google Translate can provide on the spot translation of foreign language websites, and streaming sites like Dramafever, Netflix, YouTube, or Hulu carry an extensive selection of subtitled Korean movies and dramas, in 2008 such services were still in their infancy. Our subjects watched dramas back home with their families by renting sets of subtitled DVDs from Korean video stores or on the local Korean cable channel; on campus they watched on their own computers. While some went directly to the Korean language homepages of Korean television channels, most of them instead accessed this media through English language blogs and websites like Soompi (www.soompi.com), Dramabeans (www.dramabeans.com), MySoju (www.mysoju.com) or the now defunct Noonchi (www.noonchi.com).

"We're not really into that": Racialization and Ambivalent Fandom

The women we spoke to had a complicated relationship with their status as fans. They were by all accounts avid consumers–waking up in the middle of the night to watch dramas as they aired in South Korea, buying large hard drives to store collections of video files, and sometimes being so keen to watch new episodes when they were released that they would try to use Chinese subtitles if English ones were not yet available.

Being a fan in those days required an investment in both hardware and technical knowledge. Accessing Korean dramas was technically quite challenging since Korean media companies made active attempts to deter piracy, and would regularly take down video files that had been posted online. Fans usually started with the brokering sites, where they could find links in the discussion boards to pirated episodes that Korean fans had uploaded onto other sites like Bittorrent, Crunchyroll, Veoh, MySoju and Clubbox. After downloading video files, fans had to go to other websites to download fansubs. Fansubs were produced in those days by teams of volunteers in communities like ViKi, WithS2, and Haru2subs (Jung 2013). Linking the subtitles with the pirated video file was not always easy—it required knowing which video codecs to run, which video player would work with which kind of file, how to convert files from one format to another, and how to sync the two files together. Most of our participants had bought large external hard drives to store these files, and had a substantial body of technical knowledge.

Some of our interviewees were, however, quite reluctant to disclose either the extent of their technical knowledge, the amount of time that they spent consuming Korean media, or their admiration for the genre. Interviews often began with a generic question along the lines of "So do you have an interest in Korean media?" Rachel was one participant who responded enthusiastically: "Yeah, I do, I REALLY like watching Korean dramas, even though I really suck at Korean." However, when we asked other participants this same question, they would claim that they only watched "sometimes" or "very sporadic." Jessica, for example, told us that her Korean American high school friends "kind of watch it, but not really. We're not really into that." She described her drama watching as "random…not regular," and told us she would "kind of" watch Korean movies with her boyfriend. She, like many of our interviewees, pointed to other people who were "really into drama" and she distanced herself from these figures—describing them as "acquaintances," not as "friends." When we probed further, however, it became apparent that Jessica in fact had quite an encyclopedic knowledge of both Korean dramas and contemporary Korean romantic comedies. We did not find the same kinds of distancing when our interviewees spoke about their consumption of American television shows, like Gossip Girl, The OC, or The Hills.

We understand this narrative minimization not as a description of actual drama viewing habits, but as a form of othering (Abelmann 2009; 2012, Chun 2009a, b; Park 2009a; Pyke and Dang 2003; Reyes 2007), in which second generation Asian Americans attempt to displace the stigma associated with the figure of the "drama fan." In one guise, this person was imagined as an uncool first generation immigrant peer. By pointing to some other figure--a 1st generation Taiwanese, Singaporean, Filipino, Chinese, or Indonesian student--who was, unlike them, really into drama, Korean American women attempted to preserve their own mantel of American coolness in front of a cool Korean American interviewer. In our data, this distancing happened both at the epistemic level ("I'm not really that knowledgeable" "I don't know what the important stuff is") and also in the ways fans affectively played down their engagement ("I'm not really into that"). Similarly, participants' attempts to downplay their technical expertise can be read as an effort to mark their distance from the figure of the Asian American geek, someone who is into computers and technology but is desperately uncool (and is often gendered as a sexually undesirable male) (Paek and Shah 2003). In laminating racialized stigma onto some other figure at the same time that they firmly positioned such figures as others, Korean American drama fans revealed how their consumption of Korean dramas was mediated by their racial positioning in the US.

In another guise, the "drama fan" was imagined as some other kind of Korean American who was swept up into the racializing gaze of South Koreans upon the diaspora. As interviewees located themselves and the interviewer as distant from this figure, they expressed their resentment about the presupposition that they would somehow be commensurable with, and share linguistic and cultural practices with, South Korean youth. As Sharon, a sophomore who also participated in cosplay and watched Japanese anime, put it, "I feel pressure to see [Korean media]….. 'You're Korean, right? Like you should have seen this movie.' It's my responsibility to be like all knowledgeable about the media, right?" Refusing to consume South Korean cultural products was thus positioned by these interviewees as an act of contestation against the essentializing gaze of Korean diasporic homogeneity.

For example, several of our interviewees narrated themselves as agentive consumers who refused to "go with the flow", as in this example from Sharon:

I naturally fight against like the general population. I don't think I ever like have to go with the general flow of Korea. I just watch what I think would like, you know, amuse me. I'll just pick and choose. I'll bide my time and wait and see "My Sassy Girl" at one point but not when like everyone else is telling me to. I'll do it on my own terms.

In this excerpt, Sharon locates herself as an independent agent who prefers to consume South Korean media "on my own terms." Her decision to regulate her consumption according to her own temporality ("I'll bide my time and wait and see") and also according to her own personal preferences ("I just watch what I think would like, you know, amuse me. I'll just pick and choose") can be understood here as a stand against the racializing force of a movement which sees the consumption of South Korean cultural products by Korean Americans as so natural that it hardly merits comment.

In other cases, participants narrated themselves as non-agents, locating others as people who were active consumers of South Korean cultural production. As Jessica noted, "I don't seek it [Korean media]. I just let it come to me.... There are kids who go out and seek it...but other kids like me just let it flow." We see here the same discourse of "flow" that Sharon used above. Although at first glance Jessica's narrative may seem diametrically opposed to Sharon's positioning, in that she is locating herself as specifically non-agentive, we argue that in each case interviewees are positioning themselves as not doing what everyone else is supposedly doing. Consuming by happenstance, as in Jessica's case, or in a deliberately off-kilter temporality, as in Sharon's case, are narrated as practices that distinguish Jessica and Sharon from the figure of the Korean American who blindly accepts the homogenizing presumption that they should follow South Korean popular culture.

In both this case and the one above, interviewees' narratives invoked a range of figures at several scales: the uncool immigrant drama fan, the Asian American geek, the cool Korean American, and the White American who produces Asian American uncoolness in the first set of examples; the South Korean subject who casts an essentializing gaze upon the diaspora, the Korean American who unthinkingly accepts their positioning as similar to South Korean youth, and the Korean American who pointedly marks their displeasure with that positioning in the second set. We understand these figures as refractions of one another on different scales, stemming from the ways that cool American Whiteness gets positioned as superior to uncool Asian Americaness (Irvine and Gal 2000). In each case, these fractally recursive dynamics of intraethnic othering point to the ways that Korean American women narrated dramas as heightening their sense of difference–from various Asian American, Korean American, and South Korean figures.

"They like to play": Korean American Views of South Korean Privilege

According to our interviewees, dramas that centered on the lives of young wealthy South Koreans like Couple or Trouble (환상의 커플) (Ki, 2006), featuring household servants, designer fashions, frequent international travel, and days spent golfing, shopping, and eating out provided fictionalized glimpses of the lives of leisure that South Korean Illinois undergraduates led in Seoul. Sharon, for example told us that "whatever's found on the drama is what I see within people who are interacting on campus." In contrast, Korean Americans narrated themselves in these stories as economically constrained, like many Americans in the aftermath of the 2007-8 economic crisis. For example, they told us that they had to care about grades since they had to get jobs, but grades just didn't matter for the South Koreans since they all had jobs waiting for them back home. In the Korean American gaze, South Korean undergraduates were blithely unimpacted by financial concerns, just like the young corporate CEOs or heirs to family fortunes portrayed on dramas. As Rachel commented about South Korean undergraduates on campus, "They can just pretty much throw away money for anything." In Jessica's telling, South Korean undergraduates at the University of Illinois "just liked to play a lot" (e.g. indulge and consume), and spent most of their time having fun, not studying or worrying about grades. While interviewees like Rachel imagined that the South Korean undergraduates on campus were so privileged that they did not have to work ("They own a family business or are really high up"), in fact most of the South Korean students were quite anxious about trying to find a job upon their return to South Korea.

In narratives that circulated within Korean American circles, Korean Americans portrayed themselves as figures who could only gaze awestruck upon the unreal life of this persona. Several of our participants recounted the local legend of the uberwealthy South Korean student who signed a lease at one upscale apartment complex, found another place he liked better, and just paid both rents for the full year. In marveling at this character's financial insouciance, Korean Americans located themselves as ordinary students who could never dream of having such privilege. In a similar vein, Jessica told us of the resentment that she felt when she worked as a waitress at a local restaurant. In Jessica's account, large parties of "cheap" South Korean students would spend heavily on sushi and beer, but were rude and dismissive towards her and the other 2nd generation Korean American servers, routinely shortchanging them on tips. In this story, Jessica aligns herself with the figure of the hard working, humble Korean American in contrast to the figure of the swaggering wealthy South Korean, thus illustrating how class got taken up as a sharp demarcating line.

Discrepant Cosmopolitanisms

According to our interviewees, this exceptional class privilege was what enabled South Korean undergraduate peers to inhabit a cosmopolitan subjectivity that was unavailable to Korean Americans. In stories that they told, Korean Americans depicted themselves as having to do the hard work of accommodating to American norms while in the US and South Korean norms while overseas, and being held accountable for their failures in both settings, while South Korean undergraduates could just act as they pleased no matter where they were. As they put it, coolness was supposed to be the sole prerogative of Korean Americans; the FOB was by definition a socially awkward, linguistically maladroit figure who could never aspire to the unattainable cool of the US born. They were thus taken aback by what they saw as an inversion of the customary privilege that they had thought that they enjoyed vis-a-vis so-called "FOBs."

Korean Americans cast themselves in the roles of figures those who had to labor to try to fit in in both South Korea and the US. Korean Americans alone, according to them, had to grapple with double consciousness (Du Bois 1903), making sure that they sported a "laid back" and "more Americanized" style, "like any other student that goes to the U of I who is from here" while in Illinois, but also being attentive to a White American gaze while in South Korea ("Like the shopping that I did in Korea, obviously I had to think about whether it would work in America too"). While Korean Americans depicted themselves as targets of scorn from disapproving South Koreans in Seoul ("They kind of look down on us" "I feel like Korean Americans are portrayed as just weird"), the Korean American gaze positioned South Korean undergraduates in Illinois as existing in a space apart, evidently immune to the transnational social pressures of conformity that weighed so heavily on Korean Americans both in the US and in South Korea. As Hannah put it, "The other day I was walking to [a local grocery store near campus] and I saw this Korean couple like walking down the street and I almost thought I was in Korea. They just seemed very just like natural in the setting." We can see here the yearning of the Korean American towards this figure of the utterly "natural" South Korean couple, able to live their lives apparently unchanged from Seoul to Urbana-Champaign.

According to our interviewees, South Korean students were the ultimate cosmopolitans, able to mobilize "Korean style", an emblem of South Korean privilege shared by characters on dramas and by the figure of the South Korean student on campus, wherever they went. As Rachel commented, "They dress really well.... In terms of clothes, like it's the only way you can see how much money they [South Korean students] might have....That would be the only thing between the dramas and the students I see here." Korean Americans perceived South Korean undergraduates as able to "pull off both—like, you know, the Korean trend and the American trend," in contrast with their own attempts at transnational fashion:

Hannah: (talking about being in Seoul in the summer of 2007)
I bought a t-shirt that didn't make sense the words on the front
(...)
I bought that shirt thinking that it would look cool if I wore it in America
(...)
Cause I mean it looked really cool in the store I bought it in
And I was like, I think this is an acceptable trend in America
(...)
I wore it almost every time I wanted to go out and show off
(...)
But then as soon as I came to America
I ended up shoving it to the back of my closet and never wanting to see it again
I was kind of embarrassed to show my friends even
Cause they were reading my shirt and they didn't get it
I just thought it was kind of cute
But they were like why would you buy a shirt that doesn't make sense?

Megan: Who were these friends?

Hannah: Korean Americans

Here Hannah presents herself as someone who has to think carefully about her presentation of self and how she might come off back home ("I bought that shirt thinking that it would look cool if I wore it in America" " I was like, I think this is an acceptable trend in America"). In contrast, her characterization of South Koreans depicted them as subjects who could walk around Champaign as though they were in Seoul. While Hannah narrates herself as someone who has to contend with a racializing gaze, and who finds herself humiliated by fellow Korean American peers at her failed attempts at cosmopolitanism, South Korean undergraduates, in her telling, do not bear the same burden. In framing South Korean students' ability to eschew the racist gaze of White Americans (and its counterpart at a lower scale, the disdain of other Korean Americans), Hannah here presents them as subjects who are equally at home no matter where they go, thus embodying a persona commonly depicted on dramas (Lo and Kim 2011, 2012).

This inversion can also be seen in the ways that Korean Americans spoke about multilingualism. Under most conventional readings, the English language proficiency of the 2nd generation speaker is an unassailable form of privilege, and the "accented" English of the FOB is a source of shame; commanding the English of a "native speaker" is the ever elusive goal of the South Korean migrant (Park 2009b). In our interviewees' narratives, however, it was the South Korean undergraduates, and not the Korean Americans, who enjoyed linguistic privilege.

For one, Korean Americans bemoaned the amount of linguistic labor that they had to do just to get access to South Korean media. Interviewees emphasized how frustrating it was to spend hours pursuing broken links and trying to resolve technical issues between pirated video files and fansubs. In their eyes, South Koreans peers had it so easy in this regard—they could just watch dramas whenever they wanted, in real time, from Korean sites. They didn't have to agonize while waiting for subtitling teams to try to keep current with what was being shown in South Korea, and they did not also have to participate in the laborious process of fansubbing, as some of our interviewees did, involving the coordinated hours of legions of multilingual volunteers. This delayed temporality, and access to what many English-dominant fans understood as imperfectly translated material, was experienced as a frustrating lag by our participants.

In another aspect, Korean Americans portrayed themselves as having to be careful about public displays of language, accommodating to American norms about the stigma of speaking a foreign language around English speakers ("Korean American people, you know, think this is America. [They have a] speak

English type of mentality."). However, they understood South Korean peers on campus as being entirely exempt from these social pressures. As Jessica admired, "Like they don't even speak English. They like to speak Korean, they like to dress in the Korean style.......They don't really see the need to [integrate]". Korean Americans gazed approvingly at this apparent ability to ignore American sociolinguistic norms. In Hannah's words, "Whenever I think about FOBs I always think about a flock of them just all jabbering in Korean, and just walking by, just really being to themselves." In both of these cases, it is South Koreans who are presented as enjoying linguistic privilege and Korean Americans who are disadvantaged.

This sense of awe was also leavened with scorn, as in Sharon's description of gendered interactions on dramas and on campus:

Sharon:	In Korean dramas I've noticed that the girl is more petty? … Fragile, delicate sort of? She always goes, "Awww" ((faux cute voice)) and "Whatever" ((high pitched, coy voice)) and like THIS. I don't know what this is but they go like THIS and flick their arms around like "WHOOO!" I don't know what that is! But they always do that, like "Aiguya! HAJIMA! (('Oh no! Stop it!')) I don't know" ((whining, animated)) And I'm not sure if they're more fragile or something. I don't know That's just the thing about girls. I always notice there's a weak girl and they're just like THIS: "AHhhhh!" (…)
Megan:	So when you're when you're describing like the flitting of arms and like you know the way they act sort of petty and fragile do you think this is a sort of a cultural thing or do you think--
Sharon:	Yes, it is a cultural thing at least to me from what I observe. Even daily on the school campus from the FOBs. FRESH OFF THE BOAT. They're always like THIS, you know, flitting with their boyfriends. I see them walk down the FRICKIN street, "LA LA LA LA LA LA! Aigu OPPA jinjjalo !! (('Oh honey, really!')) LA LA" ((breathless, fast paced, highly animated)). They always do that. Just so you know that really ticks me off.

Here Sharon animates the figure of the South Korean drama character pleading/chiding/flirting with her boyfriend and makes this figure's use of Korean commensurable to the grating public behavior of South Korean undergraduates on campus. Here, linguistic envy is inverted, as Sharon expresses disdain towards this linguistically gendered interaction. Indeed, several of our interviewees attempted to locate themselves as superior to South Korean peers in terms of gender relations. "There is more of an equal balance between female and male here versus in Korea," commented Sharon, observing that second generation Korean Americans would partake in "balanced [romantic] relationship[s], like the typical American relationship," while South Koreans demonstrated instead a "very paternal, masculine, culture." In this three way comparison, the figure of the Korean American gets made commensurable with "typical" Americans and set off approvingly from South Koreans on a modernist trajectory of gendered progress. The genre of Korean that Sharon attributes to both the drama characters and South Koreans on campus is known as aegyo, and is understood as a display of dependence, affection, and cuteness which involves both typified linguistic utterances (e.g. addressing one's boyfriend using a distinctive pleading contour) and physical gestures (like rubbing one's cheeks and pouting), both of which Sharon points to in her animated rendition ("They go like THIS and flick their arms around like 'WHOOO!'"). By casting South Korean students and characters on dramas as figures who are linked by a linguistic style that is culturally understood as a form of manipulating others into caring for them through staged cuteness, Korean American women elevated themselves in contrast as figures who engaged in authentic, honest, and progressive interactions with the opposite sex. In these expressions of both longing and disdain (Abelmann and Lie 1995, 62), Korean American women revealed how the fractally recursive process of intraethnic othering could take variegated forms across multiple scales.

Conclusion

In this paper, we hope to have sketched the ways that Korean American women undergraduates in Illinois drew upon Korean dramas to make sense of their relations with South Korean peers. While consumption of South Korean media is often depicted by the South Korean press as a practice that brings people across the globe together, we found that for our subjects, drama watching sharpened their sense of division from fellow South Korean undergraduates on campus. Korean American women undergraduates marveled at the seemingly effortless transnational life of the figure of the South Korean student, someone who could be at home anywhere. They located themselves as subjects who were "out of place" no matter where they were, as Hannah put it, targets of scorn by White Americans, South Koreans, and Korean Americans. Rather than seeking common cause with South Korean undergraduates, they set them apart, as possessing a degree of privilege and cosmopolitan belonging that Korean Americans could only dream of. Korean Americans cast the "Korean bubble" not as evidence of the ways that South Koreans were also subject to White racism, but as testimony to privileged South Koreans' ability to transcend racism.

As Korean Americans expressed both scoff and awe at the figure of the South Korean undergraduate, they outlined an inversion of the customary relationship between the cool second generation Korean American, and the linguistically and socially inept FOB. They also upscaled these relations on campus onto a shift between cross chronotopic frameworks of transnational Korean migration, in which the viewpoint of an earlier generation, in which the US was portrayed as the land of economic opportunity and freedom, and South Korea as a backwater, were flipped. To be sure, the imagined lives they conjured up for South Korean peers bore little resemblance to the ways that South Korean undergraduates at the University of Illinois presented their own life narratives, in which anxieties about long deferred returns to South Korea loomed large. Yet in the Korean American gaze, South Korean undergraduates led carefree lives of consumption just like characters on drama, illustrating the important influence of mediatized images of personhood upon real life encounters.

References

Abelmann, Nancy. 2009. The intimate university: Korean American students and the problems of segregation. Durham, NC: Duke University Press.

Abelmann, Nancy. 2012. "Undergraduate Korean Americans and "Korean Koreans" in the millennial American university." In Koreans in America: History, culture and identity, edited by Grace J. Yoo, 71-78. San Diego, CA: Cognella Academic Publishing.

Abelmann, Nancy, and John Lie. 1995. Blue dreams: Korean Americans and the Los Angeles riots. Cambridge, MA: Harvard University Press.

Agha, Asif. 2005. "Voicing, footing, enregisterment." Journal of Linguistic Anthropology 15(1): 38-59.

Carr, E. Summerson, and Michael Lempert, eds. 2016. Scale: Discourse and dimension

in social life. Oakland, CA: University of California Press.
Chun, Elaine. 2009a. "Ideologies of legitimate mockery: Margaret Cho's revoicings of Mock Asian." In Beyond Yellow English: Toward a linguistic anthropology of Asian Pacific America edited by Angela Reyes and Adrienne Lo. New York: Oxford University Press.
Chun, Elaine. 2009b. "Speaking like Asian immigrants: Intersections of accommodation and mocking at a U.S. high school." Pragmatics 19(1): 17-38.
Du Bois, W. E. B. 1903. The souls of black folk: Essays and sketches. Chicago: A. C. McClurg .
Gal, Susan. 2016. "Scale-making: Comparison and perspective as ideological projects." In Scale: Discoure and dimension of social life, edited by E. Summerson Carr and Michael Lempert, 91-111. Oakland, CA: University of California Press.
Goffman, Erving. 1974. Frame analysis: An essay on the organization of experience. Boston: Northeastern University Press.
Ha, Nam-hyun. 2016. "hanlyu deulama deog-e...lamyeon suchul jinanhae 2eog-1900man dalleolo sasang choedae [Thanks to hallyu dramas...Ramen exports reached $219 million last year]." Accessed March 31, 2016. Joongang Ilbo, October 6, 2016. http://news.joins.com/article/20683410.
Irvine, Judith T. 1996. "Shadow conversations: The indeterminacy of participant roles." In Natural histories of discourse, edited by Michael Silverstein and Greg Urban, 131-159. Chicago: University of Chicago Press.
Irvine, Judith T, and Susan Gal. 2000. "Language ideology and linguistic differentiation." In Regimes of language: Ideologies, polities, and identities, edited by Paul V. Kroskrity, 35-84. Santa Fe, NM: School of American Research Press.
Jung, Sun. 2013. "K-Pop beyond Asia: Performing trans-nationality, trans-sexuality, and trans-textuality." In Asian popular culture in transition, edited by Lorna Fitzsimmons and John A. Lent, 108-131. New York: Routledge.
Ki, Sang Ho (Producer). 2006. Hwansangui keopeul. Couple or Trouble. South Korea: MBC.
Kim, Nadia Y. 2008. Imperial citizens: Koreans and race from Seoul to LA. Stanford, CA: Stanford University Press.
Kim, Youna. 2011. Transnational migration, media and identity of Asian women: Diasporic daughters. New York: Routledge.
Lee, Ji-hoon. 2016. "Hanlyu kontencheue mollineun chaina meoni [China money focuses on hallyu content]." Donga Ilbo, September 26, 2016. http://news.donga.com/3/all/20160926/80468687/1.
Lee, Whi-hae. 2016. "hanlyu eob-eun 'Ksobijae', bulhwang moleunda [Due to the Korean wave, Korea wave-related goods are quite unaffected by the recession]." Chosun Biz, August 30, 2016. http://biz.chosun.com/site/data/html_dir/2016/08/30/2016083000039.html.
Lo, Adrienne, and Jenna Kim. 2012. Linguistic competency and citizenship:Contrasting portraits of multilingualism in the South Korean popular media. Journal of Sociolinguistics 16: 255-276.
Lo, Adrienne, and Jenna Kim. 2011.Manufacturing citizenship: Metapragmatic framings of language in media images of mixed race men in South Korea. Discourse

and Society 22: 440-457.

Lo, Adrienne, Nancy Abelmann, Soo Ah Kwon, and Sumie Okazaki, eds. 2015. South Korea's education exodus: The life and times of early study abroad. Seattle, WA: Center for Korean Studies, University of Washington.

Lukacs, Gabriella. 2010. "Iron Chef around the world: Japanese food television, soft power, and cultural globalization." International Journal of Cultural Studies 13(4): 409-426.

Oh, David C. 2015. Second-generation Korean Americans and transnational media: Diasporic identifications. Lanham, MD: Lexington Books.

Paek, Hye Jin, and Hermant Shah. 2003. "Racial ideology, model minorities, and the "not-so-silent partner": Stereotyping of Asian Americans in U.S. magazine advertising." Howard Journal of Communications 14: 225-43.

Park, Geun-Hye. 2013. Inaugural speech. Seoul.

Park, Joseph Sung-Yul. 2009a. "Illegitimate speakers of English: Negotiation of linguistic identity among Korean international students." In Beyond Yellow English: Toward a linguistic anthropology of Asian Pacific America, edited by Angela Reyes and Adrienne Lo, 195-212. New York: Oxford University Press.

Park, Joseph Sung-Yul. 2009b. The local construction of a global language: Ideologies of English in South Korea. Amsterdam: Mouton de Gruyterm.

Park, Joseph Sung-Yul. 2017. "Transnationalism as interdiscursivity: Korean managers of multinational corporations talking about mobility." Language in Society 46(1): 23-38.

Park, Jung-Sun. 2004a. "Korean American youth and transnational flows of popular culture across the Pacific." Amerasia 30(1): 147-169.

Park, Jung-Sun. 2004b. "Korean American youths' consumption of Korean and Japanese TV dramas and its implications." In Feeling Asian modernities: Transnational consumption of Japanese TV dramas, edited by Koichi Iwabuchi, 275-300. Hong Kong: Hong Kong University Press.

Pyke, Karen D., and Tran Dang. 2003. "'FOB' and 'Whitewashed': Identity and internalized racism among second generation Asian Americans." Qualitative Sociology 26: 147-172.

Reyes, Angela. 2007. Language, identity, and stereotype among Southeast Asian American youth: The other Asian. Mahwah, N.J.: Lawrence Erlbaum Associates.

Reyes, Angela. 2016. "The voicing of Asian American figures: Korean linguistic styles at an Asian American cram school " In Raciolinguistics: How language shapes our ideas about race, edited by H. Samy Alim, John Rickford and Arnetha Ball, 309-326. New York: Oxford University Press.

Ryoo, Wongjae. 2009. "Globalization, or the logic of cultural hybridization: The case of the Korean wave." Asian journal of communication 19(2): 137-151. doi: http://www.tandfonline.com/doi/abs/10.1080/01292980902826427.

Shim, Doobo. 2006. "Hybridity and the rise of Korean popular culture in Asia." Media, Culture & Society 28: 5-23. doi: http://journals.sagepub.com/doi/abs/10.1177/0163443706059278.

Wirtz, Kristina. 2014. Performing Afro-Cuba: Image, voice, spectacle in the making of race and history. Chicago: University of Chicago Press.

Part 3

Interest-dimension of the Korean Wave

Chapter 5

A Hybrid Model of Bridging Nation Branding and Country Image: A Case of the Korean Wave

Jaebeom Suh

Introduction

During the 1990s, people were able to experience a huge cultural surge from South Korea, which was called as the Korean Wave (or K-wave). This cultural surge was initially based on Korean pop-culture such as Korean music and Korean soap-dramas, which has earned a well-accepted popularity among East, South, and Southeast Asian countries. The Korean Wave was almost a syndrome of Korean culture consumed in those countries, and its growth is far exceeding any conceivable expectation. The Korean Wave continues to gain significant grounds throughout the world. The Korean Wave's impact is no longer limited to regional areas of Asia, but instead is expanding its influence to entities such as the United States of America, Canada, South America, Europe, and other continents alike.

The impact of the Korean Wave has been so powerful influencing many different aspects of pop-culture such as music, fashion, food, product preferences, and so forth, not only for the people in those countries experiencing the Korean Wave, but also for Korean people themselves. Because of its substantial impacts, both academicians and practitioners started to pay attention to this phenomenon to better understand why and how this surge has happened, what the consequences and impacts the Korean Wave caused, what future benefits would result from the Korean Wave, and more importantly, how one can learn the lessons of cultural surge and utilize those in building and maintaining equity, if any, associated with a specific country, which is a part of nation branding.

Diverse constituencies such as government, firms, and even individual consumers are involved in nation branding with respect to the impact of the Korean Wave. In particular, from any government perspective, a naturally arising question will be about the impacts of cultural surge like the Korean Wave on favorable contributions to nation branding. Favorable contributions to nation brand will also give a tremendous opportunity for firms involved in such a cultural surge, because favorably enhanced perceptions about a specific nation will be associated with products and services from the country where such a cultural surge initiates. In other words, I contend that the Korean Wave as a cultural surge plays a big role as a cultural ambassador from a macro-level perspective, but it also provides some kind of equity so that several industries and business from a micro-level perspective can take advantages of the phenomenon. Given the dynamics and complexity of cultural impacts and related underlying cultural dimensions, one important thing to note, from a managerial perspective, is that Korea as a nation brand has gained "unintended equity" associated with the Korean Wave surge and its unintended equity is likely to be spilled over to the firms that are involved in the Korean Wave.

In this sense, the purpose of the current study is to propose a new conceptual framework to understand the effect of the Korean Wave on nation branding and its brand equity by combining two concepts of nation branding and brand equity, based on both macro- and micro-level perspectives. Specifically, I'd like to address how the Korean Wave positively can influence Korean nation brand with respect to country image and overall attitude toward country.

The Korean Wave

The Korean Wave is essentially the influx of popularity for South Korean culture on a global scale. In the 1990s, across mainly Asian countries, there was a rise in interest about the Korean culture, in particular Korean dramas (K-dramas) and Korean pop-culture. The term Korean Wave was coined from the Korean phrase "Han Ryu". The words "Han" for "Korean" and "Ryu" for "wave," were combined, literally meaning the wave of Korea. Starting out as an Asian regional spread of Korean culture, the Korean Wave phenomenon gains a more global presence over time.

Given the growing popularity of Korean pop-culture in many countries, it is no wonder to see the Korean government's proactive involvement in the Korean Wave. The government itself supports relevant cultural industries via subsidies and grants for start-up firms for the diffusion and additional development of the Korean Wave. Such efforts result in a very promising consequence in that the Korean Wave allowed Korea itself to become one of the leading exporters of pop culture (Hong 2014). For instance, total value of cultural exports of Korea in 2008 and 2009 is $1.8 billion (The Economist, January 25, 2010) and $2.6 billion (Oliver 2012), respectively. In other words, the Korean Wave provided an opportunity for Korea to position itself as the world's coolest brand through the diffusion of Korean culture (Leong 2014), which, I believe, becomes an important source of nation branding as a soft power (Potter 2009) and/or as a brand equity (Keller 1993). Therefore, I contend that the understanding of the Korean Wave should not be limited to the simple diffusion of Korean pop-culture; its impacts should be re-examined as a potential source to generate economic benefits in many different industries and positive public diplomacy aspects of a country from a macro perspective as well as firms' competitive advantages from a micro perspective.

Shifting the Focus of the Korean Wave

The scope of the Korean Wave is somewhat limited at the early stage of the wave. Some areas of Korean culture such as K-dramas (Korean film and television), K-pop (Korean music and dance), K-cuisine (Korean food), and K-beauty (Korean fashion) have gained significant regional awareness and reputations. Yet, its spread is not on a global scale and its scope is also limited to Asia. As Nye (2009) refers the concept and scope of the Korean Wave to "the growing popularity of all things Korean, from fashion and film to music and cuisine," the Korean Wave should be able to encompass every possible area if global audiences are consuming the Korean cultural products.

During 1990's, the Korean Wave can be characterized as a simple flow and diffusion of diverse areas of Korean culture to different countries. However, given the powerful influence of cultural impacts and related interaction effects with diverse areas of economic entities, one should go beyond of simple diffusion of the wave, take advantages of the Korean Wave and transfer its impacts to different dimensions of nation branding. In other words, instead of simple diffusion and spread of cultural impact of the Korean Wave, one should be able to proactively create, manage, and revise nation branding based on favorable brand association, which will lead to country equity as a nation brand.

In terms of diffusion of the Korean Wave, there are two eras of the Korean Wave. The first era, often labeled as the Korean Wave 1.0, is mostly based on the export of local cultural goods and services to East and Southeast Asia between 1990's and 2007 (Jin 2012). Thus, it is literally a simple flow or wave of Korean pop culture into regional areas of Asia. The second era, labeled as the Korean Wave 2.0, is fundamentally different from the first era due to the development of digital technology and social media. Digital technology and social media have changed the arena and degree of the Korean Wave from local regions to the globe itself; global audiences are experiencing the Korean Wave and related K-pop culture. In particular, Korean online gaming and K-pop music industry enjoy a global presence. As Jin (2012) argued, the Korean Wave as a cultural genre can be an important source for creative industries rather than simple cultural industries. In this light, I would argue that a cultural surge like the Korean Wave plays an active role not only for a simple cultural exporter, but also for a crucial medium of cultural production in creative industries via the convergence of technology and social media usage. Because of such roles, the Korean Wave has been an important underlying and hidden antecedent of nation branding to create nation brand equity.

Global Presence of the Korean Wave

A Korean singer, PSY becomes a world-recognized icon for Korean pop culture with his song, Gangnam style. The total number of views are more than 2.7 billion throughout the world at Youtube. People start to ask, "Where is Gangnam?" Many tourists from Asian countries visit the district of Gangnam, Seoul, Korea to experience its culture and related K-pop music. It is a by-product of the Korean Wave directly influencing on place branding (Kotler and Gertner 2002).

PSY's record-breaking views provide significant opportunities for the related industries in Korea and a bridge to world audiences. The Korean Wave is now a worldwide global phenomenon instead of a regional cultural fever. For instance, a K-pop star, boy band "Big Bang" is one of the most well known bands in Korea. When Big Bang came to New York for its concert, New York Times (Oct 12, 2015) described the boy band Big Bang as "an extreme, intense, overwhelming Korean pop carnival." Singer's excellent dance, performance, and appearance attract American audiences and K-pop is well accepted even in the USA. The image of K-pop is perceived as being cool from the US audience's eye.

K-drama, called Dae Jang Geum (translated into Jewel in Palace) in Iran, 2007, was an extraordinary success with its TV average rating over 90%. Obviously the sudden increased purchase of "Made in Korea" including cellphone and automobile can be tied to the popularity of K-dramas in Iran at that time. Regardless of product categories, many Korean products gained unexpected and unintended country equity because of the Korean Wave in Iran.

In Brazil, its effect goes beyond K-Pop and dance. In fact, many Brazilian want to learn Korean language, history, and its culture to get jobs at Korean firms in Brazil.. The Korean Wave Community Clubs or fan clubs are also one of intriguing outcomes of the Korean Wave. According to Yonhap News Agency (12/18/2015), by 2014, 21 million people are expected to be members of such groups. That number transfers to potential economic effect of $14.8 billion, and by 2016, the goal is 40 million people with an estimated economic effect of $17.4 billion.

Korean Creative Content Agency (KOCCA) conducted an online survey in China during October 2014 with 2,304 respondents with respect to the number of hours watching K-Drama. It turned out that 53.2% of respondents watched over 7 hours per week. In USA, Netflix bets on Korean drama for expansion to reach global audience in 2018 (Tan 2017).

Economic Effect of the Korean Wave

The effect of the Korean Wave on economic sectors in Korea is beyond expectation and a big success. Based on the report by KOTRA (Korean Trade-Investment Promotion Agency), the Korean Wave effect generated more than $10 billion in 2015. Specifically, online gaming industry was the most beneficiary one, generating $2.08 billion, which is 3.2% increase compared to that of previous year. Tourism industry takes the second place in total money generated with $1.95 billion (13.5% increase). Food and beverage industry get $1.68 billion (4.7% increase).

The six place is cosmetics industry. It generates $0.82 billion in total dollar amount; however, its increase is 56.6% compared to the previous year, which is the largest increase out of all the industries. This result is particularly interesting because the Korean Wave generates economic benefits for related industries, but also drives some industries by creating a totally new venue based on cultural elements such as esthetics and beauty, which is believed to be very local and culture-specific.

Moreover, the effect of the Korean Wave is not limited to business industries and firms; it is influencing Korean people themselves. Many Korean people start to find jobs directly related to the firms and industries benefiting from the Korean Wave. The Korean Wave helped create as many as 103,326 new jobs in 2014 in Korea (KOTRA).

Understanding Nation Branding

The Korean Wave as a cultural ambassador and its successful impacts open up prolific discussions regarding its potential role for contributing to nation branding for Korea. A lesson one should learn would be that such cultural surges should be handled with a more systematic framework, if any, to fully take advantages of such impacts on nation image. In this paper, I propose a hybrid approach combining traditional brand equity model from micro-level perspectives and nation (country) branding model from macro-level perspectives.

Definition of Nation Branding

Several researchers have attempted to define nation branding differently depending on their disciplines. For instance, Kerr and Wiseman (2013, 354) define nation branding as "the application of corporate marketing concepts and techniques to countries, in the interests of enhancing their reputation in international relations." Anholt (2007) proposes a similar argument contending that the understanding of reputations of countries is analogous to that of brand images of companies. These two conceptualizations of nation branding are not much different from traditional customer-based brand equity concept (Keller 1993), which is based on micro-level firms' perspectives.

Compared to the micro-level understanding of nation branding, Aronczyk (2013, 16) defined it as "the result of the interpenetration of commercial and public sector interests to communicate priorities among domestic and international populations for variety of interrelated purposes," emphasizing public sectors and macro-level perspectives. Similarly, Potter(2009) attempts to understand nation branding as its soft power via public diplomacy. Despite its importance, a consensus has not been established to develop unified theoretical frameworks. One thing to note is that many governments put significant and systematic efforts to create a stronger, more positive, and more cohesive national identity (Aronczyk 2013), which can be tied to brand association approach (Keller 1993) for the case of Korean Wave.

Kaneva (2011) proposed three different perspectives on nation branding: economic, political, and cultural approaches. The main goal of economic approach is to seek a country's competitive advantage for economic growth whereas the goal of political approach to understand nation branding is to corporate government efforts to strengthen economic and political position to promote tourism, foreign relations, investment, and so on. The third perspective is cultural approach focusing on people's perceptions of self and national identity (Kaneva 2011), which can be strongly tied to the effect of the Korean Wave.

Measurement of Nation Branding

When it comes to the measurement of nation branding, Anholt (2002) originally developed the Nation Brands Index (NBI) to measure perceptions of countries on the basis of six dimensions: cultural heritage, governance, people, exports, tourism, investment and immigration, called nation brand hexagon (Anholt 2002). This Nation Brands Index has been used to help involved constituencies such as governments and businesses to identify the current country image and ultimately build a strong, favorable, and unique national image and reputation.

A potential problem with this measurement is that the NBI does not incorporate a micro-level of brand equity approach in its measurement. More importantly, most individuals may not know the details of six elements of nation brands index for specific countries, which will lead to incongruent understanding of certain countries compared to individual's assessment. To overcome such possible incongruence and bias, a hybrid model of utilizing both elements of macro-level and micro-level dimensions should be proposed in the development of theoretical framework and measurement alike. Such a hybrid model would capture the essence of nation brand and county image more precisely and accurately to enhance the validity and reliability of measurement.

Cultural Perspective on Nation Branding: A Case of the Korean Wave

The concept of nation brand or country equity refers to the country's intangible assets without any explicit links with a product category (Fan 2006). In other words, nation brand is not bounded to product category because there is no specific referent. For instance, Korean pop-music is not necessarily a specific product or brand; instead it should be interpreted as a multidimensional cultural entity, generating certain amount of equity that all the related industries can benefit from.

K-pop's increase in popularity has partially defined the Korean Wave, which has contributed to a positive image of Korea from cultural perspective as well as economic one (Kaneva 2011). Adopting Fan's (2006) approach, one should be able to apply marketing and communication theories and methods to the development of nation branding to promote a nation's image without explicit link to product categories. Therefore, cultural impact on nation branding can be a very critical method to achieve sustainable competitive advantages not only for regional scale, but also for a global scale, as is evidenced with the case of the Korean Wave in terms of cultural influence and economic impacts.

Country Image and Country of Origin Effect Revisited

Country Image

Country image is not much different from nation branding. Roth and Romeo (1992, 480) define country image as "overall perception consumers form of products from a particular country based on their prior perceptions of the country's production and marketing strengths and weaknesses." Kotler, Haider, and Rein (1993, 141) contend that country image is a set of people's beliefs, ideas and impressions about a certain country. These two definitions are fundamentally different in that the former has a specific referent and the latter does not.

When linked with a certain specific product category, country image may have a stronger effect and consumers may have developed a special association between a certain product category and a country. For instance, people can easily associate Japan with consumer electronics during 1980's, France with wine, and so forth. This association is product category-specific, which means it has a referent. This type of conceptualization of country image is very similar to that of country-of-origin effect. Country image and country-of-origin are often interchangeably used as long as both have product-specific referents.

The second conceptualization of country image does not have product-specific referents and is simply an overall image about country reflecting the entire aspect of a country including people, government, natural environment, political and legal environment, technology level, and importantly economic status. A country is utilizing its image to promote and increase sales and exports of physical products, services, and even cultural products. For instance, Chinese tourists in Korea spend large sums of money on Korean cosmetics during their stay in Korea. Up to 84% of Chinese tourist buy some form of cosmetics (Lee 2016). Chinese tourists spend, on average, $2,000 on shopping during their stay in Korea (Yonhap News Agency, 2016/7/7).

A likely reason for the seemingly "must buy" cosmetic products is the positive association of Korean cosmetics and Asian beauty standards. Stereotypes associated with certain countries affect the buying behavior of consumers as the perceived quality is likely to shift based on these stereo types. Thus, the Chinese tourists are attracted to not only the products themselves, but also the positive image of beauty using Korean cosmetics in particular. Thus, enhanced country image aligned with place or destination branding (Kotler and Gertner 2002) becomes more important because the enhanced country image can directly influence willingness to visit specific country.

Country of Origin Effect

The consumer perceptions of a product's quality can be strongly associated with a country name, which is country-of-origin (COO) effect (Han and Terpstra 1988; Nebenzahl, Jaffe and Lampert 1997). A main argument of COO is that consumers tend to evaluate products first on the perception of the country and then product attributes. In other word, consumers may develop a stereotype for a product category for a certain country and its stereotype can be very robust and persistent. Consumers purchase accordingly based on the available information regarding the country and product's image. The Korean wave has facilitated this information to be more readily available, which can account for the increase in popularity for the Korean branded cosmetics. However, the products are not necessarily limited to the beauty aspect of the Korean Wave.

Korea has experienced increases in exports of information technology products such as digital TVs and cell phones. With a wide array of products that are being exported, Korea is able to gain a leverage in the global market because of country image and COO from the Korean Wave. Fan (2006) states that nation branding is an efficient method to differentiate a country's product from international competitors, which ultimately targets a broader international audience and I contend such nation branding is tied to COO influenced by cultural surge like the Korean Wave.

Measurement Issues and Problems

I contend that researchers need to revisit the current definition and measurement of country image, because it is generally limited to product quality perception even though the definition is relatively broad. Also COO effect based on specific product category would be very myopic simply because the perception is bounded to specific product categories.

Roth and Romeo (1992) emphasized the relevance of actual country experience and product usage for measurement to better evaluate country image rather than the self-assessments. Nebenzahl et al. (1997) suggest that generalizations and perceptions about a country influence a person's evaluations of the country's products and/or brands. A major flaw for those definitions of country image is that most studies are univariate and treat country image as the only cue affecting product evaluations. Given complexity and dynamic characteristics of country image over time, such definitions and corresponding measurement would face serious validity and reliability issues.

With respect to COO, one needs to clearly differentiate country of manufacturer, country of assembly, consumer's home country, and country of design as moderating variables. For instance, consumer's home country is also a part

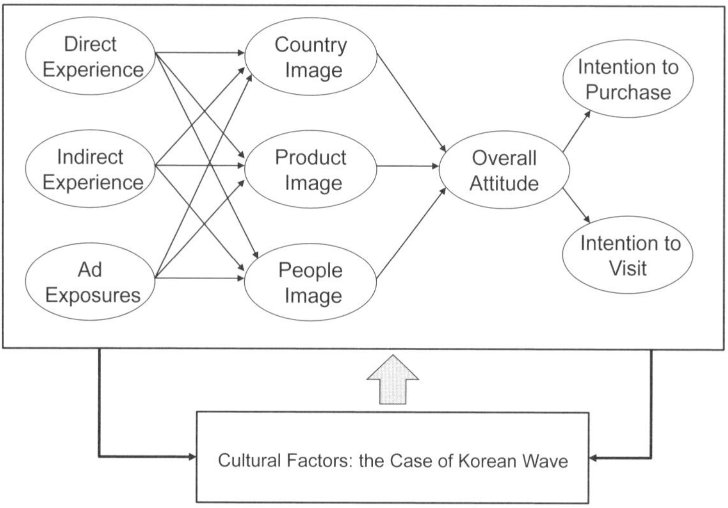

Figure 1. A New Hybrid Framework

of country image. Such an inherent consumer's home country bias has been identified in the previous literature (Cattin, Jolibert, and Lohnes 1982; Sharma, Shimp, and Shin 1995).

Bilkey and Nes (1982) viewed country image as a halo effect that consumers infer product quality of foreign brand on the basis of country name. As was mentioned, such perceptions are typically product category-specific (Etzel and Walker 1974). While country image as a halo effect seems reasonable for most cases, but this approach has a serious limitation in that consumers are assumed to use country image as a halo even when they are not familiar with a country's products (Han 1989). Based on the discussion so far, one needs to develop a new framework to resolve issues such as micro and macro level of country image, presence of product category specific referent, direct experience of product use, home country nationality, and so on.

Empirical Evidence

Micro-Level Brand Association: First Thought

During October-December 2015, KOFICE (Korea Foundation for International Culture Exchange) conducted a survey regarding the effect of Korean Wave using an association question item: What first comes to your mind when you hear "Korea"? More than 6,500 respondents participated in the survey and these responses were from 14 countries including China, USA, and Brazil. The result showed that 20.1% of respondents mentioned K-pop. The second and third one was K-food (12.1%) and IT industry (9.7%), respectively.

This is a surprising result considering the reputation and dominant power of Samsung electronics (e.g., Samsung Galaxy) in Korea and in the world. K-pop, not Samsung, is the first thought that comes to global audience's mind. The finding implies and confirms the importance of nation branding from a cultural perspective as well as economic benefits that the Korean Wave generates

I conducted a similar survey during April to May 2002 and want to show the results for comparison. I had sent out a questionnaire to the adult residents of the New York state and respondents' inputs were returned in sealed envelopes. A total 424 respondents were contacted based on quota sampling of different age groups. 45% of respondents are females. Ethnicity distribution of respondents is as follows: 70% White, 9% Black, 5% Hispanic, and 6% Asian.

I was interested in understanding what typical American consumers think of the following countries: England, Mexico, China, Japan, and Korea. If respondent's ethnicity is England, Mexican, Chinese, Japanese, or Korean, he or she was not allowed to participate in the survey to prevent respondent's home country nationality bias. As an association question item, I used a similar approach that has been done in many studies. The main question was, "What comes to your mind when you think of the following country? Please list the very first thought or image that comes to your mind." After this association item, I asked country image, attitude toward country, purchase intention, and so on, using a self-administered questionnaire. The summary table is as follows:

Table 1. Survey Result of Country Image Based on Association Method

England The Legacy Land		**Mexico Taco and Cactus**		**Japan Cutting Edge**		**China Chopstick Crowd**		**Korea Survive or Succeed?**	
Queen & Royals	76	Taco	59	Sushi	71	Chinese Food	60	War	94
London	36	Cheap or Poor	41	Cars with brand names	48	Many People	52	Kimchi	16
Tea	32	Mexican Food	32	High-tech	42	Communism	49	Korean Food	11
Big Ben	26	Cancun	31	Electronics	40	Rice	48	North Korea	10
Weather	24	Sombrero	20	Pearl Harbor or WW II	18	Great Wall	27	Olympics	10
British Accent	18	Immigrants and workers	13	Sony	14	Chinese imports	26	World Cup	8
Beatles	17	Bad water	12	Atomic Bomb	12	Cheap Labor	14	Hyundai	8
No response	8	No response	13	No response	8	No response	16	No response	43

The results are amazing in that survey participants' responses cover most of dimensions, variables, areas of nation branding and country image. For instance, Cancun for Mexico and Great Wall for China are evidence directly related to the association of place or destination, which is an important topic for tourism as destination branding. Big Ben and Sombrero are deeply related to cultural heritages, which is an element of nation branding index. Technology, bad water, weather, cheap labor are measurements of country image measurement adopted by Roth and Romeo (1992). One of interesting findings is about food. Tea, taco, sushi, Chinese food, Kimchi are ethnic food with cultural backgrounds to specific countries. Most people are exposed to easily to different ethnic food, which implies a very important aspect of cultural heritage, and thus food should be included in measurement of country image.

In addition, only cars and electronics (like SONY) for Japan, and Hyundai car for Korea are product-specific associations. This result implies that product-specific country-of-origin effect is important, but may not be a prevalent concept when most people associate with countries. Rather, overall country image could play a more critical association with specific countries.

Empirical Evidence of Country Image and Attitude

I further investigate Americans' perceptions/images of and attitudes toward five countries: England, Mexico, Japan, China (Mainland), and Korea (South). My research goal was to identify informational foundations of country images and attitudes. In particular, through a survey, I attempt to identify the effects of advertising along with those of other relevant information sources. There are three types of information sources that influence the country images and attitudes: direct experience, indirect experience, and advertising exposure. As previously described, a total of 424 adult residents of New York State (46% aged over 40) participated in the survey by completing a six-page-long self-administered questionnaire.

Measurements of direct experience included travel (I have I traveled this country), ethnic food (I eat the ethnic food of this country very often), and product (I buy products made in this country very often). The indirect information sources included mass media (I have watched many television programs or read news articles featuring this country), movies (I have watched many movies featuring this country as the background), travelers' word-of-mouth (I heard about the country from people who have been there), and immigrants (I know many people who are originally from this country). Two items measuring advertising exposure were included: products ads (I have seen many advertisements for products made in this country) and travel ads (I have seen many advertisements promoting travel to this country). I also measured, for each country, overall attitude (three items), country image (economy, politics, technology, and so on), product image (quality, reliability, etc.), and stereotypes associated with the people (efficient, educated, etc.).

Multiple regression analyses indicated that the role of advertising in determining the country attitudes depend on the specific country. For England, indirect experiences such as exposures to mass media, move, and travelers' word-of-mouth had significant positive effects on the attitude toward the country. However, exposures to either products ads or travel ads did not affect the attitude toward England. By contrast, exposures to both product ads and travel/tourism ads significantly improved the attitudes toward all other countries (Mexico, Japan, China, and Korea). It appears that, because our respondents were most familiar with England (i.e., the highest subjective knowledge ratings), advertising might not have significant incremental effect on their attitude toward England. The same analyses also showed that product purchase experience enhances the attitude toward England and Japan only. Likewise, travel experience enhanced the attitude toward a subset of countries (Mexico, Japan, and China). In sum, factors affecting country attitudes depend on the focal country.

Correlation analyses also indicated that advertising exposures are significantly correlated with most facets of country image (e.g., perceptions of economy, political system, product quality, and people stereotypes). In general, the greater the advertising exposure, the more positive were the images across the five countries.

The findings underscore the importance of international advertising (both travel ads and product ads) in enhancing the perceptions, images, and attitudes. Of all the sources of information (direct or indirect), advertising has the most consistent, positive effects on the country image.

A New Hybrid Framework

The above discussion so far provide a guideline for a hybrid model combining mirco- and macro-level factors to conceptualize nation branding and country image. Product specific country-of-origin effect, overall country images based on product and people, country's location and tourism as destination marketing, and even public diplomacy as a soft power in diplomacy and political context, influence successful nation branding and country image. As such, a new model should cover all the aspects of nation brand and country image. In particular, based on the three dimensions of nation branding previously mentioned, I propose a new hybrid framework in Figure 1.

First of all, an overall moderating effect of the Korean Wave on the entire framework is proposed. The Korean Wave is hypothesized to shift the perceptions of Korea as a nation brand in multiple facets such as country image, product image, and people image through its overarching influence both regionally and globally. Intention to purchase and intention to visit would be two outcome variables that any firm and country would be interested in from a marketing perspective. Given a well accepted theoretical explanation for the relationship between attitude and behavioral intention (eventually behavior itself), the core of this new framework is overall attitude toward country.

Compared to a broader definiton of country image and nation branding, and a narrow definion of country-of-origin, a new hybrid conceptual framework is proposed to cover both approaches. Specifically, I use three images that should be explicitly included in the model: (1) country image based on a macro-level factors such as economy, technology, environment (Remeo), (2) product image, aligned with country-of-origin, (3) people image, based on an element of nation branding index.

These will be influenced by three information sources. First, direct experiences of and interactions with country, product, and people will be strongest factors to influence overall attitude toward country. However, the direct expereines may be limited in terms of acutal exposures. Second, indirect experience is also an important information source to develop country image and eventually attitude toward country. Mass media, movies, travelor's word-of-mouth, and immigrants are example sources of indirect experience. In addition, information such as nation brand index (NBI), country reports, blog, and social network services like Facebook, Tweeter, Youtube, and other relevant technology become sources for indirect experiences that should be included in the measurement. Third, from firm's viewpoint, advertising is a controllable variable and one of 4 P's (product, price, promotion, and place). Product ads and travel ads are common information sources for global audiences.

Conclusion

Nation branding, if generating equity associated with a specific country, can be a powerful tool to make economic, social, and cultural impacts to other countries, which will in turn give significant advantages to the focal country in various ways. Country as brand, thus, nation brand is a very complex, dynamic, and multidimensional entity. It is extremely difficult to create and maintain a favorable, strong, and unique perception in people's minds. However, with successful associations of nation brand to any constituencies such as government, firms, non-profit organization, people, or even products, it can be a huge potential source for sustainable competitive advantages for the country, firms, and people from the same country. One should develop a proactive course of action to carefully design, develop, and create a nation brand, thus generate positive attitude toward the country with corresponding behavioral intentions.

For the case of Korean Wave as an example of cultural surge to different countries, related industries and people in Korea have harnessed the popularity of the Korean Wave in different countries. Korea as a country has exponentially benefited from the Korean Wave in terms of overall economic impacts. Therefore, both countries and firms need to constantly search and monitor such cultural trends if already created. Recognizing the importance of cultural trends, one should be able to connect such cultural trends to nation branding and favorable attitude toward country. Finally, nation branding as an increase in soft power and diplomacy is another important area. Its increase is likely to elicit favorable public opinions from other countries. The Korean Wave can particularly play a big role in this soft power, which is an unintended, but very consequential and promising result.

In conclusion, a viral cultural trend like the Korean Wave will directly and/or indirectly make impacts on nation branding and country image, which will provide tremendous opportunities in the format of sustainable competitive advantages, increase in economic growth, and increase in soft power. I hope the proposed new hybrid model in this paper be used as a reference for a better understanding how to create nation branding and country image.

References

Anholt, Simon. 2002. "Foreword." Journal of Brand Management 9: 229–239.

Anholt, Simon. 2007. Competitive Identity: The New Brand Management for Nations, Cities and Regions. New York: Palgrave Macmillan.

Anholt, Simon. 2011. "Beyond the Nation Brand: The Role of Image and Identity in International Relations." Exchange: The Journal of Public Diplomacy 2(1): 6-12. http://surface.syr.edu/exchange/vol2/iss1/1.

Bilkey, Warren and Erik B. Nes. 1982. "Country of Origin Effects on Product Evaluations." Journal of International Business Studies 13(1): 89-100.

Aronczyk, Melissa. 2013. Branding the Nation: The Global Business of National Identity. New York: Oxford University Press.

Cattin, Philippe, Alain Jolibert, Alain, and Colleen Lohnes. 1982. "A Cross-Cultural Study of "Made in" Concepts." Journal of International Business Studies 13(3): 131-141.

Economist. "South Korea's Pop-cultural Exports." Economist, January 25, 2010. http://www.economist.com/node/15385735

Etzel, Michael J. and Walker, Bruce J. 1974. "Advertising Strategy for Foreign Products." Journal of Advertising Research 14: 41-44.

Fan, Y. 2006. "Branding the Nation: What is Being Branded?" Journal of Vacation Marketing 12(1): 5-14.

Han, C. Min. 1989. "Country Image: Halo or Summary Construct?" Journal of Marketing Research 26: 222-229.

Han, C. Min, and V. Terpstra. 1988. "Country-of-Origin Effects for Uni-national and Binational Products." Journal of International Business Studies19(2): 235-55.

Hong, Euny. 2014. The Birth of Korean Cool: How One Nation Is Conquering the World Through Pop Culture. New York: Picador.

Jin, Dal Young. 2012. "Hallyu 2.0: The New Korean Wave in the Creative Industry." International Institute Journal 2(1). http://hdl.handle.net/2027/spo.11645653.0002.102

Kaneva, Nadia. 2011. "Nation Branding: Toward an Agenda for Critical Research." International Journal of Communication 5: 117–141.

Keller, Kevin L. 1993. "Conceptualizing, Measuring, and Managing Customer-Based Brand Equity." Journal of Marketing 57(1): 1-22.

Kerr, Pauline, and Geoffrey Wiseman. 2013. Diplomacy in a Globalizing World: Theories and Practice. New York: Oxford University Press.

Kotler, Philip, Donald Haider, and Irving Rein. 1993. Marketing Places: Attracting Investment and Tourism to Cities, States and Nations. New York: Free Press.

Kotler, Philp, and Gertner, David. 2002. "Country as Brand, Product, and Beyond: A Place Marketing and Brand Management Perspective." Journal of Brand Management 9: 249-261.

Lee, S. 2016. "Chinese group travel." BNK Investment Securities, February 26, 2016.

Leong, Melissa. 2014. "How Korea Became the World's Coolest Brand." Financial Post, August 2, 2014.

Nebenzahl, Israel D., Eugene D. Jaffe, and Shlomo I. Lampert. 1997. "Towards a Theory of Country Image Effect on Product Evaluation." Management International Review 37(1): 27-49.

Nye, Joseph S. 2009. "South Korea's Growing Soft Power." Harvard University, Kennedy School, Belfer Center for Science and International Affairs, November 11, 2009. http://www.belfercenter.org/publication/south-koreas-growing-soft-power

Oliver, Christian. 2012. "South Korea's K-pop Takes Off in the West." Financial Times, February 10, 2012.

Potter, Evan. 2009. Branding Canada: Projecting Canada's Soft Power through Public

Dipolomacy. Montreal: McGill-Queen's University Press.

Roth, Martin S., and Jean B. Romeo. 1992. "Matching Product Category and Country Image Perceptions: A Framework for Managing Country-of-origin Effects." Journal of International Business Studies 23(3): 477-497.

Sharma, Subhash, Terence A. Shimp, and Jeongshin Shin. 1995. "Consumer Ethnocentrism: A test of Antecedents and Moderators." Journal of the Academy of Marketing Science 23(1): 26-37.

Tan, Huileng. 2017. "Netflix Bets on Korean Drama for Expansion." CNBC, January 9, 2017. http://www.cnbc.com/2017/01/09/netflix-bets-on-korean-drama-for-expansion.html.

Chapter 6

Yet to Crest: The Korean Wave and Korean Language Learning

Yeonhee Yoon

Introduction

Thanks to the Korean Wave, there is a growing desire for Korean language proficiency across the globe. Korean learners are increasing with the rising popularity of Korean dramas and K-Pop music, and Korean language learning is becoming a very popular pursuit.

As general interest in learning Korean is on the rise, the number of foreign students studying at the King Sejong Institute, a governmental body dedicated to fostering Korean language education, has increased, and the number of applicants to the Korean language proficiency test (TOPIK • Test of Proficiency in Korean) is surging. The Test of Proficiency in Korean (TOPIK) is designed by the Ministry of Education and the National Institute for International Education to evaluate the language ability of foreigners who do not speak Korean as their native language. On April 16, 2016, 74,295 people registered for/took the 46th TOPIK, which was administered in 164 cities in 45 countries including China, France, Australia, Argentina, and South Africa (The Chosun Ilbo April 19, 2016). By comparison, in the first test administered in 1997, 2,692 test-takers applied from four countries including Korea, Japan, Uzbekistan and Kazakhstan; the number of applicants for one test increased 27 fold in 20 years. In the second half of 2017, tests are also being administered in Bolivia, Jamaica, and Poland.

As of 2015, the King Sejong Institute established 138 schools in 54 countries, and in 2016 it expanded to 144 schools in 68 countries. By region, there are 89 schools in 23 countries in Asia, 18 schools in 10 countries in North America, 28 schools in 17 countries in Europe, 5 schools in 5 countries in

Africa, and 4 schools in 2 countries in Oceania (The King Sejong Institute Foundation 2017). In 2015, the number of students at the King Sejong Institute was 43,308, and the number of students enrolled online was 61,155.

Especially considering that the number enrolled in beginning Korean courses is rapidly increasing in relation to the proliferation of Korean media culture worldwide, it can be argued that most of these students came to be interested in and to pursue Korean language learning due to the influence of the Korean Wave.

Correlation between the Korean Wave and Korean Language Learning

Using Korean culture in Korean language education can foster enthusiasm in language learners to study and learn further. For example, Korean media can play a role in enhancing the motivation to learn Korean by stimulating and satisfying the learners' intellectual curiosities. Thus, the Korean Wave and its cultural productions can exert a positive influence on the whole process of learning Korean. In addition, cultural affinity with the Korean Wave improves foreign learners' perceptions of Korea and leads to their enjoyment of Korean culture (Korea Creative Content Agency 2010).

A survey of learners who are studying Korean at language schools in Korea revealed that popular culture was the second most motivating reason for having interest in Korea (Im 2005). In Japan, more than 70% of Korean learners responded that their motivation to study Korean was Korean popular culture and that they also learned to speak Korean through popular culture (Jung, Yoon, Kang 2007). In a survey of 100 Chinese university students in Beijing, 94.5% of the respondents said they accessed Korean language through Korean popular culture, and 52% of the students said they wanted to learn Korean. According to a questionnaire surveying Chinese and Japanese students who are already studying Korean, 19.5% of respondents said that they were influenced by Korean popular culture to learn Korean, and 33% said that they were influenced significantly (ibid., 167-206).

The number of foreign students studying at educational institutions in Korea has been rising exponentially since the Korean Wave boomed in 2000; it increased from 12,134 in 2003 to 49,270 in 2007; 63,952 in 2008; 75,850 in 2009; 83,842 in 2010, 89,537 in 2011; 86,878 in 2012; 85,923 in 2013; 84,891 in 2014; and 91,332 in 2015.[1] A survey of 950 international students residing in

1 Korea Foundation for International Culture Exchange (KOFICE), 2012, *Korean Wave NOW*, 2-3 quarter of 2012, Korea Foundation for International Culture Exchange (KOFICE); Since 2010, the

Korea revealed that 61.5% of Japanese students and 51.7% of all Asian students were influenced by the Korean Wave in their decision to study abroad in Korea (Korea Foundation for International Culture Exchange 2012).

The Korean Wave has also affected overseas enrollment in Korean language classes in elementary, middle and high schools. Schools with Korean language classes have seen enrollment growth by an annual average of 10% over the past three years, breaking 1,000 in 2013. In 2014, 1,111 schools were open with a total of 93,144 students enrolled.

The country with the highest number of Korean classes is Japan. By 2014, there were 511 schools in Japan offering Korean classes with 17,718 students. In Thailand, the number of schools adopting Korean classes was smaller than that of Japan (75 schools), but the number of students was as high as 24,000, demonstrating the high enthusiasm of Thai people to learn the Korean language.

The Number of applicants for TOPIK (Test of Proficiency in Korean)

(Ministry of Education 2017)

Year	Test	Applicants	Successful applicants
1997	1st	2,692	711
1998	2nd	3,227	1,011
1999	3rd	3,926	2,513
2000	4th	5,976	2,920
2001	5th	7,475	3,364
2002	6th	8,788	4,534
2003	7th	12,187	6,362
2004	8th	17,545	9,558
2005	9th	26,611	14,548
2006	10th	34,028	16,456
2007	11th	13,247	7,655
	12th	36,886	19,112
2008	13th	31,796	17,449
	14th	42,497	18,881
2009	15th	39,658	21,216
	16th	46,262	21,525
2010	17th (in Korea)	3,552	1,840
	18th	41,865	1,840
	19th	41,865	18,558
	20th (in Korea)	13,964	5,711

statistics are based on "The Current Status of International Students", *National Index System* (Source of Statistics for International Students in Korea: Basic Statistics on Education (Approval No. -33401)). http://www.index.go.kr/potal/main/EachDtlPageDetail.do?idx_cd=1534

2011	21st	8,233	4,417
	22nd	46,797	24,065
	23rd (in Korea)	14,710	7,598
	24th	51,810	24,972
2012	25th (in Korea)	15,983	7,018
	26th	53,613	26,587
	27th	19,344	10,432
	28th	62,226	27,964
2013	29th (in Korea)	18,702	11,578
	30th	58,637	30,418
	31st (in Korea)	22,919	12,108
	32nd	67,595	31,766

The number of applicants for the Test of Proficiency in Korean (TOPIK) and the number of registrants for Korean language classes are both continuously increasing every year, and the region of interest is spreading beyond Asia to North America, Central and South America, Europe and Oceania. Global interest in the Korean Wave has given rise to widespread Korean language interest, instruction, and an educational infrastructure (Korea Foundation for International Culture Exchange 2016, 461-463).

The TOPIK (Test of Proficiency in Korean) is administered by the National Institute for International Education. Test applicants are typically foreigners or people who do not speak Korean as their first language. Since 1997, the number of test takers, test frequency, and test sites has increased significantly due to the spread of Hallyu culture and the expansion of overseas investment by Korean companies.

TOPIK is administered in two forms: TOPIK I and TOPIK II. Its results are used as an important basis for assessing the qualifications of foreign and non-native students to enter Korean universities and graduate schools; in the special selection of overseas Koreans; for granting Korean permanent residence status; for issuing work visas; and for examining the qualifications of foreigners as Korean teachers (The Kyunghyang Newspaper April 18, 2016).

The 46th TOPIK test in 2016 attracted the largest number of applicants ever recorded, with 72,295 applicants taking the test at 164 sites in 45 countries. By contrast, the number of applicants in the first year of the test was only 2,692 in 1997, but after reaching 12,187 in 2003, the number of applicants increased to 74,293 by 2008, then 106,953 in 2010, 167,853 in 2013, 179,000 in 2014, and 206,768 in 2015. More than 200,000 students currently take the TOPIK each year.[2]

2 For statistics up to 2013, please refer to the following Ministry of Education data. "Yearly Sta-

In 2014, the TOPIK was first administered in Cuba, which still has no diplomatic relations with South Korea. In 2016, the first TOPIK test was administered in Morocco in April and in Jamaica and Poland in the latter half of the year. Lastly, though the TOPIK was initially administered just once a year, the number of examinations held per year increased from 2 times in 2007 to 4 times in 2011 and to 6 times in 2015. The number of test sites has increased from just 4 countries in 1997 (Korea, Japan, Uzbekistan, and Kazakhstan) to 71 countries in 2016.

Considering that the phenomenon of the rapid increase of applicants for the TOPIK nearly coincides with the period of the wider global expansion of the Korean pop culture, it is possible to deduce that a significant and positive relationship exists between the Korean Wave and increased general interest in Korean language learning.

The Korean Wave appears to be functioning as an incentive to learn Korean. In many cases, students describe being motivated to learn Korean or to study abroad in Korea out of a desire to understand and follow the meaning of television dramas, movies, and songs that they came into contact with through the Korean Wave.

The Korean Wave and Potential Korean Learners

The spread of culture is broader, faster, and more powerful than the spread of language. It can allow those who are foreign to a given culture to experience that culture from a distance through its artifacts and productions and to develop a positive attitude towards the society of that culture's origin. As the desire to enjoy the culture intensifies, those individuals may feel inclined to learn the language (Cho, 2013).

However, a major disconnect between the interest sparked by the enjoyment of popular culture and the actual process of language learning lies in the question of authenticity and persistence of learning motivation. For example, following the spread of the Korean Wave to Japan, the audience of Korean learning broadcasting programs and sales of Korean language textbooks in Japan increased greatly, but the number of students who regularly took Korean

tistics on TOPIK (Test of Proficiency in Korean) Candidates", Ministry of Education, accessed Jan 15,2017. Http://www.moe.go.kr/newsearch/search.jsp# ; For statistics since 2014, please refer to the following data:"Korean Language Proficiency Test Candidates, 70-fold increase over 20 years", *The Kyunghyang Newspaper*, April 18, 2016. Http://news.khan.co.kr/kh_news/khan_art_view.html?artid=201604181148001&code=940100#csidxc9489e366d99c279cc52251afc89db8

language classes at high schools or universities did not increase significantly.

The spread of the Korean Wave has created a large number of potential learners, but there remains the challenge of retaining potential learners as true or long-term learners (ibid 2013). “Potential learner” here is used to mean a casual or initial-stage learner who is enthusiastic about the Korean Wave, as opposed to a genuine, long-term Korean language learner (Baek 2008, 133-4).

Korean learners emerged in Japan, where they grew up and acculturated independently to Korean culture through interaction with K-Pop and Korean-related clubs within Japanese high schools and universities. As a result, potential Korean learners who study Korean as something like a hobby appeared. A survey of Japanese college students studying Korean showed that their main reason for doing so was because of their affinity for Koreans and Korean popular culture (Ogoshi 2004, 151-162).

Since the start of the new Korean Wave in 2010, Korean idol singers such as TVXQ and 2PM have appeared in the NHK (Nippon Hoso Kyokai, Japan Broadcasting Corporation) Hangul (Korean) course program in Japan, and the volume of content related to the Korean Wave such as dance, music, and drama included in the program has increased dramatically. According to the Korean Cultural Center in Japan, the NHK Korean Course Program’s annual textbook sales volume is currently about 300,000 copies including 220,000 copies of TV Korean language programs and 80,000-90,000 copies of radio Korean language programs. The number of people watching and listening to these programs without textbooks is three to four times more than those who study Korean lanuguage with having textbooks. More than one million people have joined the NHK Hangul course program over the past 5 years.

It is evident that the Korean Wave is influencing Korean language studies through the increasingly widespread availability of Korean popular culture. NHK is actively utilizing Korean language dramas and songs as examples of Hangul and as instructional texts in Korean course programs. Shimizu Chuichi, who is charge of the Korean cultural service in the South Korean Embassy in Japan, said, “High school students who are attracted to Korean musical artists BoA and Girls’ Generation also learn Korean as a foreign language instead of English.” (Korea Economic Daily May 14, 2010).

In China, the number of potential Korean learners is increasing in relation to the influx of Korean popular culture. In a survey of 400 Chinese students pursuing Korean language learning, 25.9% of respondents responded that they were studying Korean because they wanted to travel to Korea or wanted to expand their knowledge of the language, and 25.6% responded they are studying Korean because of the Korean Wave. These reasons were divided somewhat along generational lines; university students generally stated their interest in travel to Korea and in the Korean language as their primary reason for learning Korean while other older respondents identified the Korean Wave as the most important motivating factor (Jung, Yoon, Kang 2007).

However, the transition of potential learners to true learners remains limited. In 2002, the number of people who expressed interest in Korean language learning increased following the release of the Korean drama "Winter Sonata". While the number of Japanese high schools that established Korean language courses nearly doubled from 219 in 2003 to 426 in 2007, the number of students who took Korean language classes has seen relatively limited growth from 6,476 in 2003 to only 8,865 in 2007 (Korea Economic Daily May 14, 2010). While it is true that the number of potential learners has greatly increased due to the Korean wave, potential learners have not consistently developed into true Korean learners.

Conclusion: Hallyu-based textbook for potential Korean learners

The Korean learner, who has been caught in the Korean Wave, has great potential to learn the language actively. The spread of culture is more powerful than the spread of language. However, potential Korean learners often lack the motivation and support to ensure the continuity of their learning. Therefore, with an eye to the increasing globalization of the Korean language, it is necessary to actively promote policies and research efforts towards converting potential Korean learners into true Korean learners.

To this end, potential learners should be provided with culture-based language teaching and a digital environment accessible from anywhere in the world. A Korean language learning support system that emphasizes popular culture-based language teaching, delivered through a digital learning environment, can meet these goals of cultural relevancy and accessibility and lead to continuous learning among potential Korean learners. In particular, it is imperative to develop a Korean-language textbook based on the communicative approach using Korean popular media as examples and cultural gateways.

A survey of Chinese and Japanese people showed a positive attitude towards the development of Korean textbooks that incorporate elements of Korean popular culture, such as Korean dramas, movies, and music videos starring their favorite entertainers. Therefore, elements of Korean culture such as Korean dramas, Korean movies, and entertainment programs should be introduced into Korean textbooks based on pedagogics, which can foster learning motivation for foreign learners.

Korean pop culture-based textbooks should focus on improving the Korean learner's communicative competence. For communicative skills, Korean dramas, movies, music, current and realistic contents should be included in Korean textbooks so that learners can actively participate in their education by modeling their communication on familiar and interesting content. These media can also be helpful in improving students' nonverbal communicative skills, leading to a more integrated Korean language education.

In addition to basic textbooks capitalizing on the Korean Wave, reading, listening, speaking, and practice materials need to be developed in the form of multimedia available on the Internet. Potential Korean learners who come into contact with the Korean Wave that initially spread through the Internet can learn the Korean language from anywhere in the world using these online multimedia materials. Therefore, it would be prudent to develop Korean textbooks geared towards fostering integrated communicative competency and to create versatile learning materials made available online and used in the classroom based on the media of the Korean Wave.

References

Baek, Bongja. 2008. Evaluation Report of the King Sejong Institute.

Ogoshi, Naoki. 2004. "Image Formation toward Korea and Korean and Korean Language Learning." Korean Language and Culture Studies l(2): 151-162. (In Korean)

Im, Mi-Kyung. 2005. "A Comparative Needs Survey for Learner-Centered Cultural Education." Master's thesis, Yonsei University Graduate School of Education. (In Korean)

Jung, Hye Kyung, Yoon Seok-im, and Kang Mi-ok. 2007. Acceptance of the Korean Wave and Korean Language Education- China, Japan, Seoul: Pakijong. (In Korean)

Cho, Hang Rok. 2013. A Study on Strategies of Supporting Korean Language Education. Korean Ministry of Culture, Sports and Tourism (In Korean)

Ministry of Education. 2017. "Yearly Statistics on TOPIK (Test of Proficiency in Korean) Candidates", Accessed Jan 15, 2017. Http://www.moe.go.kr/newsearch/search.jsp#

The King Sejong Institute Foundation. 2017. "King Sejong Institute of Worldwide", Accessed Jan 14, 2017, Http://www.ksif.or.kr/business/locSejong.do

The King Sejong Institute Foundation. 2015. "World King Sejong Institutes. " Annual

Report of the King Sejong Institute Foundation.

Korea Foundation for International Culture Exchange (KOFICE). 2012. Korean Wave NOW 2-3 quarter of 2012. Korea Foundation for International Culture Exchange (KOFICE).

Korea Foundation for International Culture Exchange (KOFICE). 2015. 2015 Hallyu White Paper. Korea Foundation for International Culture Exchange (KOFICE).

Korea Creative Content Agency. 2010. Contents Industry Trend, Korea Creative Content Agency.

The Chosun Ilbo. 2016. "Thanks to the Korean Wave ... TOPIK craze in the world." The Chosun Ilbo, April 19, 2016. http://news.chosun.com/site/data/html_dir/2016/04/19/2016041900099.html.

The Korea Economic Daily. 2010. "I Want to Talk like 'Yonsama'." The Korea Economic Daily, May 14, 2010.

http://stock.hankyung.com/news/app/newsview.php?aid=2010051444231&skin=print&sid=0102.

The Kyunghyang Newspaper. 2016. "The Korean Language Proficiency Test Candidates, 70-fold increase over 20 years." The Kyunghyang Newspaper, April 18, 2016.

http://news.khan.co.kr/kh_news/khan_art_view.html?artid=201604181148001&code=940100.

Part 4

Power-dimension of the Korean Wave

Chapter 7

The Anti-Korean Wave in Japan: Identity Clash

Yeonhee Yoon

Introduction

Cultural conflicts are inevitable phenomena that accompany the process of cultural globalization. They often occur when the nations that receive another country's popular culture and media attempt to protect their popular culture and industries or when the values of one culture collide with those of the other. For example, anti-Hollywood sentiment emerged in Korea as a form of resistance to the dominant American media distribution system and as an expression of antipathy against its portrayals of political issues, particularly its negative portrayals of Korean culture. It also signaled anxiety over the influx of American cultural values into the Korean cultural sphere (Korean Culture and Tourism Institute, 2009). When Japanese comics (Manga) arrived in Korea, it provoked similar backlash given pre-existing anti-Japan sentiment in South Korea and general wariness of cultural encroachment in Korea, especially around the issue of its oftentimes graphically violent and sexual content.

R. Robertson (1992) presents the dual cultural processes of the 'particularization of universalism' and the 'universalization of particularism.' He argues that globalization accelerates and institutionalizes the interpenetration of these parallel phenomena and that they are complementary (Robertson 1992, 98-105).

According to Robertson, conflicts between Western culture and non-Western cultures, based on the assumption made by cultural imperialism, will eventually disappear or languish. That is, globalization incurs cultural complexity, compatibility, and hybridity.

This paper discusses the cultural conflicts that have arisen in the international spread of Korean culture through Robertson's framework of the interpenetrating processes of universalization and particularization. This paper analyzes the causes and characteristics of the anti-Korean wave and pro-nationalist sentiment in Japan following the emergence and global proliferation of South Korean culture. The difference between the Anti-Korean Wave in Japan and the same phenomenon as expressed in China can be explained in light of these countries' differing responses to a clash in national identities and values.

The Korean Wave

The Korean Wave (*hallyu*) refers to the phenomenal popularity of South Korean popular cultural products and industries ranging from television dramas, movies, popular music (K-pop) and dance, and tourism to food, gaming and technology, and fashion which began in East Asia in the early 2000s.

The South Korean government exercises "soft power" in promoting the rise and spread of the Korean wave (hereafter, *hallyu*). The regime of former president Kim Young Sam (YS) (1993-1998) was the first to focus government attention on cultural phenomena. The YS regime established a division of cultural industry and thereafter, the regime of former president Kim Dae Joong (1998-2003) prioritized policymaking that affected the cultural industry. As a result, South Korean big business groups (chaebol) such as Samsung, Hyundai, and Daewoo established cultural content-producing divisions and started to invest in recording, movie production, and the multimedia industries. President Kim Dae Joong emphasized that cultural influence is the most important asset for securing the power of the future of South Korean society. Owing to the South Korean government's policy of promoting cultural industries and investing in major companies, Korea's cultural industry achieved rapid growth during this time (Kim 2014).

The total export of the cultural industry increased from 3.19 billion dollars in 2010 to 5.7 billion dollars in 2015, showing about 80% of export growth within six years. The economic impact of the Korean Wave was not limited to a massive increase in the availability and popularity of Korean cultural products, but it also led to a vastly increased global awareness of Korea's national brand image. Accordingly, the Korean Wave also incurred secondary economic effects through the increase in tourism revenue and the popular consumption of Korean goods, including food and beverage, cosmetics, and clothing. In other words, it is said that the Korean Wave induced a ripple effect in the Korean economy by production inducement, value-added inducement effects, and employment creation. Table 1 shows the increase in Korea's content industry exports from 2010 to 2016 (Korea Foundation for International Culture Exchange 2016).

<Table 1> Exports of South Korean Content Industry (2010~2015)

1million USD

Business Sectors		**2010**	**2011**	**2012**	**2013**	**2014**	**2015**	**Percentage of business sectors as of 2015**
Publication	Export Amount	358	283	245	292	247	255	4.5%
	Variation Rate (%)	-	-20.9%	247.0%	19.2%	-15.4%	3.1%	
Cartoon	Export Amount	8	17	17	21	26	27	0.5%
	Variation Rate (%)	-	112.5%	0.0%	23.5%	23.8%	5.4%	
Music	Export Amount	83	196	235	277	336	361	6.3%
	Variation Rate (%)	-	136.1%	19.9%	17.9%	21.3%	7.3%	
Game	Export Amount	1,606	2,378	2,639	2,715	2,974	3,220	56.5%
	Variation Rate (%)	-	48.1%	11.0%	2.9%	9.5%	8.3%	
Movie	Export Amount	14	16	20	37	26	29	0.5%
	Variation Rate (%)	-	14.3%	25.0%	85.0%	-29.7%	13.1%	
Animation	Export Amount	97	116	113	110	116	124	2.2%
	Variation Rate (%)	-	19.6%	-2.6%	-2.7%	5.5%	6.9%	
Broadcast	Export Amount	185	222	234	309	336	367	6.4%
	Variation Rate (%)	-	20.0%	5.4%	32.1%	8.7%	9.2%	
Advertise-ment	Export Amount	76	102	97	103	76	75	1.3%
	Variation Rate (%)	-	34.2%	-4.9%	1371.4%	-26.2%	-0.9%	
Character	Export Amount	276	392	416	446	489	551	9.7%
	Variation Rate (%)	-	42.0%	6.1%	7.2%	9.6%	12.7%	
Knowledge Information	Export Amount	368	432	445	457	480	527	9.2%
	Variation Rate (%)	-	17.4%	3.0%	2.7%	5.0%	9.8%	
Contents Solution	Export Amount	119	146	150	155	168	168	2.9%
	Variation Rate (%)	-	22.7%	2.7%	3.3%	8.4%	0.0%	
Total	Export Amount	3,189	4,302	4,612	4,923	5,274	5,700	100.0%
	Variation Rate (%)	22.20%	34.9%	7.2%	6.7%	7.1%	8.1%	

There are various reasons why Korean popular culture proliferated rapidly in Asian countries. In the first place, this phenomenon can be explained in light of cultural proximity and similarity. In other words, Korean popular culture in large part reflects familiar, if not common, values of Asian cultures generally, so the cultural discount rate[1] is low (Jang, Kim, Kim 2012, 696). Secondly, Korean media often presents an appealing model of modernization through which people in developing Asian countries can vicariously visualize their own futures. Thirdly, Korean pop culture is widely considered to be a fresh and novel alterntive to the dominant cultures of the United States and Japan (Mukasa 2011). For example, Korean dramas such as *My love from the star* (2014) and *Descendents of the Sun* (2016) captivated viewers in most of Asian countries for its attractive stars, inventive storylines, and storytelling format (Wong 2016).

This favoritism is not unilateral or uniform, however. The results of a survey conducted in 2015 by KOFICE (the Korea Foundation for International Culture Exchange) and KOTRA (Korea Trade Investment Promotion Agency) show that the Korean Wave decreased in popularity in Japan, Iran, and India. This trend does not portend an optimistic portrayal of the Korean wave's trajectory in other target countries of similar development and international prominence such as China and Taiwan. However, the popularity of Korean popular culture and the growth of the Korean Wave phenomenon is predicted to increase in the emerging Southeast Asian market in countries such as Indonesia, Malaysia, and Vietnam.

The factors that have hindered the popular spread of the Korean Wave phenomenon vary by country. In China, for instance, the government instated regulatory measures on the import of Korean media, in conjunction with public sentiment that Korean popular culture might negatively influence Chinese culture. Similarly, in Taiwan, there is anxiety over the possibility that Korean popular culture might negatively influence Taiwanese youth. Unlike the anti-Korean Wave sentiments in China and Taiwan, however, the decline of the Korean Wave in Japan results from political factors that sway the attitudes of Japanese consumers and which contribute to the persistence of a pessimistic view of Korean culture (Korea Foundation for International Culture Exchange 2015).

1 The term "cultural discount" has been coined to capture the notion that a particular program (or feature film) rooted in one culture, and thus attractive in that environment, will have diminished appeal elsewhere as viewers find it difficult to identify with the styles, values, beliefs, institutions, and behaviour patterns being portrayed (Hoskins, Rolf 1988, 499-515).

The Korean Wave and Perceptions of Korea in Japan

South Korea and Japan began exchanging popular culture in earnest in the early 2000s. The South Korean government first decided to open the popular culture markets toward Japan in 1998 when the Korea-Japan summit adopted the Korea-Japan Joint Declaration, which promised to work toward building future relations between the countries (Goh 2007). In addition, Korea and Japan decided to co-host the 2002 FIFA World Cup in 1996.

In December 2001, the word "*Hallyu*" appeared for the first time in the Japanese national newspaper *Asahi Shimbun*. In April 2003, the Korean drama *Winter Sonata* was first broadcast in Japan, and the actor Bae Yong Joon became so popular that the phenomenon was called "Yon-sama" (translated to Emperor Yon) and thus the Korean Wave craze in Japan was ignited. After this craze, *Dae Jang Geum (Jewel in the Palace)* was broadcast in Japan in October 2004 and became popular among both middle-aged men and women (Jung 2013, 138). On the whole, Japanese viewers who had previously been indifferent or critical of Korean people and culture became newly interested in and began to develop a favorable impression of Korea. Accordingly, the economic impact of the Korean Wave in 2004 was considerable, amounting to 1.4 trillion KRW and thus effectively raising Korea's GDP by 0.18% (Goh 2007, 80-81).

The results of surveys among Japanese subjects regarding the impact of Korean popular culture on general attitudes towards Korea can be broadly classified into three types: positive, neutral, and negative (Lim 2012, 415-433).

The positive regard for the Korean Wave phenomenon reported by these results can be summarized as follows. First, the Korean Wave phenomenon promoted a positive relationship between Korea and Japan. Its media offered up a positive, modernized portrait of Korea to Japanese viewers, which allowed Japanese viewers to reappraise their stance on contemporary Korea and revisit the history of Korean-Japanese international relations. In particular, Japanese audiences were able to realize that many Korean people harbor anti-Japanese sentiment due to Japan's colonization of Korea in the early 20th century.

Second, the neutral view accounts for the possible difficulty facing Japanese viewers in accepting the Korean Wave phenomenon in a wholly positive manner, given that some Japanese people harbor negative views on Korean popular culture and pride themselves on their own culture. Moreover, not all people in contemporary Japan are equally aware of the historical conflicts and tensions between Korea and Japan.

Third, the negative view on the Korean Wave phenomenon by survey participants reported that some Japanese people hold the opinion that Japanese popular culture has lost momentum in other Asian countries directly due to the incursion of the Korean Wave phenomenon and related intentional business practices. These Japanese participants who hold these negative views on the Korean Wave maintain that the dominant narratives and contents of the Korean wave were manipulated to keep Japanese consumers largely ignorant of historical conflicts, North Korean issues, or the social issues facing *Zainichi* (Japanese-acculturated Koreans residing in Japan).

Overall, however, the Korean Wave has generally improved the Japanese perception of Korea. In 2001, the Cabinet Office of Japan conducted a poll on foreign affairs and examined how Japanese people perceive Korea. 50.3% of Japanese respondents indicated they feel friendly towards Korea. The next year, when the two countries co-hosted the World Cup in 2002, that figure rose to 54.2%. In 2003, when *Winter Sonata* was broadcast in Japan, it rose again to 55%, and when *Dae Jang Geum* was released in 2004, to 56.7%. According to the same annual poll conducted between 2008 and 2011 – during which time the second boom of the Korean wave took place, this time through the import of music through K-pop "idol" artists and groups – the percentage of respondents indicating positive affinity was recorded at 57.1% in 2008, 63.1% in 2009, 61.8% in 2010 and 62.2% in 2011. Accordingly, between 2001-2011, the percentage of Japanese respondents who did not feel amicably towards Korea diminished, recorded as 45.5% in 2001, 40.5% in 2002, 41% in 2003, 39.2% in 2004, 40.9% in 2008, 34.2% in 2009 and 36% and 35.3% in 2011. These statistics indicate that the Korean Wave and the co-hosting of the World Cup coincided with and may even have brought about a significant improvement in the Japanese cultural imagination and reception of Korea and the feelings of the Japanese people toward Korea in general (Cabinet Office of Government of Japan, 2014).

What is noteworthy in these poll results, however, is that the perception of Korea also significantly declined in 2006, 2012, 2013 and 2014. Interestingly, specific geopolitical events corresponded with these downturns; the first was the flare-up of diplomatic tension over the territory of Dokdo, an island between the two countries. In a special statement regarding this conflict, then-president of South Korea Roh Moo-hyun (2003-2008) said on April 26, 2006: "Dokdo is a land of deep grief that has been carved through history for forty years. Japan must be honest and humble before the truth of history and the conscience of human society." Additionally, six years later in 2012, then-president Lee Myung-bak (2008-2013) visited Dokdo and publicly referenced the necessity that the Emperor of Japan apologize, which further deteriorated Japanese feelings for South Korea over this matter. In addition, the Japanese perception of South Korea was negatively influenced by three major political events in the past five years: firstly, former President Park Geun-hye (2013-2017)'s hard-line diplomacy regarding the issue of Korean 'comfort women'; secondly, Japan's antipathy toward South Korea's political approach to China; and thirdly, the speech made by former President Park at the March 1st independence movement ceremony in 2013, in which she stated that the historical position of the perpetrators and victims could not be changed even after a thousand years of history (Kijo, 2015). In this final instance, Park was referring to and incisively describing the irreversibility of conflict between Japan and Korea.

Japan's Anti-Korean Sentiment

Historical Background of Anti-Korean sentiment

Ogura Gijo (2015) identifies the cause of anti-Korea attitudes in Japan as feelings of defeat in light of the rise of Korea and China. In addition, he argues that factors such as "apology fatigue" – referring to the exhaustion and exasperation experienced by Japan that feels it has already fully apologized for historical wrongdoings – a deep-seated contempt for Korean people, aversion towards pan-Asian rhetoric and nationalism in Japanese politics, the media strategies of anti-Korean groups as well as culture-wide complaints about conscientious Japanese liberals all further influence and exacerbate anti-Korean sentiment.

Moreover, recent speeches by former Presidents Lee Myung-bak and Park Geun-hye have also contributed to the deterioration of Japan's positive regard for South Korea. Under these circumstances, anti-Korean groups in Japan started a full-scale anti-Korea campaign, expressing opposition to the "Korean-Japanese Friendship Frame" broadcast over Japanese media and the "Korean Wave" boom that began in 2003 when the two countries co-hosted the 2002 World Cup.

Anti-Korean phenomenon in Japanese publishing and journalism

In 2005, when Yamano Shirin published the book *Manga Kenkanryu (Hating the Korean Wave)*, it sold 650,000 copies in two months. By 2011, it had been reprinted four times. Yamano Shirin had previously written solely for the Internet and had been unable to publish his writings in print, but he was able to reach a wider audience through the publisher Shinyusha in the spring of

2004, the coinciding period of anti-Japanese demonstrations in South Korea and China. While superficially, the content of the book is a reaction against the trend of Korean popular culture, upon closer reading, the book consists of a criticism of Korea itself rather than criticism of its popular culture. In other words, the subject of Shirin's work is not solely an 'instance of the so-called anti-Korean Wave' that takes aim at the rise of Korean popular culture; rather, it also takes an 'anti-Korean' approach that hates what is 'Korean' more generally (Itagaki 2006, 405-423).

Several other books criticizing and denigrating the Korean Wave were published following the release and popularity of *Manga Kenkanryu*. According to one Japanese weekly magazine, its issue sales exceeded 100,000 copies even if only the word "Korean" was included in the title on the cover page, which was a great boon to Japanese weekly magazines in crisis (Lim 2014, 217-223).

The word *kenkan (Hating the Korean Wave)* first appeared in the *Mainichi Shimbun* in 1992 and largely disappeared from use thereafter, but it resurfaced and was frequently used in 2005 and 2006; usage increased dramatically once again in 2014 (Park 2009; Tawaragi 2015, 113-140). According to a study by Tawaragi (2015), the *Sankei Shimbun* generally argued that the Korean people themselves were responsible for Japan's anti-Korean sentiment, while the editorial stance of the *Asahi Shimbun* maintained that the Japanese government was responsible for Japan's anti-Korean sentiment by tolerating speeches that irritate anti-Korean sentiment in the Japanese population.

Factors of Japan's anti-Korean sentiment

Following the arrival of a foreign culture on domestic soils, reactions in the receiving culture can be quite heterogeneous; the coexistence of positive and negative opinions in the process of accepting a foreign culture is a universal phenomenon. How, then, did the phenomenon of a seemingly unified anti-Korean sentiment arise in Japan and spread so rapidly and virulently? Following the framework of Jung Min Ju (2013), we can analyze the causes of this spread of anti-Korean sentiment through the dimensions of culture, nationalism, and media (Jung 2013, 140).

First, in terms of culture, anti-Korean sentiment in Japan can be seen as arising from the debate over 'cultural originality,' a competitiveness stemming from national pride, and an internal cultural crisis. The controversy of cultural originality has grown fierce in Japan, especially as the status of Sout Korea has improved and attracted global attention. For example, efforts to rename green tea as 'Japanese tea' and to coin a new Japanese term 'kimuchi' for the Korean staple food 'kimchi' indicate efforts to assert national pride and proprietariness. In 2009, the South Korean TV drama series "*Iris*" was broadcasted by a Japanese commercial TV network in Japan during prime time; the success of this South Korean TV drama series reportedly hurt the cultural pride of the Japanese because South Korean TV drama series were so popular. As the craze for learning about Korean culture has accelerated in Japan, some netizens in Japan and the press have expressed an increasing sense of cultural crisis and the hopeful view that they may be able to promote Japanese culture against Korean culture.

At the national level, minority groups in Japan dissatisfied with the intensifying Korea-Japan conflict and with mainstream Japanese society itself are increasingly expressing their political and social grievances in a way that targets and opposes the Korean Wave. These few marginalized groups have increasingly taken up anti-Korean sentiment when various political problems between Korea and Japan have arisen in recent years such as in the North Korean abduction issue, the Yasukuni shrine controversy, the territorial conflict over Dokdo Island, and the grievances of comfort women. These groups express their dissatisfaction with the existing social structure through the rhetoric of anti-Korean sentiment.

One such group is the "*Zaitokukai*" (Association of Citizens against the Special Privileges of *Zainichi* Koreans), one of the primary radical groups in Japan opposing the Korean Wave and *Zainichi* Koreans more generally. On December 2, 2006, the *Zaitokukai* was first established with the aim of proclaiming that *Zainichi* and other foreigners in Japan unfairly enjoy privileges that, in their estimation, only Japanese citizens should receive. The *Zaitokukai* expanded its influence with information strategies using the Internet, radical street demonstrations, and overly straightforward, self-centered claims. Most of the people who align themselves with the *Zaitokukai* belong to the socially and economically disadvantaged, and their general discourse consists of complaints about the economic and social landscape in the terms of anti-Korean sentiment. The zaitokukai opposes such measures as free education in Korean schools, foreigners' suffrage, Korean recovery of annexed territory, and subsidies for the livelihood protection of foreign nationals. They insist that Korean entertainers withdraw from Japan. When Korean entertainers talk about the Dokdo issue in Japanese broadcasts, the group actively advocates for deportation proceedings (Lee 2014, 72-80).

Thirdly, the Japanese conservative media, publishing houses, and the Internet are inciting and spreading anti-Korean sentiment. The expansion of conservative journalism in Japan, the function of nationalist discourse in the media, overtly patriotic discourse, and the actions of the Japanese publishing industry reproduce and affirm anti-Korean sentiment. For example, *Shinyusha* published the first volume of *Manga Kenkanryu* at the time of the anti-Japanese demonstrations in Korea and China and published the second edition of the cartoon on the "Takeshima Day" established by the Japanese local government to claim the sovereignty of Dokdo (Takeshima) Island. Moreover, websites such as *2ch* form digital epicenters of anti-Korean sentiment. Exploiting the possibility for anonymity that the internet provides, netizens can freely attack or criticize dissenters to their 'media nationalism'. On such sites and forums, anti-Korean nationalists in Japan are free to pour out aversion and discrimination against North Korea and the *Zainich* Koreans (Japanese-acculturated Koreans residing in Japan) (Jung 2013, 151).

Conclusion: Identity Clash?

John Storey (2003) argues that identity does not come from nature but from history and culture. Differentiated cultural characteristics are related in their origin and development to history, which in turn differs by nation or territory and accumulates over a long period of time. Nationalism seeks to form a specific culture that differentiates itself and its constituents from other peoples through the reinterpretation and reproduction of a nation-based culture. If culture lies at the core of identity, the identity of modern society is undoubtedly in part constructed from consumption of media and popular culture available in the market.

Why does cultural conflict occur at the national level in tandem with the process of universalizing and diffusing a particular culture? I assert that it originates from the duality of nationalism. Nationalism, which wants to protect its own culture, is predicated on the territorialization of culture. Nationalism that seeks to project its culture outward pursues de-territorialization and re-territorialization.

From this point of view, the Korean Wave phenomenon can be understood as involving a process of de-territorialization—in which a particular (Korean) culture is universalized in the process of globalization—and re-territorialization, in which that home culture thus expands its cultural territory. The anti-Korean Wave phenomenon in Japan arises out of the clash between the re-territorialization of Korean popular culture, which seeks to expand its cultural territory, and the reactive territorialization of Japanese nationalism to protect its own cultural territory.

In Japan, however, the anti-Korean Wave is also linked to the clash of national identities respective to both countries. The proliferation of the Korean Wave in Japan has triggered a clash between the identity of a Korean nationalism based on anti-Japanese colonialism, whereas the identity of Japanese nationalism is in large part predicated on the memory of the Empire. Japanese nationalism recognized the proliferation of Korean popular culture in Japan as a challenge from Korean nationalism and as a result experienced a crisis of identity. Contrary to the expectation that globalization can lead to the deterritorialization of culture and the weakening of nationalism (Tomlinson 1999, 106-149; Appadurai 1990, 295-310), in the case of Japan it has stimulated cultural conflicts while strengthening nationalism (Antony 1990, 171).

In terms of the clash of nationalistic identities, we can explain the difference between the anti-Korean Wave phenomenon in Japan and the anti-Korean Wave in China. In China, the anti-Korean Wave is not connected with nationalistic identity but rather expressed in the form of 'cultural competition', or the economic competition of respective government-led cultural industries. On the other hand, the anti-Korean Wave in Japan, linked to the immaterial competition of national identity, fomented due to cultural conflict and identity clashes fueled by the Japanese popular culture industry and media. The case of South Korean actress Kim Tae-hee and singer Lee Seung-cheol - both of whom were outspoken critics of the Japanese position on the Dokdo conflict - provide representative examples of the present-day confluence of popular culture and nationalism. This is why *Kenkanryu (Hating the Korean Wave)* evolved into an anti-Korean sentiment beyond the anti-Korea Wave in Japan. The propagation and diffusion process of popular culture is easily and often fused with conflicts over history and diplomacy.

References

Appadurai, Arjun. 1990. "Disjuncture and difference in the global cultural economy." *Theory, culture and society* 7(2): 295-310.

Goh, Gil-Hee. 2007. "The Relationship between Japan and Korea as seen in 'Korean Wave' and 'Anti-Korean Wave'- Searching for 'Diversified Nationalism'." *The Japanese Modern Association of Korea* 17.

Han, Young Kyun. 2013. "The Reality of the Phenomenon of Anti-Korean Sentiment in Japan." *Japanese Cultural Studies* 48: 433-456.

Hoskins, Colin, and Mirus Rolf. 1988. "Reasons for the U.S. Dominance of the International Trade in Television Programmes." *Media, Culture and Society* 10: 499-515.
Itagaki, Ryuta. 2006. "Two Perspectives of Japanese Society Looking at the Korean Wave." *The Quarterly Changbi* 34(2): 405-423. (In Korean)
Jang, Won-ho, Kim Ik-ki and Kim Ji. 2012. "Analysis of Cultural Industries on the Expansion of the Korean Wave- Focusing on the Korean Wave in Japan." *Journal of Korean Economic Geography* 15(4).
Ju, Jung Min. 2013. "Causes and Responses of the Phenomenon of Anti-Korean Wave to the Korean Wave Contents." *Diaspora Study* 7(2).
Kim, Pyeon Soo. 2014. *Basic Theory of Cultural Industry*. Seoul: Communication Books.
Kim, Ik-Ki. 2013. "Modes of the Korean Wave Consumption in East Asia." In *A New Flow of East Asian Pop Culture Consumption*, edited by Hyunjin Lim and Myung-gu Kang. Seoul: Nanam Press.
Lee, Kyu Soo. 2014. "Japanese Zaitokukai's Anti-Korea, Foreignism." *Japan Studies* 38: 72-80.
Lee, Yoon Kyung. 2009. *Analysis of the Anti-Korean Wave and a Study on Countermeasures*. Korea Culture & Tourism Institute.
Lim, Sang Gyun. 2014. "Anti-Korea in Japanese Journalism." *Kwanhun Journal* 130: 217-223.
Lim, Young Eun. 2012. "The Koreanism of the Korean Wave Culture and its impact on Koreatown Japanese." *Japanese Language and Literature* 55: 415-433.
Ogura, Kijo. 2015. What are the Anti-Korean Nationalists in Japan Claiming. Seoul: J & C.
Park, Soo Ok. 2009. "Japan's Anti- Korean Sentiment and Media Nationalism- Focusing on *2ch* and the Four Japanese National Newspapers." *Korean Journal of Press Information* 47.
Robertson, R. 1992. *Globalization: Social theory and Global Culture*. London: Sage.
Smith, Antony D. 1990. "Towards a Global Culture?" *Theory, Culture and Society* 7(2).
Storey, J. 2003. *Inventing Popular Culture : From Folklore to Globalization* (Blackwell manifestos). Malden: Blackwell Pub.
Tawaragi, Harumi. 2015. "A Study on the Meaning of Anti-Korean Discourses in the Japanese Newspapers." *The Japanese Modern Association of Korea* 50: 113-140.
Tomlinson, John. 1999. *Globalization and Culture*. Chicago: University of Chicago Press
Cabinet Office. 2014. *Government of Japan. Public Opinion Survey on the Diplomacy*. Http://survey.gov-online.go.jp
Korea Foundation for International Culture Exchange (KOFICE). 2016. 2015 *Hallyu White Paper*. Seoul: KOFICE.
Korea Foundation for International Culture Exchange (KOFICE). 2015. *A Study on the Economic Effects of the Korean Wave*.
Korean Culture and Tourism Institute. 2009. *Analysis on the Status of Anti-Korean Waves and Countermeasures*.
Mukasa, Edwina. 2011. "Bored with Cowell Pop? Try K-pop." *The Guardian*, December 15 2011. http://www.theguardian.com/music/2011/dec/15/cowell-pop-k-pop

Tan, Huileng. "Descendants of the Sun Smash Hit Prompts Beijing to Warn on South Korean Dramas." CNBC, 16 March 2016. http://www.cnbc.com/2016/03/16/descendants-of-the-sun-smash-hit-prompts-beijing-to-warn-on-south-korean-dramas.html

Wan, William Wan. "Chinese Officials Debate Why China Can't Make a Soap Opera as Good as South Korea's." The Washington Post, 7 March 2014. https://www.washingtonpost.com/world/asia_pacific/chinese-officials-debate-why-china-cant-make-a-soap-opera-as-good-as-south-koreas/2014/03/07/94b86678-a5f3-11e3-84d4-e59b1709222c_story.html

Wong, Tessa. "Descendants of the Sun: the Korean Military Romance Sweeping Asia." BBC News, 26 March 2016. http://www.bbc.com/news/world-asia-35888537;

Chapter 8

The Korean Wave as a Soft Power

Kiwoong Yang & Maddalena Ciesa

Introduction

Global interest in the Korean Wave is bigger than interest in Korea itself. According to a survey of 46 branches of the King Sejong Institute in 29 nations in 2013, about 34 percent of enrolled students attributed their desire to learn Korean language to Korean pop culture, while approximately 20 percent of them cited interest in the country.[1]

For example, the Korean drama Dae Jang Geum (Jewel in the Palace)[2], showcasing the traditional plates of Korean royal court cuisine, drew the attention of the world to Korean food more effectively than the actions of diplomats or public advertisements.

The Korean government is using the Korean Wave as a basic asset for public diplomacy. In order to increase intimacy with Korea and promote the export of its cultural goods, MOFAT(Ministry of Foreign Affairs and Trade) has continued to support overseas broadcasting of Korean TV dramas, especially in areas where private broadcasters have found difficulties in gaining access(Ministry of Foreign Affairs, Republic of Koera 2012).

By strategically utilizing popular culture, South Korea has become rich in

1 "King Sejong Institute promotes Korean education", The Korea Times, October 23, 2013. The King Sejong Institute is the overseas educational institution of the Korean language and Korean cultures. The name of the institute originates from King Sejong of the Joseon-era, who is revered because of his contribution to the creation of "hangeul," the Korean alphabet.

2 A plot synopsis of *Dae Jang Geum*: "In the Joseon-era when women held little influence in society, a young apprentice chef strives to learn the secrets of Korean cooking and medicine in order to cure the King of his various ailments." I would like to thank Maddalena Ciesa for generously sharing her ideas and works. Much of the content and ideas in this chapter depend on her thesis. She is a de facto co-author.

"soft power". While hard power involves the use of coercion and payment, soft power aims to change the behavior of others through the means of attraction and persuasion. Joseph S. Nye has pointed to three primary sources of soft power: culture, political values, and foreign policy. In a soft power context, culture is defined as the "set of practices that create meaning for a society" (Nye 2004). Culture includes literature, art and education as well as media such as television, cinema and pop music. Political values such as transparency, justice, and equality are also function as important tenets of soft power. Soft power refers to the ability to achieve political ends through attraction.

South Korea has garnered impressive potential for soft power. In addition to its stunning economic success, it has achieved democratization and developed a truly democratic system, characterized by an emphasis on human rights, free elections and the transfer of power between different political parties (Kim 2013). Even the mass candlelight vigils that imposed the impeachment of President Park during the winter of 2016 may be considered an attraction of Korean democracy.

In the shadows of Japan, China, and North Korea, South Korea has been underestimated by the international community despite its phenomenal success. However, the Korean Wave has heightened South Korea's visibility around the world and captured the imagination of a new generation. This visibility has changed foreign perceptions of the country.

What is Soft Power?

Soft power uses means other than direct force—such as the demonstration of shared values and justice—to engender political cooperation. Nye emphasizes the importance of influence of a positive national image that derives from a number of intangible sources such as domestic and foreign policies, the actions that the country undertakes, and cultural production. "A country may obtain the outcomes it wants in world politics because other countries admire its values, emulate its example, and aspire to its level of prosperity and openness. This soft power getting others to want the outcomes that you want co-opts people rather than coerces them. Soft power rests on the ability to shape the preferences of others" (Nye 2004). Favorable perception generates respect and admiration which in turn endears countries with soft power to other nations.

The growing importance of soft power is related to globalization, which deepens interdependence among nations and reduces the utility of hard power.

In such a globalized world, where there is a high degree of interdependence among countries, punishing or threatening other nations is equal to self-punishment (Gallarotti 2010). The emergent importance of soft power is also linked to the rapid progress of the information age. Power in the information age will come not from the application of strong hard power, but from the connections built through sharing. As we share with others, we develop common outlooks and approaches that improve our ability to deal with new challenges (Nye 2004). Sharing not only enhances the ability of others to cooperate with us but also increases their inclination to do so. Lastly, the development of democracy also reduces the utility of coercion as the people bearing the greatest burden of such coercion and force (the people) gain political power over decision makers (Gallarotti 2010, Ch.1).

With the rise of global interdependence, a sharing-based information economy, and the spread of democracy, national leaders will increasingly place a high priority on international cooperation to economic growth and employment and avoid hard power policies that could undermine this goal.

The soft power of a country depends heavily on three fundamental attributes: a charming culture, favorable national political values, and a foreign policy with legal and moral authority (Nye 2011).

The values that a government advocates greatly affect the preferences of other people For example, the notions of democracy at home, cooperation in the international community, and the promotion of peace and human rights in foreign policy can be linked as tenets of the same core values. Nye cites Norway as a nation with political power that supersedes its military or economic power. Norway demonstrates its national interests as inclusive of attractive causes such as generous economic aid and peacemaking. Norway has participated in peace talks in the Philippines, the Balkans, Colombia, Guatemala, Sri Lanka, and the Middle East. Positioning itself as a global peacekeeper identifies Norway with values shared by other nations and enhances Norwegian soft power (Nye 2011).

The assets of hard power, such as military strength, are strictly governmental. Other resources of hard power, such as oil and mineral deposits, also belong to government control. In contrast, many soft power resources are distinct from the policies and actions of a nation's government and only partially serve government objectives.

The opportunity to achieve the country's political objectives cannot be considered independently of the image of that country created and spread by its media. For this reason, some analysts treat soft power as a force of popular culture (Nye 2004).

We can suggest three major antecedent conditions that affect soft power (Kim and Ni 2011, 132-154).

First, on a macroscopic level, collective perceptions and assessments of a given country formed by the mass media can lead to positive or negative perceptions and assessments about that country among foreign peoples.

Second, the collective perception and evaluation of a country is further generated and influenced by interpersonal communication. Yun calls this relational approach "citizen diplomacy", which refers to the interactions among ordinary citizens who are represented on behalf of the country (Yun 2012, 2199-2219).

Third, soft power can be influenced by the consumption of cultural commodities by foreign masses. Especially given the trends of globalization, people are increasingly seeking and consuming foreign cultural products such as movies, dramas, music, and literature. Continuous cultural consumption could potentially stimulate and amplify positive perceptions and assessments of the cultural goods' country of origin.

South Korea's Soft Power

In the IFG-Monocle Index, which shows the world rankings of soft power, South Korea ranked 19th place in 2010. In 2011 it came in 14th and in 2012, 12th. In 2011, South Korea ranked 10th in the domain of education, and 9th in business and innovation; in 2012, 9th in education, and 10th in culture. Overall, South Korea ranked 15th in 2014-15 and 2015-16 (Monocle Soft Power Survey 2015).

Since the late 1990s, a new wave of Korean culture has changed the status of the South Korea in Asia to such an extent that the foreign Ministry spoke of of a "Hallyu Diplomacy". Viral K-pop hits such as "Gangnam Style" by PSY have contributed more to the soft power of the country than any marketing campaigns. According to a 2013 editorial in The Guardian, "Hallyu has erased South Korea's regional reputation as a brutish emerging industrial nation where everything smelled of garlic and kimchi, and replaced it with images of prosperous, cosmopolitan life"(Linskey 2013).

The Korean Wave has fundamentally improved the cultural image of the nation worldwide, causing a "halo effect" that revises people's images and ideas of Korea's political, economic and social identity. "I used to think that Korea was a feudalistic, male-centered society", a 22-year Taiwanese girl said in an interview with The New York Times. "Now I don't have the same image as I had before. It seems like an open society, democratic" (Onishi 2005).

The Korean Wave has changed the way people from neighboring countries look at Korea. As viewers in Taiwan, China, Hong Kong, and Japan share in the rise of capitalism across Asia, Koreans are increasingly characterized as fellow "urban, global, and middle-class" citizens thanks to media representation by "sophisticated and individualistic Korean stars" (Cho 2005, 147-182).

On the other hand, many teenagers in countries like China, Thailand, and Vietnam are becoming enthusiastically heavy consumers of the messages offered through Korean-style block-busters and soap operas, with the desire to live in a world like that (Onishi 2006).

Foreign people as the new Korea's ambassadors

The global sharing of culture has considerably spurred peer-to-peer interactions and created groups of people who keep the Korean flag flying across the world. Foreign tourists visiting Korea and Korean tourists traveling overseas have a very important role in sustaining Korea's soft power. Foreign tourists, once they return to their home countries, become ambassadors of South Korea and are able to share their knowledge and experiences—potentially even mitigating or altering negative perceptions of Korea. Furthermore, direct interpersonal interactions, thanks to the element of tourism, empower the average Korean citizen to become an ambassador of their country when approaching the foreign public. The interaction between Koreans and foreigners creates a higher reputation towards the foreign countries and, at the same time, a stronger national brand .

International students also play a very important role in creating soft power. A plethora of research on international exchange student programs gives empirical evidence for the gains in the reputation of a host country when foreign students return home (Atkinson 2010, 1-22). The attractiveness of a nation's education system can boost its soft power capacity: when students go and learn in host countries, they gain broadened cultural understanding and familiarity. When they come back home, they usually have a more positive view of the country in which they studied and the people with whom they interacted. Their positive perceptions have been shown to have beneficial "ripple effects" (Nye 2011) on the opinions and attitudes of those surrounding the exchange, such as family and friends. For all these reasons, exchange students can play a beneficial role in improving the reputation of a nation abroad—serving, as S.H. Yun articulates, as "middle-class multipliers of the ideas, values, and institutions of the host country" (Yun 2012).

South Korea's re-branding as a favorable place for quality education stems in part from the Korean Wave. The government of Korea and its education institutions have looked to capitalize on the popularity of cultural products, establishing Hallyu-centered programs targeted at international students (Allen 2013). Thus, Korea has been able to reinvent itself as a young and trendy destination where people can go to study, a shift affirmed by enrollment statistics: by 2004 Korea had enrolled 16,832 international students, and by 2012 this figure was increased fivefold, reaching 86,878 foreign students (The Korean Association of International Educators 2013).

Hallyu for a creative economy

The digital industry was one of the most important supporting factors in the success of the new Korean wave. Social media has played an important role in spreading popular genres, especially K-pop, in many regions, including Europe and North America.[3] Moreover, Korea has the potential to develop creative content using new technologies in K-pop music, video games and animation. The spread of the Korean wave around the world was facilitated by the combination of social media, their customs, and the uses and assets they offer, and this innovation was made possible because of Korea's strong development of digital technology (Jin 2012).

Hallyu has been able to turn this new and powerful creative nexus of media and technology into one of the most successful contributors to the national economy. As such, Korea has become an advanced economy that today rates highly across several internationally-recognized indicators and measures of innovation. In 2012, Korea placed as the third country in the world for the highest investment in expenditure on R&D (in media technologies?), representing 3.74% of the GDP, one of the highest percentages among OECD member economies. Korea is a prolific source of ICT-related patents—an important indicator of the quality of its innovation— capabilities and home of one of the strongest internet infrastructures of any country (Connell 2013).

The Benefits of Hallyu as a Soft Power

Political ties with culture

Hallyu has provided a meaningful chance for the Korean government to take advantage of a newly emerging space for cultural and public diplomacy to restore the country's global standing.

The Vietnamese have long remembered that the Korean army helped fight

3 Gangnam Style craze in Youtube.

against the Vietnam Liberation army during the war. The Taiwanese were also betrayed by South Korea when its government suddenly broke diplomatic relations with Taipei in 1992 to establish a new diplomatic relationship with China.

In these scenarios, the Korean Wave has served to mollify deteriorated foreign relations. Korean actors Jang Donng-gun and Kim Nam-ju have gained such popularity in Vietnam that the Vietnamese have labeled them their "national" stars. The Korean President Kim Dae Jung even invited the pair to the dinner he hosted for Vietnamese President Tran Duc Luong when the latter visited Korea on 23 August 2001 (Shim 2006) .

Sung, S.Y., (2010, 25-45) reports that with the burgeoning "Korean fever" in Taiwanese society, Taiwan could no longer hold onto long-held negative views of South Korea. Thus, a negative impression has been transformed into the positive image of a nation with confidence and strong nationalism, two features extensively represented in Korean pop culture and both highly favored by the Taiwanese people. Many Taiwanese started referring to South Korea as a role model in its being an advanced and modernized country with an honorable position in the globalized world.

The South-Korea pop star BoA, who was featured on the cover of French newspaper Le Monde in July 2002 as an icon of cultural exchange between Korea and Japan, was invited to the two countries' summit conference in June 2003 in Tokyo (Zehngut 2009).

The Korean Wave has become a tool for 'indirect cooperation' in conflict resolution. Indirect co-operation occurs in conflict resolution when contact between the interacting parties occurs through various cultural means such as film, music, literature and other forms of art (Zehngut 2009). From this perspective, cultural consumption can be seen as an effective means of promoting peace in the aftermath of conflict.

Additionally, South Korean cultural imports serve as vectors of political and social change even outside the context of South-East Asia. In the Middle East, many are calling on the Israeli's and Palestinians' mutual love of Hallyu to be used as a tool for peace, addressing the estimated 5,000 Israeli and 3,000 Palestinian K-pop fans to find common ground over their mutual obsession (Wi and Lee 2013). An article in the BBC describes this phenomenon: "While Israeli and Palestinian negotiators make renewed efforts to find common ground for a lasting peace, youngsters in the region are reportedly taking their minds off the conflict with "K-pop" (BBC Monitoring 2013).

This is not the first time South Korean cultural imports have been used for peace in the Middle East. In 2005, the Korean TV drama Winter Sonata hit airwaves in Iraq. That same year, the South Korean government reported that producers had signed a broadcast agreement with Kurdistan Satellite Channel. The underlying goal of these international broadcasts was to generate positive feelings in the Arab world towards the 3,200 South Korean soldiers stationed in northern Iraq during the Iraq War (Kim 2013).

Thae Yong-Ho, a North Korean official who defected to South Korea in August 2016, talked about daily life in North Korea on December 27, 2016 and said, "I do not know anyone who didn't watch a Korean movie or drama in North Korea." Thae had been North Korea's deputy ambassador to the United Kingdom prior to defecting with his family to South Korea in 2016. It was reported that, from the UK, he exiled to South Korea via the US military Rammstein air base in Germany. Mr. Thae is likely the highest-ranking North Korean official ever to defect.

Mr. Thae said, "During the day, I cried out 'Kim Jong-un, Hurray!' but I spent the evening in bed watching Korean movies... Educated people like historical dramas and movies. I wached the Immortal Yi Sun-shin and Jeong Do-jeon. Ordinary people enjoyed drama such as Winter Sonata or Autumn in My Heart." He also reported that movies and drama about North Korean defectors are among the most popular in North Korea. It is said that the drama Blow Breeze, aired recently at the time of writing, and entertainment programs such as 'Moran Bong Club' and 'I am going to see you now' are a few such popular examples.

Thae articulated his belief that North Korea will collapse on the day when such external information comes into the country. As the international community imposes continued sanctions on North Korea, the regime of Kim Jong-un is in crisis and the North Koreans feel a great deal of agitation (Chun 2016).

Mr. Thae argues that the advent of new technologies has broken Pyongyang's grip on information flow to its population, deterring the Kim regime's ability to control its peoples' awareness of the outside world. Experts say that North Koreans are now able to easily consume South Korean soap operas and news reports through smuggled flash drives and cell phones (Chen 2017).

According to investigations based on surveys and interviews with 100 North Korean defectors,the spread of Hallyu to North Korean people and throughout North Korean society impacted their decision to defect (Chung 2012). Admiration for South Korean society inspired by the cultural productions of Hallyu contents was very influential in their decision. Almost all study respondents said they obtained a positive image of South Korea by watching South Korean TV. Of these, 85% said that the Korean Wave's visual media acted as an incentive for them to escape North Korea. More than 90% of the surveyed participants who were in their twenties grew up watching South Korean TV dramas, became accustomed to Korean culture, and were able to share more of the Korean Wave content through newer information technologies and equipment. The so-called 'Rush of Defect' is not directly led by the South Korean government, but by the independent determination of North Koreans themselves, instigated by the attractiveness of the Korean Wave's. The Korean Wave seems to impress more people in North Korea than in any other country because of the cultural proximity between the two Koreas. As North Korean authorities use increasingly a hard power to oppress people's desires, the soft power of the Korean Wave, which attracts North Koreans to South Korea, grows larger and larger. The Korean Wave is able to draw citizens of this closed society out of isolation, spurring North Koreans to defect, and helping North Koreans adapt to South Korean culture.

Conclusion

South Korea was one of the poorest countries in the world in the 1960s, relying on the assistance of the OECD Development Assistance Committee. It has since grown to become the 11th largest economy in the world and was ranked as the world's 5th largest exporter (4 percent of world trade, excluding intra-EU trade) as of 2015 (World Trade Organization 2015). Korea has also become a member of the world's donators' club, the OECD DAC. Korea has become an important middle power in world affairs. As Goldstein (2013) notes, Korea has attained global competitiveness in robotics, electronics, and automotive technologies and industries. Korea is also an important participant in international governance (Korea.net N.d.).

South Korea's stellar rise is not exclusively a result of its hard powers such as economic growth. Today, Korea is increasingly producing scientific knowledge, the world rankings of its universities are rapidly climbing, and its arts and culture industry is the most active in Asia. In order to create an ecosystem for the cultural and digital industries, the Korean government has allocated significant funding towards promoting and consolidating the success of K-pop. Korea aims to become a "soft powerhouse".

The Korean Wave is a product of the hybridization of global and local forces. The physical size of the United States and China are both nearly 100 times larger than that of South Korea, and Japan is also 3.7 times larger than South Korea. The size of South Korea is approximately the same as the state of Indiana in the United States. However, Korea has created a uniquely potent soft power in the form of its popular culture, which has had a profound impact on the country's global status. As such, Korea has gained a reputation as an economy worth establishing a business in, a destination worth visiting, and a culture worth experiencing in various forms. Due in large part to the reputation of its pop culture, Korea has acquired almost the same level of trust, soft power, and influence as major larger countries.

The national "brand" of Korea was a private commodity born of the entertainment industry's entrepreneurial spirit. In the form of the Korean Wave, this competitive advantage surpassed commercial utility and eventually became a "public good" that could benefit the entire nation. Korea's self-branding and cultural diplomacy projects have relied on the Korean Wave to show the image of a positive and modern nation. The private sector of the entertainment industry was able to utilize the charm of Korean celebrities and cultural attractions to create branding strategies that promote the export of Korean products and increase the influx of foreign tourists. Moreover, this phenomenon opened the possibility for ordinary Korean citizens to connect with more of the world through interpersonal exchange.

References

Articles and Books

Atkinson, Carol. 2010. "Does soft power matter? A comparative analysis of student exchange programs 1980–2006." Foreign Policy Analysis 6(1): 1–22.

Cho, Hae-Joang, 2005. "Reading the Korean Wave as a sign of global shift." Korea Journal 45(4): 147-182.

Chung, Ka Young. 2012. "The Soft Power of Hallyu, the Korean Wave in North Korea." M.A. thesis, Seoul National University. 2012.

Ciesa, Maddalena. 2014. "The South Korea case study." M.A. thesis, the University of Verona.

Connell, Sean. 2013. "Building a Creative Economy in South Korea: Analyzing the Plans and Possibilities for New Economic Growth." Korea Economic Institute of America Academic Paper Series (December). http://keia.org/sites/default/files/publications/kei_creative_economy.pdf

Gallarotti, Giulio. M. 2010. Cosmopolitan Power in International Relations: A Synthesis of Realism, Neoliberalism, and Constructivism. New York: Cambridge University Press.

Jin, Dal-Yong. 2012. "Hallyu 2.0: The New Korean Wave in the Creative Industry." International Institute Journal 2(1). Ann Arbor: University of Michigan. https://quod.lib.umich.edu/i/iij/11645653.0002.102/--hallyu-20-the-new-korean-wave-in-the-creative-industry?rgn=main;view=fulltext

Kim, Jeong-Nam and Lan Ni. 2011. "The Nexus between Hallyu and soft power: Cultural public diplomacy in the era of sociological globalism." In Hallyu: Influence of Korean popular culture in Asia and beyond, edited by Do-Kyun Kim & Min-Sun Kim, 132-154. Seoul: Seoul National University Press.

Kim, Youna. 2013. The Korean Wave: Korean media go global. New York: Routledge.

Nye, Joseph. S. 2004. Soft Power: The Means to Success in World Politics. New York: Public Affairs.

Nye, Joseph.S. 2011. The Future of Power. New York: Public Affairs.

Shim, Doobo. 2006. "Hybridity and the rise of Korean popular culture in Asia." Media, Culture & Society 28(1): 25-44.

Sung, Sang-Yeon. 2010. "Constructing a new image. Hallyu in Taiwan." European Journal of East Asian Studies 9(1): 25-45.

Yun, Seong-Hun. 2012. "Relational Public Diplomacy: The Perspective of Sociological Globalism." International Journal of Communication 6: 2199–2219.

Zehngut, Rafi Nets. 2009. "Passive healing of the aftermath of intractable conflicts." International Journal of Peace Studies 14(1): 39-60.

Government & International Organizations

Korea.net, "The Korean Economy-The Miracle on The Hangang." Korea.net. Accessed May 07, 2018. http://www.korea.net/AboutKorea/Economy/The-Miracle-on-The-Hangang

Ministry of Foreign Affairs, Republic of Koera. 2012. "Promotion of the Korean Wave" In Diplomatic White Paper, Ch.3. http://mcms.mofa.go.kr/trade/data/whitepaper/english/index.jsp?menu=m_30_210_40&tabmenu=t_2

Monocle, Soft Power Survey. 2014-15 & 2015-16. https://monocle.com/film/affairs/soft-power-survey-2014-15/; https://monocle.com/film/affairs/soft-power-survey-2015-16/

The Korean Association of International Educators. 2013. Study Korea 2020 Project. November 27, 2013. http://www.jafsa.org/uploads/20131127KAIE-JAFSA1.pdf

World Trade Organization. 2015. "Leading exporters and importers of merchandise trade exluding intra-EU (28) trade." https://www.wto.org/english/news_e/pres16_e/pr768_e.htm

Newspapers

Allen, Ryan M. 2013. "Far East aims high for international student numbers." University World News, March 23, 2013. http://www.universityworldnews.com/article.php?story=20130318165323246

BBC Monitoring. 2013. "Middle East: Korean pop brings hope for peace." BBC News, August 7, 2013. http://www.bbc.com/news/blogs-news-from-elsewhere-23606319

Chen, Jonathan. 2017. "North Korean Defector Says Kim Jong Un Can't Last." The

Wall Street Journal, Jan. 26, 2017. http://www.wsj.com/articles/north-korean-defector-says-kim-jong-un-cant-last-1485346155

Chun, E. 2016. "Mr. Thae, North Korean People like Korean Dramas and Movies". SISA News People, Dec. 28, 2016. http://www.inewspeople.co.kr/news/articleView.html?idxno=14738

Chung, H. 2013. "King Sejong Institute promotes Korean education", The Korea Times, October 23, 2013. http://www.koreatimes.co.kr/www/news/culture/2013/10/386_144799.html

Lynskey, Dorian. 2013. "Britain's soft power is greater than Gangnam Style – so appreciate it." The Guardian, June 19, 2013. https://www.theguardian.com/commentisfree/2013/jun/19/britain-soft-power-greater-gangnam-style

Onishi, Norimitsu. 2005. "Roll over, Godzilla: Korea rules." The New York Times, June 28, 2005. http://www.nytimes.com/2005/06/28/world/asia/roll-over-godzilla-korea-rules.html?_r=0

Onishi, Norimitsu. 2006. "China's Youth Look to Seoul for Inspiration." The New York Times, Jan. 2, 2006. http://www.nytimes.com/2006/01/02/world/asia/chinas-youth-look-to-seoul-for-inspiration.html

Wi, Tack-whan and Lee Seung-ah. 2013. "Israeli and Palestinian youths find common ground: K-pop." Korea official website, August 14, 2013. http://www.korea.net/NewsFocus/Culture/view?articleId=111369

Part 5

A Rivalry with the Korean Wave

Chapter 9

Between Fans: History and National Identity in Online Debates on Axis Powers Hetalia

Kathryn Hemmann

Transnational fan communities have become a hot topic in Media Studies scholarship due to their increasing influence on the mainstream media of numerous countries around the world. Partially because of the success of international crowdfunding platforms such as Kickstarter and the awe-inspiring efforts of social media users to promote various project campaigns, anime and manga fans have begun to exert a powerful influence on mainstream media properties. For instance, in the United States, we can see clear traces of the landmark anime series Revolutionary Girl Utena (1997, Shōjo kakumei Utena) on Rebecca Sugar's designs and storyboard work for the wildly successful Adventure Time animated television series. To give another example, based on the overwhelming popularity of her animated YouTube short Bee & PuppyCat, which also exhibits an obvious anime influence, Adventure Time's Studio Frederator helped creator Natasha Allegri launch her own highly successful Kickstarter campaign. The convergence of anime and manga influences on mass-market media in America with the rise of crowdfunding as a legitimate method of media production is illustrative of a global media landscape in which fans shape media mix ecosystems through their involvement and participation in transnational fandom cultures.

Fandom communities are far from frictionless, however, and differences arising from historically weighted national identities still manifest themselves in supposedly borderless online discussion forums. As Sandra Annett (2011) reminds us, "Transnationalism is not simply another word for postnationalism, or the flow of information and people across the fading borders of a globalized world, just as a transnational fan community is not necessarily a blissfully multicultural group where people of all nations are (supposedly) united in equality" (p. 173). In the context of anime fandoms in particular, attitudes towards Japan and Japanese history have the potential to become an especially fraught point of contention, as many fans in the United States and other countries outside of Asia may express sentiments regarding Japan that occupy a spectrum between respectful and worshipful (Napier 2007, Schodt 2013). Japan is a site of longing and a perceived country of dreams, after all, and it is the home of everything from Studio Ghibli to Hello Kitty to the Honda Accord. In contrast, to citizens of Japan's neighbors in East Asia, the appealing aspects of Japanese popular culture that Susan Napier, following Arjun Appadurai's theory of mediascapes, has dubbed "fantasyscapes" (p. 11) cannot remain entirely separate from Japan's past military aggressions and more recent economic imperialism.

In this essay I will demonstrate how South Korean and Korean-American fans, as a loosely linked community, have emerged as a major voice in the critique of Japanese popular media among North American and European fan communities. Online debates surrounding the media franchise Axis Powers Hetalia (Akushisu Pawāzu Hetaria), which humorously lampoons the nations that acted as major players in World War II, have emerged as a watershed moment in this process. Although the Hetalia franchise contains many subversive themes and can easily be read as a bonfire of the militaristic grand narratives that shaped the rise and clash of nations over the course of the twentieth century, Korean and Korean-American commenters have encouraged their fellow fans to break out of the pattern of postmodern play that characterized fan activities inspired by the franchise at the height of its popularity from roughly 2009 to 2011. In doing so, they alerted fan communities to several of the more problematic aspects of contemporary Japanese and American historiography, including the consequences of erasing the Korean peninsula from our understanding of the stakes, causalities, and casualties of the Pacific War. I will first offer a brief summary of the Hetalia franchise before summarizing its initial fan reception. I will then outline the history of the controversies surrounding the franchise while invoking specific comments that served as catalysts for online debates. Finally, I will widen the scope of the essay to include several related online debates in order to outline a sketch of how active fan engagement has changed and shaped mainstream discourse concerning the portrayal of Asian national identities and the legacies of the Pacific War in contemporary popular media.

Rich Nations, Strong Armies, and Public Outrage

In the manga Axis Powers Hetalia, World War II is a game played by two teams of handsome men. The Hetalia franchise, which began as an amateur webcomic written by Himaruya Hidekaz, anthropomorphizes the major world powers of the early twentieth century as attractive young men. America sports a bomber jacket and guzzles hamburgers, Germany enjoys making cuckoo clocks and is serious to a fault, and Italy, the namesake of the series,[1] is a pasta-loving coward who depends on Germany to protect him. Although the original webcomic plays with national stereotypes and caricatured reenactments of historical events, later incarnations of the franchise (such as several seasons of an animated series, a feature-length film, and drama CDs featuring the voice actors of the anime) focus less on historical jokes and references and more on the homoerotic tensions that arise between the masculine representations of countries in heated competition with one another.

In Between Men, Eve Sedgwick argues that the intense relationships of the men involved in the creation and administration of the British Empire were characterized by homosocial desire, a "pattern of male friendship, mentorship, entitlement, [and] rivalry" (p. 1). The members of many fandom communities[2] centered around Hetalia have interpreted the international homosocial rivalries and conflicts between the men of the twentieth century as overt homoeroticism between anthropomorphic avatars of national identity. Germany defends Italy like an senior student with a crush on an incoming freshman in a boarding school novel. England, having introduced America to the allure of international politics, is now frustrated to find himself in position of subordination to his younger charge, a situation that parallels the triangular relationships common in Victorian romances. In the eyes of fans, these character dynamics directly allude to forbidden longings and stolen kisses behind closed doors.[3] The Heta-

1 The title is a portmanteau of *heta*, a Japanese word meaning "incompetent," and "Italia." "Hetalia" also plays on the word *hetare*, meaning "loser." These connotations are appropriate, as the manga portrays Italy and his buddies Germany and Japan as being highly idiosyncratic, if not overtly antisocial.

2 Although anecdotal evidence suggests that the majority of members of *Hetalia* fan communities tend to identify as female, there are a number of male fans in Japan and other countries who participate in the slash fan cultures associated with *Hetalia*, as demonstrated by their participation in practices such as cosplay masquerades (in which fans dress up as anime characters and enact dramatic performances or dance routines in front of an audiences at a fan convention) and the production of AMVs (anime music videos).

3 The fan response to *Hetalia* calls to mind Henry Jenkins's assessment of the "slash" subcultures of female fans in America who create homoerotic parodies of popular television shows. According to Jenkins, "Slash confronts the most repressive forms of sexual identity and provides utopian alternatives to current configurations of gender; slash does not, however, provide a politically stable or even consistently coherent response to these concerns" (1992, 190). The artists drawing romances involving the

lia anime in particular, which targets the demographic of adult women who enjoyed "shipping" the characters of the original webcomic,[4] plays on and emphasizes the homoerotic themes of homosocial modernity to such a degree that they are apparent to even a casual viewer.

The levity with which the major events of modern history are portrayed in Hetalia betrays a surprisingly liberal understanding of history. Not only does the franchise render the supposedly great deeds of men as trifling, but it also critiques the ambitions of homosocial modernity. For example, by representing the Sino-Japanese Wars as a series of quarrels between two brothers (or lovers) who can't communicate properly, Hetalia and its fans are not engaging in a process of forgetting or downplaying the impact of historical events, but rather of gently mocking the grave seriousness of masculine-gendered modernist pursuits such as colonization, war, and the formation of national identity. In effect, by highlighting the textual homoeroticism that arises between the anthropomorphized nations of Hetalia, fans use the franchise as a vehicle for queering the notion of history itself. By discrediting both heterosexuality and conventional masculinity (especially as it is represented by military ideals) as the basis of normative identity, Hetalia fans challenge the heteronormative phallocentrism underlying the construction of history as it is presented in state-sponsored narratives such as secondary school textbooks and period dramas serialized on public television.

Nevertheless, Hetalia has frequently come under criticism for reinforcing national and ethnic stereotypes and turning a blind eye to wartime atrocities such as the Holocaust and the Japanese occupation of Nanking. There has been a significant outcry against the franchise on Korean-language internet discussion boards, where posters decry the treatment of Japan's wartime history as a laughing matter. Online commenters have also been offended by Korea's characterization as nursing a one-sided crush on Japan in the Hetalia webcomic. In January 2009, this online activity escalated into a formal petition, reported to have gained over ten thousand signatures in three days, being issued to the Japanese satellite television channel Kid's Station, which specializes in animation and had, in the July of 2008, announced its plans to

countries represented in *Hetalia*, like the women publishing slash fiction in America, are not attempting to make an overt political statement, but I might argue that, based on so-called "meta fandom" posts on fannish social networking sites such as Pixiv and Tumblr, many fans are fully aware of the social and historical critique of their activities.

4 The expression "to ship" describes the fannish activity of imaging two (or more) characters in a romantic or sexual relationship. The Japanese linguistic equivalent of "shipping" is *kappuringu*, or "coupling."

air an animated version of Hetalia (Anime News Network, 2009). In a January 14, 2009 diplomacy council of the South Korean Congress, congresswoman Jeong Mi-Kyeong stated that she considers the comic Hetalia "to be a crime on a private level.[5]" The Japanese producers of the Hetalia animation took these protests quite seriously, eventually resolving to completely delete South Korea from the anime altogether, which was to be broadcast online instead of on television.

Fandom Wank and Social Justice

Despite South Korean protests regarding the historical and cultural insensitivity of the Hetalia webcomic, the franchise continued to grow in popularity throughout 2009, aided in no small part by the successful launch of the anime on January 24.[6] Due to the efforts of fans posting unofficial translations of the Hetalia webcomic and unlicensed subtitled versions of the Hetalia anime, the franchise attracted a large international English-language fanbase. Roughly speaking, until around the end of 2012, the most active English-language Hetalia fan communities were hosted on the blog-based social networking site LiveJournal. Even despite the decline in fan participation on the site, the main Hetalia community on LiveJournal had almost forty thousand members as of April 2014, with an additional eighteen thousand watchers.[7] There were also dozens of branch communities across LiveJournal and its sister site Dreamwidth that focused on one particular character or romantic pairing between characters in Hetalia.[8] Although fans came together from all corners of the world when these communities were first created, the number of active

5 Jeong's speech was posted onto YouTube, along with an English translation, at http://www.youtube.com/watch?v=yo_btds9-kM .

6 Due in part to the aforementioned backlash against the webcomic, the television broadcast of the animation was cancelled, but the show, which consists of five-minute self-contained episodes, was still made available to viewers through various online and mobile platforms. Being removed from television airwaves did not seem to impede the popularity of the anime, as three more seasons were produced in 2009 and 2010. In early 2010, the North American distributor Funimation acquired the rights to all of the seasons of the animation, which it streams on its website, as well as on Hulu, an online television subscription service.

7 This data was collected on April 25, 2014, from the LiveJournal "Hetalia" community's profile information page at http://hetalia.livejournal.com/profile. In a community on LiveJournal, a "member" has posting access, while a "watcher" merely receives community updates through the site's internal feed tracking service.

8 The pairing between America and England was quite popular, as were the pairings between Germany and Northern Italy, between Spain and Southern Italy, between France and England, and between America and Canada.

participants who could understand Japanese was relatively small, and the number who could understand Korean was even smaller. As a result, many people found it difficult to understand the South Korean protest against Hetalia, especially since the Chinese-language fandom seemed, to the many English language fans who found pirate translations of the manga, anime, and drama CDs on Chinese websites, to have enthusiastically embraced the series.

This lack of linguistic proficiency and historical context led to the sort of ill feelings that may easily arise over seemingly arbitrarily criticism. In an August 2010 post titled "Korea and China" on the LiveJournal community Hetalia Wank ("wank" meaning, in this context, "unpopular or problematic opinion"), user Galael wrote that Hetalia creator Himaruya Hidekazu did not, to my knowledge, address the topic of Korea's colonization by Japan. No, he probably won't. Why? Because Hetalia is a funny comic. Such a recent event, which continues to tear apart the two countries and include the death and suffering of hundreds of people, is not funny. The fact that Hidekaz acknowledges Japan's aggression and bad behaviour toward China is already a big thing, but he is seeking to make people laugh and love the characters – not to address such big issues, especially with characters that are, explicitly, stereotypes. Showing Japan and Korea as enemies would have constantly reminded the reader of hate, death and war.

Galael thus justifies the webcomic's lack of acknowledgement of Japan's colonial past by stating that topics directly portraying "the death and suffering of hundreds of people" are not appropriate for the humorous tone of the four-panel gag comic, and that, by not making light of Japan's wartime atrocities, Hetalia's creator is in fact demonstrating respect. This post attracted dozens of comments offering explanations and putting the reaction into the context of disputes over Japanese textbooks and the Dokdo/Takeshima islands. More abrasive posts, such as an essay titled "Korea Is Retarded" on the blog Anime Might, attracted hundreds of comments, with commenters debating each other and clarifying their positions across lengthy comment threads, which included scattered links to global news media outlets such as The Guardian, Al Jazeera, and Haaretz.

Commentary on the relationship between Korea and Japan as expressed through Hetalia continued throughout early 2012 in online essays such as "Why Hetalia is bad and you should feel bad," in which the author decries the reduction of the complexity of history to shallow anime stereotypes. She introduces her post by stating that "the fact that [the nations involved in World War Two] are characterized as shallow little giggly turdlets instead of deep characters with complex relationships and varying motivations is [...] insulting to the reality of the countries and history."[9] This post also attracted hundreds of comments, which ranged from lighthearted jokes about Sarah Palin to strongly worded personal attacks. Commenters defending Hetalia as "nothing more than entertainment" that "wasn't meant to be offensive" were met with a range of well-considered responses concerning the legacy of the Pacific War in Asian countries, especially Korea. Other responses challenged the privileged position Japan seems to occupy as a producer of popular media. As one anonymous commenter points out, Hetalia is a good example, that Japan is allowed to be more ignorant than other countries. I'm sorry, but that's what it is. When a POP star mistakes Chinesse traditional clothes with Japanese – we have a [media] war. When Japan shows Victorians dressed as kawaii lolitas exposing almost all their legs or shows other countries as nothing but mix of awfull stereotypes- it's completly okay. That's not fair, is it?[10]

Although the verbally aggressive and scornfully mocking attack-and-counterattack format of these discussions may not seem to lend itself to either Henry Jenkins's (2006) model of the "scholar-fan" or Matthew Hills's (2002) model of the "fan as intellectual," fans contributing comments such as the one quoted above to online debates on Hetalia are engaged in forcibly inserting an awareness and acknowledgement of history and national identity into discourses surrounding Japanese cultural products.

Online discussions concerning Hetalia were intense, informative, and far from limited to the Pacific Theater of World War II, ultimately delving into topics such contemporary ethnic conflicts and racial representations in entertainment media. These discussions occurred within the broader awareness of social justice issues within online communities sparked by the infamous "RaceFail 2009" debates on the representation of otherness and people of color in English-language science fiction and fantasy novels, especially those

9 The tone of this statement, which has been edited to remove its more caustic profanity, is typical of the blog, a forum on which readers are invited to mock the more ridiculous tropes of *yaoi* (homoerotic) anime, manga, and English-language slash fan fiction. The title of the blog, *Rape Is Kawaii!*, refers to one such trope, wherein nonconsensual sex is equated with overpowering romantic love, *kawaii* being a Japanese word well-known to anime fans as meaning "cute" or "adorable." Although the prevailing attitude of the blog and its commenters is sarcastic amusement, both the original post on *Hetalia* its comments are quite serious.

10 The spelling mistakes of the original comment have been preserved in this quotation. Although English is the lingua franca of many anime blogs, even those not hosted or maintained by people from territories in which English is a dominant language, the English language proficiency of readers and commenters can vary widely, and "perfect" English is neither expected nor even necessarily desired in such discursive spaces. This is not to say that all or even most online discussion of anime outside Japan is in English (as a great deal of said discussion occurs in Chinese or Russian), but rather that popular anime blogs and news sites attract a range of readers from all over the world.

originating in the United States.[11] Over time, such online discussions and debates have resulted in a shift in fandom attitudes towards racism and cultural insensitivity, a trend that has escalated as fans have jumped aboard social media platforms like Twitter and Tumblr, which enable instant sharing of information and opinions across interrelated fandom communities.

To give an example, on April 21, 2014 the Canadian pop star Avril Lavigne released a music video for her new single "Hello Kitty," a mishmash of Japanesque nonsense words and decontextualized pop culture images that Billboard magazine's Jason Lipshutz wrote "is an embarrassment in any language" (2014). The backlash against the "positive racism" of the video was immediate and overwhelming, which serves as a significant contrast to the positive reception of Gwen Stefani's 2004 single "Harajuku Girls," which featured an almost identical presentation of "Japaneseness" as something unique yet culturally odorless and ready for consumption. The online uproar in response to Lavigne's video was not an isolated occurrence, as Justin Bieber also found himself in hot water after visiting the Yasukuni Shrine two days later, on April 23. According to The Washington Post, Bieber received thousands of angry messages in English on his Facebook post commemorating his visit, which shocked fans from around the world (Taylor 2014). The vehemence of the outcry was startling to many critics tracking the pop star's career, as even his unfortunate behavior at the Anne Frank Museum in April of 2013 was not met with the same degree of outrage and disappointment (Duke 2013). These two incidents demonstrate a strong awareness of the social, political, and historical issues implicit in mainstream media generally considered to be harmless, even among fans in their early teens.

The roots of this broad shift in fan attitudes are deep and tangled. Regardless, because of the spread of international fandom communities over various social media platforms, no single debate on issues concerning cultural sensitivity and social justice occurs in a vacuum. As fans jump from one fandom community to another, and as they shape the emerging communities through which younger fans enter online fandom, they carry their knowledge regarding social justice with them. While discussions of issues such as the international controversy over the Yasukuni Shrine may have once been limited to academic journals, university classrooms, and second-page news stories, they now take place on heavily trafficked webpages and fan blogs, which can be accessed at all times via popular smartphone apps. The popularity of the Hetalia franchise has faded, but it engendered debates that are representative of an important

11 For a summary of these debates, a selection of key quotations, and a list of relevant links, see the "RaceFail '09" page of the *Fanlore* wiki.

moment in transnational fandom communities surrounding Asian popular cultures. These discussions are illustrative of how fans who work together across national borders are able to challenge received knowledge, address gaps in what they have learned about history and culture, and influence public discourse concerning problematic representations of nationality and national history.

References

Anime Might. 2009. "Hetalia: Korea is retarded." January 28, 2009. http://animight.wordpress.com/2009/01/28/hetalia-korea-is-retarded/

Anime News Network. 2009. "Korean protests call for Hetalia anime's cancellation (update2)." January 13, 2009. http://www.animenewsnetwork.com/news/2009-01-13/korean-protests-call-for-hetalia-anime-cancellation

Annett, S. 2011. "Imagining transcultural fandom: Animation and Global media communities." Transcultural Studies 2: 164-188.

Duke, A. 2013. "Justin Bieber hopes Anne Frank 'would have been a belieber.'" CNN, April 16, 2013. http://www.cnn.com/2013/04/14/showbiz/bieber-anne-frank/

Fanlore Wiki. N.d. "RaceFail '09." http://fanlore.org/wiki/RaceFail_%2709

Galael. 2010. "Korea and China." Hetalia Wank, August 3, 2010. http://hetalia-wank.livejournal.com/4982.html

Hills, M. 2002. Fan cultures. New York, NY: Routledge.

Jenkins, H. 1992. Textual poachers: Television fans and participatory culture. New York, NY: Routledge.

Jenkins, H. 2006. Fans, bloggers, and gamers: Media consumers in a digital age. New York, NY: NYU Press.

Lipshutz, J. 2014. "Avril Lavigne 'Hello Kitty' video is an embarrassment in any language." Billboard, April 22, 2014. http://www.billboard.com/articles/columns/pop-shop/6062836/avril-lavigne-hello-kitty-video-is-an-embarrassment-in-any

Napier, S. J. 2007. From impressionism to anime: Japan as fantasy and fan cult in the mind of the West. New York, NY: Palgrave Macmillian.

Schodt, F. L. 2013. "The view from North America: Manga as late-twentieth-century Japonisme?" In Manga's cultural crossroads, edited by J. Berndt & B. Kümmerling-Meibauer, 19-26. New York, NY: Routledge.

Sedgwick, E. K. 1985. Between men: English literature and male homosocial desire. New York, NY: Columbia University Press.

Taylor, A. 2014. "How Justin Bieber inadvertently stepped into one of the world's greatest geopolitical controversies." The Washington Post, April 23, 2014. http://www.washingtonpost.com/blogs/worldviews/wp/2014/04/23/how-justin-bieber-inadvertently-stepped-into-one-of-the-worlds-greatest-geopolitical-controversies/

Yourfapsendhere. 2012. "Why Hetalia is bad and you should feel bad." Rape Is Kawaii!: Riffing bad yaoi comics for great justice!. Accessed June 2, 2012. http://cry-some-more.demon-sushi.com/?p=1339

Chapter 10

Lost and Found in "Cool Japan"

Heather Bowen-Struyk

Ōtomo Katsuhiro's epic anime *Akira* (1988) is set in Neo Tokyo in a dystopian future in which neglected youth blow off school, drag race and get into fights with other biker gangs while corrupt adults including scientists, religious leaders, the military, politicians and business men fight among themselves for the power to control a world collapsing in uncertainty. The year is 2019, one year before Japan is due to host the Olympics in the anime as in real life. In the anime, Tokyo proper had been destroyed during WWIII in 1988 by a great power called Akira, a power that is at once reminiscent of a nuclear explosion but also described as a psychic power cultivated by scientists who lost control of it. The young antihero Tetsuo randomly encounters one of the escaped psychic test subjects and this unlocks his own extraordinary psychic and physical transformation. As teenaged Tetsuo's power grows, not only does he turn against his girlfriend Kaori and best friend Kaneda who had befriended him at the orphanage when they were younger, he also unleashes destruction on Neo Tokyo and by the end, apparently causes a new star system to be born.

Fig. 1. Poster for Akira

Metaphor for adolescence, Tetsuo's monstrous transformation is a pushback against the protection offered by his surrogate big brother Kaneda. However this is no conventional bildungsroman: the idea of growing up and becoming a proper adult is foreclosed a priori by a setting in which adults are all represented as corrupt. There is no version of an "adult" for Tetsuo to grow up to be: instead, he grows up and explodes and apparently initiates a new planetary system. *Akira* was a watershed anime. Exquisitely hand-drawn, viscerally engaging, and thematically dark with exquisite attention to the gritty underside of society, *Akira* announced to the world that Japanese animation was an alternative to Disney hyper-cheerfulness or Hollywood happy endings, with high production values and fresh ideas.

In 2002, American journalist Douglas McGray famously wrote that post-industrial Japan may not make any*thing* anymore, but it does make *cool*, referring to the enthusiasm of international fans of Japanese popular culture like anime, manga, video games, television dramas, pop music, figurines. Calling this "Gross National Cool," McGray posed the question of whether and how Japan would be able to cash in on this soft power (McGray 2002, 53-54). McGray's formulation struck a nerve. Inspired by Tony Blair's 1997 Cool Britannia, a glib nod to imperialist Rule Britannia, in 2004, the Content Industry Promotion Law was passed to further promote already profitable popular culture, called Cool Japan. Kukhee Choo writes, "the Japanese government shifted its focus from a century-long practice of promoting traditional arts to supporting the popular culture industry under the banner 'Cool Japan'" (Choo 2012, 85). Formerly dismissed as disposable child's play, the content industries were suddenly promoted to both drive economic growth and represent a national brand. While it has not been as economically successful as hoped, Cool Japan has been much celebrated as a successful national rebranding. For the first time since WWII, a generation of youth in Asia and the rest of the world is growing up with affection for Japanese cultural products.

But there are costs to "cool" as economic driver and national brand, costs that are hidden in plain sight within the products and production of Cool Japan itself. Anticipating both the major themes and forms of Cool Japan, *Akira* expresses the angst of youth who have inherited a harrowing, precarious world rendered unstable by the self-centeredness of adults who failed to create safe, nurturing places for children to thrive and grow up to become adults themselves. Moreover, *Akira*'s production was extremely labor-intensive and costly including a staff of seventy working round the clock to produce 150,000 cels ("*Akira*: Production Report (1988)" 1990), a model of producing cool that is unsustainable except for blockbusters.

In the 1980s, Japan—as Japan Inc.—represented the successes of capitalism in its cities, technological development, brand-name export commodities, and economic power. Nearly three decades of high economic growth had made Japan the second strongest economy in the world, and Japan Inc. was associated with salaryman masculinity—fearsome to the west for its apparently unstoppable hive-dedication and efficiency. In sharp contrast, "cool" reflects a detachment from the compulsory logic of productivity so associated with the economic successes of Japan Inc. In particular, it is the rejection of uncool salaryman adult society with its numbingly strict gender expectations. By contrast, the exemplars of Japanese cool—from Hello Kitty to *Neon Genesis Evangelion*, *Sailor Moon* to *Gundam* and Pokemon and beyond—are produced for youth, about youth.

Youth and Nonregular Employment

For the now twenty-five years of recession in Japan, the securities associated with adulthood during the period of high growth—lifetime employment and stable, reproductive marriages—have become precarious. Although Japan famously has a low unemployment rate, youth are disproportionately in nonregular employment. Kingston and Osawa write that "from 1995 to 2008 the number of regular workers decreased by 3.8 million, while the number of nonregular workers increased by 7.6 million" (Kingston and Osawa 2015, 60). The trend mitigates against nonregular employees becoming regular: "Future career prospects hang in the balance because only about 20 percent of nonregular workers are able to switch over to regular jobs" (Ibid., 60). This poses a problem for youth who find it harder and harder to "grow up." Anne Allison writes, "Without steady employment, fewer youth are marrying, having children or leaving parental homes. Moving from job to job and getting stuck in time without the means to become 'adults', youth are futureless—a state they also get blamed for" (Allison 2009, 90). The "crucial dividing line" of salary? ¥3 million (or ~$30,000 USD) annually. Kingston and Osawa write that "below that income level, only 8 to 10 percent of men in their twenties and thirties were married, while above ¥3 million, the proportion of married rose to 24 to 40 percent, rising with income" (Kingston and Osawa 2015, 70).

Early in the recession, the neologism "freeter" emerged to describe young educated people who opted out of corporate society, choosing instead part-time or contract work to allow them to live a supposedly freer life. Much criticism was directed at freeter, for failing to grow up and assume the adult responsibilities that would supposedly have saved Japan from the ongoing recession. But the discussion has changed, and it is now widely recognized that secure jobs are disappearing as neoliberalism demands a flexible work force. In a brilliant formulation, Anne Allison writes, "So, when such a construct of youth sells commodities, it is claimed as 'gross national cool.' But when real youth fail to get steady jobs or reproduce, as did their parents, they are castigated for not assuring Japan's future—what gets rendered as a crisis in reproduction" (Allison 2009, 91).

Producers and consumers of Cool Japan are among those living in uncertainty. The government is aware of the problem and recently the Agency for Cultural Affairs, a branch of the Ministry of Education, Culture, Sports, Science and Technology (MEXT), commissioned a report on the living conditions of animators. The survey was conducted by Japan Animation Creators Association (JAniCA) in 2014 and published in 2015; they received 759 responses, just 28.6% of those polled, but the results reveal long hours, low wages and precarity (JAniCA 2015, 10). Just over 16% of respondents have regular employment; 23.1% are contract employees, 14.9% are self-employed and 37.7% are freelancers (Ibid., 34). They average eleven hours a day (Ibid., 39) and 262.7 hours a month (Ibid., 40)—that is more than one hundred hours a month more than a forty-hour work week. Despite the fact that 67.7% call themselves the primary income in the household (Ibid., 15), the average wages for 2013 were a paltry ¥3.328 million (just over $30,000 USD) (Ibid., 44), the "crucial dividing line" indicated by Kingston and Osawa.

Animation is costly to produce: imagine having to draw 24 frames per second. One of the significant ways that anime differentiated itself from Disney was the development of "limited animation," a variety of techniques to cut down on drawn images which became part of the esthetic. Even so, it requires long hours by highly skilled artists. Once associated with the "freedom" in "freeter," cool industries attracted young talented artists. But most animators do not become famous or even make a decent living. Of the lowest paid animators, "dōgaman," about 90% of them last less than five years in the field (Mōri 2011, 35). And 80% of all animators leave the field eventually. Mōri Yoshitaka writes, "The anime industry demands these disposable and cheap young labor forces because it cannot carry on without them" (Ibid., 36). Disposable, cheap labor is necessary for the production of animation.

To further complicate things, China, Korea, and Hong Kong have played important, albeit often overlooked, roles in producing so-called Japanese anime. In the 1960s, Japanese animation studio Daiichi Animation used a Korean subcontractor to produce *Ōgon Bat* in 1967 and then *Yōkai Ningen Bem* in 1968 (Ibid., 32-33). Mōri writes: "From then on, Toei Animation began to contract Korean anime studios, while Toei Movie worked with Taiwanese studios. . . [I]t was said that more that 30% of the anime were produced in Korea" (Ibid.,

33). In the 1980s, bases for outsourced anime production were moved to China, such as the Shenzhen Cartoon and Animation Centre, "a business complex for subcontractors of anime and animation production in Japan, the USA and China, including Hong Kong and Taiwan" (Ibid., 32). In many cases, Chinese studios were not credited and there are is no official data of how much work was done in Chinese studios. Workers in the animation industries in Japan have much in common with their peers in Korea and China—despite nationalist rhetoric.

The Protest of Cool Japan

Because of economic considerations, cultural products tend to appear first as serialized manga, then a book, possibly figurines and serialized TV, then feature-length anime and possibly live action TV or film with a theme song by a popular boy band or girl band. This logic is determined by capital. However, the creative workers producing these products often reflect the insecurities facing youth.

Matsumoto Taiyō's *Tekkonkinkreet* (manga 1993-94, anime 2006) is a dark picaresque of two homeless boys navigating the violence of a mythical city, Treasure Town, being redeveloped for profit. Ironically, the older boy, Black, is upset that part of "his" town once full of strip joints is being turned into a kiddie amusement park. While the boys are shown going to the park and enjoying the amusements with stolen money, still, Black is upset that "his" town is being wrecked in this way by a returning yakuza boss trying to control redevelopment. Black is often poised on a roof or atop an electric pole with a bird's eye view of the city (and he seems to be able to fly down) inverting the conventional idea that children have limited views of what is really going on. Instead, Black sees the corruption and violence carried out by the adults who are fighting over economic power to redevelop the city. This kiddie amusement park ought to be a pleasure for children in the logic of capitalism, but instead, it is called out by Black as part of that corruption.

Like *Akira*, *Tekkonkinkreet* focuses on the boys and readers are left to guess how the boys ended up abandoned in a world of adults who have failed to take care of them. Also like *Akira*, despite the fact that youth are thematized, the content is rife with vulgar sexuality and violence which proper adult society would deem inappropriate for youth—but in these worlds, there are no adults to protect the young people. White, the mentally stunted younger boy, is defined by his innocence, a sharp contrast to the violence of the world the boys inhabit. And yet, he, too, is capable of startling violence.

The drawing style is rough, suggesting an adolescent hand, which rhymes

Fig. 2. Matsumoto Taiyō, "Skirmish 2: Paving the Road to Hell," *Tekkonkinkreet*, 31

form and content. This rough edginess defines the way the boys see their town, and Matsumoto shows us how these down-and-out youth have a unique position from which to view corruption. Only once White is stabbed by an assassin do any adults (the police) step in to help him by putting him in protective custody. But Black, left on the streets by himself and hunted by assassins, becomes increasingly violent and deranged. Only White can save him from utter moral decrepitude—but it's not by rehabilitation into a comforting world regulated by adults. These coming-of-age tales do not allow for a progression to adulthood.

Across the media mix of popular culture including novels and live action films, we see excessive and gratuitous violence unleashed on and by youth, mostly for the entertainment of readers/viewers, but also, as a critique on this very logic, for the entertainment of a diegetic audience. Kōshun Takami's *Battle Royale* (novel 1999; live action film 2000) presents a dramatic case: 9th graders are taken to a deserted island and forced to kill each other off in an epic class school trip from hell. Diegetic television audiences throughout Japan are able to follow the contest as the children's terror is both entertainment and a form of insurance that others don't protest too loudly.

In one of prolific director Sono Shion's most recent films, *Tag* (2015), based on *Riaru Onigokko* (2004) by Yamada Yūsuke, wind literally as sharp as knives slices through a busload of girls on a school trip, sparing only one girl, whose identity morphs as she struggles to escape the horrors that follow her. At the end we learn that this is all an elaborate "real" video game with live characters created from DNA. Young people are subjected to extreme violence—but

Fig. 3. Poster for *Tag* (Dir. Sono Shion, 2015)

for what? The youth within these narratives hardly understand why they are called to be so violent and so punished. Is this just for fun or does it mean something? Is it a critique of the violence youth are subjected to or just more of the same?

In the 2015 manga, *High Mobility Unemployed: Neetenberg*, youth experience the threat of violence as a call to join the Indentured Employment Army. This manga parodies the bestselling mecha Gundam franchise with a NEET antihero. NEET stands for "Not in Education, Employment or Training," and the NEET must fight with the Jobless League against "the oppressive corporate slaves of the Indentured Employment Army" (Nakamura 2015). The antihero is Fudō Yū (literally, No-work Play), a 17-year-old unemployed high school dropout who plays video games and speaks disrespectfully to his mother, but not without remorse.

Yū is dragged away by a member of the Forced Labor Army (aka Desu Māchigun, Death March Army) and threatened with severe working conditions. While unwilling to work, Yū is willing to fight, especially for a pretty young woman whose life seemed to be in trouble. Turns out she was sent to rescue him, as a member of the Jobless League. She invites him to climb inside the mechanical Work Man and join the resistance movement, after assuring him that he will not have to work. Yū senses he is being mocked when he is referred to as

Fig. 4. Panel from *High Mobility Unemployed: Neetenberg* (2015)

a special NEET, but the pretty Neru (whose name means "sleep") explains that in this case, NEET stands for "Next Evolution Exceed Type," a type of person with "special powers" to "breath life into the engine of Neetenberg" (Aoki 2015, 59). Cue giant robots fighting. Cultural products are engaging the problem of precarity and youth, but even in the most direct critique, such as this, there is the possibility that it ends as nothing more than yet more gratuitous violence that youth are subjected to for entertainment value.

Youth Activism

In addition to the protests in cultural products themselves, there have been new youth activist groups that have arisen in the past decade such as SEALDs, Amateur Riot (Shirōto no ran), and the independent freeter movement. The newest group, SEALDs (Students Emergency Action for Liberal Democracy), has emerged to protest the reinterpretation of the Constitution which weakens the "no-war" clause, Article 9. SEALDs is a university student movement, "overwhelmingly from elite, private universities." These students are aware of their socio-economic privilege, Robin O'Day writes, and "seek to use some their cultural capital to push their political agenda forward. Their privilege is in fact part of their politics, as they self-consciously use it as a platform from which they feel empowered to speak" (O'Day 2015). These youth are the privileged who expect to secure regular employment: "They talk openly about getting regular jobs and integrating into mainstream society once they graduate from university, and often worry that their involvement in political activism could jeopardize this professional future" (Ibid.)

By contrast, there are youth movements by those who have been excluded by the exclusive "regular" employment opportunities. These groups focus on issues related to precarity and embody the cluster of values of the recession generation, not least their rejection of inherited models of adulthood. O'Day writes:

To oppose neoliberal capitalism, Ono [Toshihiko, founding member of The Freeter Union Fukuoka] suggests, is at the core of his understanding of the freeter movement. As Ono describes it, freeter movement politics is effectively an oppositional politics by those who feel pushed out of the mainstream by corporate and state interests that prioritize economic growth over individual wellbeing, particularly at the expense of young workers struggling to gain a foothold in the labor market (*Ibid.*).

Both the message and the tactics of the freeter movement mesh with the critique of works like *High Mobility-Unemployed: Neetenberg.*

Amamiya Karin, an advocate for the precariat, writes: "It is an opposition movement against the fact that people all over the world are forced into instability because of neo-liberalism, which is advancing globalization" (Amamiya 2010, 254). Amamiya is a prolific and topical speaker and writer. She tackles issues related to youth in poverty, including bullying, social withdrawal, and suicide, but also NATO and the G10, and the problems associated with nuclear power and weapons. She resists being called a leftist, not least because she is committed to thinking compassionately about those on the right, and she recalls with gratitude how it was the right wing that first gave her a sense of community and opportunities to think about the relation between individual suffering and social structure.

Articulate and self-aware, she speaks for and to a generation of youth who feel disenfranchised from economic power. Her fashion sense is deliberately youthy and provocative: from Lolita goth to faux schoolgirl to a frilly white babydoll dress, she presents herself as a representative of youth. She is sensitive to the media mix of popular culture, producing music, film, blog, tweets, fiction, non-fiction and demonstrations in a style that combines a well-rehearsed emotional vulnerability with a hard-core defiance.

In 2012, I joined the Freedom and Life May Day March in Tokyo. The Freedom and Life May Day March was in its ninth year (sixth since Amamiya joined), so it has acquired its own sense of historical mission, one that grows and changes from year to year. It is an independent May Day demonstration, organized in conjunction with the All-Japan Freeter Union. The Indies Freedom and Life May Day is an attempt to redefine May Day by organizers at the All-Freeter Union, a union that allows anyone, regardless of employment, to join, and therefore, initiate new forms of community. A "Freedom and Life May Day 2012 Planning Committee" was responsible for a well-organized march and a two-page list of "slogans." Corralled into a single lane by police, the 2012 march moved energetically in a circuit through the busy streets of Shinjuku (despite a downpour that began midway) as Amamiya Karin issued call-and-response slogans like "Liberate Shinjuku!" and "Let's make some noise in the streets!" with a danceable, syncopated rhythm. Headed by a sound car with a live DJ and a banner that read, "Dance is not a Crime," this was not your parents' May Day March, and it represents both the transformation in protest culture and consciousness of the recession generation.

The numbers may have been relatively small, but the march more than made up for that in spectacle: dance beat sound car; the photogenic Amamiya in a lacy white babydoll dress and bullhorn; several participants in cosplay (costume play) giant animal costumes; and a general celebration of nonconformity hardly dampened by the rain.

The theme of the 2012 march was "The aspirations of a motley crew" with a focus on respecting diversity of background, nationality, sexuality, schooling. When Amamiya called out, "We oppose labor," it was in a string of "We oppose…," which also included "We oppose overtime" and "We oppose sexual harassment" and tellingly, "We oppose getting up early." As we have seen, this resistance to labor is characteristic of the precariat. Guy Standing writes, "Besides labour insecurity and insecure social income, those in the precariat lack a work-based identity. When employed, they are in career-less jobs, without traditions of social memory, a feeling they belong to an occupational community steeped in stable practice, codes of ethics and norms of behaviors, reciprocity and fraternity" (Standing 2011, 12). In a 2011 book on the rising freeter union movement in Japan, sociologist Hashiguchi Shōji (b. 1977) describes the movement in terms of the contradiction between "let us work" and "we won't work" (Hashiguchi 2011).

Part of the appeal of Amamiya as a spokesperson-mascot for the precariat is the way she appears to function independently of all the organizations, including the family, school (she withdrew), and corporations, etc., that have been contaminated by association with Japan Inc., but also, interestingly, of old-school organized politics. Working within the same culture generative of capital represented by Cool Japan, Amamiya's affective labor insists on affirming non-productivity. Undoubtedly she profits from her productivity in the sense that she makes a living as a writer; still, she parlays that into an appeal for those without the same benefits.

Conclusion

"Precariat," a neologism combining precarious and proletariat, was first used in the 1980s by French sociologists, but with decades of intervening neoliberalism, the 2008 economic crisis, and the 2016 Brexit shock, it has gained new traction. Guy Standing sees the precariat as a global phenomenon, consisting of people who lack labor-related security including labor-market security, employment security, job security (within one's employment), work security (protection against harm at work), skill reproduction security, income security and representation security (Standing 2011, 10). While this is inflected differently in different cultures, there are several key features of the global precariat: "it consists of people who have minimal trust relationships with capital or the state, making it quite unlike the salariat. And it has none of the social contract relationships of the proletariat, whereby labour securities were provided in exchange for subordination and contingent loyalty" (Ibid., 8). The securities sought by post-war social democrats, labor parties and trade unions have been diminished by the transformations wrought by a flexible economy, a reliance on temporary workers and the resultant loss of social support.

"Cool Japan" has received a lot of attention from scholars studying anime, manga, popular music, video games, etc. with the same kinds of critical attention once only afforded to objects of high culture. However, the focus on these cultural products alone fails to engage compassionately with the widespread reality of the youth whose very culture is being celebrated. The loosening of labor markets brought about by neoliberalism and the ongoing recession have produced a generation with fewer opportunities to "grow up" and become adults in the ways that were available to their parents during the period of high economic growth that followed WWII.

References

Akira: 25th Anniversary Edition. Directed by Ōtomo Katsuhiro. 1998. Funimation, 2013. DVD.

Akira: Production Report (1988). Directed by Shintani Yuichi. 1990. Akira Committee Company Ltd. DVD.

Allison, Anne. 2009. "The Cool Brand, Affective Activism and Japanese Youth." *Theory Culture & Society*, March/May. Vol. 26, no. 2-3: 89-111. doi: 10.1177/0263276409103118

Amamiya, Karin. 2010. "Suffering Forces Us to Think beyond the Right-Left Barrier." Translated by Jodie Beck. In *Mechademia 5: Fanthropologies*, edited by Frenchy Lunning. Minneapolis and London: University of Minnesota Press. Original publication: Amamiya Karin. "Ikitzurasa ga koesaseru 'sayū' no kakine: Baburu no hōkaigo no 'yakenohara' nite." Migi to hidari wa te o musuberu ka [Can the left and right join hands?]. Special issue of *Rosujene / Lost Generation*, May 2008: 44–53.

______.2007. *Ikisasero!: nanminkasuru wakamonotachi* [Survive! The Refugeeization of Young People] Tokyo: Ōta Shoin.

Aoki, Hayato. 2015. *Kōkidō Mushoku: Neetenberg* [High Mobility Unemployed]. Kadokawa Comics A. Vol. 1.

Battle Royale. Directed by Fukasaku Kinji. 2000. DVD.

Brinton, Mary. 2011. *Lost in Transition: Youth, Work, and Instability in Japan*. Cambridge: Cambridge University Press.

Cassegard, Carl. 2014. *Youth Movements, Trauma and Alternative Space in Contemporary Japan*. Leiden, Boston: Global Oriental.

Choo, Kukhee. 2012. "Nationalizing 'Cool': Japan's Global Promotion of the Content

Industry." In *Popular Culture and the State in East and Southeast Asia*, edited by Nissin Otmazgin and Eyal Ben-Ari, 85-105. London and New York: Routledge.

"Furīta hyōrū: monotsukuri no genba de" [Freeters adrift: where things are made]. 2005. NHK. Broadcast February 5.

Hashiguchi Shōji. 2011. *Wakamono no rōdō undō: "Hatarakaserō" to "Hataranakai" no shakaigaku* [Labor Movements of the Youth: Sociology of "Let us Work" and "We Do not Work"]. Tokyo: Seikatsu Shoin.

Ishida, Hiroshi and David Slater, eds. 2011. *Social Class in Contemporary Japan: Structures, Sorting and Strategies*. Routledge.

Japan Animation Creators Association (JAniCA). 2015. "Animēshon seisakusha jittai chōsa hōkokusho 2015" [Report on the survey on the actual conditions of animation creators 2015]. *Geinōjitsuenka, sutaffu no katsudō to sekatsu jittai, Chōsa hōkokusho 2015*, no. 9, special edition, 1-123. http://www.janica.jp/survey/survey2015Report.pdf

Kingston, Jeff and Machiko Osawa. 2015. "Risk and Consequences: The Changing Japanese Employment Paradigm." In *Japan: The Precarious Future*, edited by Anne Allison and Frank Baldwin, 58-96. New York: New York University Press.

Matsumoto, Taiyō. 2006. *Tekkonkinkreet: Black & White*. Translated by Lillian Olsen. San Francisco, CA: Viz Media. Originally published 1993-1994, Biggu Komikku Supirittsu; 1994 Shogakukan Inc.

McGray, Douglas. 2002. "Japan's Gross National Cool." *Foreign Policy. The Magazine of Global Politics, Economics, and Ideas*, May 1: 44-54.

Mōri, Yoshitaka. 2011. "The Pitfall Facing the Cool Japan Project: The Transnational Development of the Anime Industry under the Condition of Post-Fordism." *International Journal of Japanese Sociology*. No. 20: 30-42.

Nakamura, Toshi. 2015. "The Willfully Unemployed of Japan Have Their Own Mecha Manga." *Kotaku*. November 26.

O'Day, Robin. 2015. "Differentiating SEALDs from Freeters, and Precariats: The Politics of Youth Movements in Contemporary Japan." *The Asia-Pacific Journal*, Vol. 13, Issue 37, No. 2, September 1.

Slater, David, Robin O'Day, Satsuki Uno, Love Kindstrand and Chiharu Takano. 2015. "SEALDs (Students Emergency Action for Liberal Democracy): Research Note on Contemporary Youth Politics in Japan." *The Asia-Pacific Journal*, Vol. 13, Issue 37, No. 1, September 14.

Standing, Guy. 2011. *The Precariat: The New Dangerous Class*. London: Bloomsbury Academic.

Tag [Riaru onigokko]. Directed by Sono Shion. 2015. Shochiku. DVD.

Takami, Kōshun. 1999. *Battoru Rowairu* [Battle Royale]. Ōta Shuppan. English edition: Translated by Yuji Oniki. 2009. Haika Soru, 2nd ed.

Tekkonkinkreet. Directed by Michael Arias. 2006. Studio 4°C Co., Ltd.. DVD.

The Korean Wave in the World Seen through Statistics

Kiwoong Yang, Kyungeun Lee and Jeounghwa An

Introduction

In this chapter, we will analyze the recent trend of the Korean Wave, introducing important statistical data that will be useful to researchers interested in the Korean Wave by presenting the '2015 Korean Wave White Paper'. The introduction of this document summarizes contemporary trends in the contents industry in the world and Korea. We introduce the statistics of major trends by category as follows: trends in the global content industry, trends within the Korean content industry specifically, trends in the exports of the Korean content industry, consumer trends, and lastly, we present these trends in relation to the economic and political effects of the Korean Wave.

The Trend of the World Content Industry

The global content industry is expected to maintain steady growth over the next five years. We expect to see a stable annual growth rate of 5% through 2019 due to an increase in content subscribers, content consumption, and worldwide investments in network upgrades. The world content market is dominated by the United States, which comprises one-third, followed by Japan and China. The US, the world's top content market, is expected to grow at a Compound Annual Growth Reat (CAGR) of 4.8% through 2019, leading in the global content market. In addition, the respective content markets of emerging economies such as Indonesia, Vietnam, China, India, and Brazil are expected to maintain a high CAGR of over 10%. All four major regions of the global content market into four regions—the Americas, Europe, Asia, and the Middle East / Africa—are expected to grow steadily from 2014 to 2019. The overall market for the four major regions is projected to grow at an average annual rate of 5%, reaching $ 2.4 trillion in 2019. The Asian market is expected to grow at a CAGR of 5.7%, largely on the strength of economic growth in emerging Asian economies. The European market, on the other hand, is expected to plateau and grow slowly.

The Trend of Korean Content Industry

The information and knowledge industry, which includes education, media in Korea presents one of the most noticeable cases of economic growth in recent history. The information and knowledge industry grew 12% annually to one worth 12.7 trillion won, thanks to the development of information technology and the growth of virtual-reality related industries. In 2015, Korea's content industry exports are expected to grow at an average annual rate of 8.1%, to about $5.7 billion. Thanks to the explosive popularity of Korean media overseas in the Chinese market, the overall export of Korean video content has increased. In addition, the exports of Korea's knowledge and information industry—competitive because of its use of highly advanced information and communication technologies—has contributed significantly to the export growth of the content industry as a whole. For 2015, steady growth is predicted for all sectors of Korea's content industry except the advertising industry. While in the past, cultural exports were boosted by the explosive growth of the Korean broadcasting, movies, and music industries, overall exports will increase even further in 2015. The game industry, worth about $ 3.22 billion, accounts for 56.5% of the total information and knowledge industry exports from Korea. After the game industry, the character industry (9.7%) and knowledge and information industry (9.2%) generate the next largest portions of cultural exports.. These two industries are also making significant contributions to the growth of content export, not only in terms of the volume of their exports but also in annual growth rate.

Export Trends of Korean Content Industry

Exports of Korean broadcasting content to China in 2014 were up 213% year-on-year. As the media distribution environment of China improved, the popularity of Korean broadcasting contents spread rapidly, largely through social media networks and communities, generating increased demand for and consumption of media content. In 2014, music-related exports from Korea also increased by 418.3% to US $ 52.8 million. Film exports also grew 176.4% year-on-year to about $ 10.96 million, with similar growth expected in 2015.

Japan was the highest overseas consumer of Korea's content exports, accounting for 31.2% of Korea's total content exports that year. In particular, 70% of Korean music and 30% of television broadcasting were exported to

Japan. However, the decline in exports of films and broadcast to Japan in 2014 is a bad signal for the entire Korea's content market. This is largely due to the fact that the domestic content market in Japan has stagnated and that there have been no works produced to the taste of Japanese consumers exported. In addition, a weak yen, diplomatic disputes between Korea and Japan, and the rise of anti-Korean sentiment in Japan have all negatively influenced the growth in Korean cultural exports to Japan.

With a population of 600 million people and increasing purchasing power due to rising incomes, Southeast Asia is expected to become a significant avenue of new growth for the global export of Korean cultural productions. Moreover, in contrast to Japan and China, the embrace of multiculturalism and plurality in the Southeast Asian market may prove a boon to its reception of the Korean Wave's content.

Korean cultural productions do not enjoy widespread popularity in North America. American consumers and enthusiasts of the Korean Wave organize mainly around clubs and communities and exchange and consume Korean content mostly within these closed networks.

Europe is the smallest market for the Korean Wave, accounting only 6% of Korea's content exports, but this may indicate that the potential for exports is great. A strategic approach to the unexplored European market will be necessary in order for the export of Hallyu contents to continue its worldwide growth.

Export Trends of Korean Content Industry by Product

The total exports of the Korean film industry increased steadily between 2010 to 2014, decreasing slightly in 2015 due to a corresponding decline of service sector exports. Exports to Asia comprise the largest proportion of total film exports, followed by exports to North America. Since 2014, China has been the highest consumer of Korean cultural exports generally. In 2015, exports to China grew 12.8% from the previous year, and the Chinese market accounted for 31.5% of total exports—double the proportion of exports to Japan, which comprises the second-largest market.

Broadcast content exports increased at a CAGR of 19.9% from 2011 to 2014. After 2012, the export and import balance of the broadcasting industry showed a surplus, and thereafter, the amount of surplus continues to increase each year. The broadcasting content exports to China and Hong Kong combined comprise 42.8% of the total exports, exceeding Japan's share by 30.8%. This is a result of the explosive expansion of the Chinese market and the decline of Korean broadcasting exports in the Japanese market.

Analyzing the growth of Korean content exports by genre, K-dramas lead by accounting for 73.8% of total broadcasting exports.

Chinese market demand for Korean music content is predicted to drive growth in cultural due to the size of the market and increase in consumer purchasing power. Currently, Japan is the leading importer of Korean music exports, accounting for 70% of music content exports.

Approximately 60% of current Korean game content exports are online games and 30% are mobile games; mobile games are expected to increase

The knowledge and information industry shows the most growth in sales within the content industry. Exports of knowledge and information content are expected to surge to $ 500 million by 2015. The "smart learning" market platform is among the industry's leading exports, especially to the Chinese market, and mobile-oriented businesses are driving overseas expansion. In 2014, Southeast Asia accounted for the largest share (45.8%) of total knowledge and Information industry exports.

Consumer Trends of the Korean Wave (Hallyu)

Between 2010 and 2014, the United States (14.8%) exhibited the highest number of internet searches for 60 highly-rated Korean dramas, followed by the Philippines, Malaysia, and Indonesia with similar search volumes of about 13 to 15 percent each. These top four countries accounted for more than half of the worldwide volume of Korean drama-related internet searches. In 2015, the total search volume has surged, and these top four countries moved rank—Indonesia now leads the group, followed by Malaysia, the United States and the Philippines.

In 2015, global search volume for 'K-Pop' rose 40% compared to the previous year. The largest search volume occurred in the US, which accounted for 25% of the total. In 2015, search volume increased significantly in the Philippines while search volume in the UK and Vietnam decreased slightly.

In the United States, which accounts for the largest percentage of internet searches related to Korean movies, the volume of searches increased from 25% in 2014 to 30% in 2015. Additionally, in 2015, the proportion of other countries' searches increased, which indicates that Korean movies are being increasingly searched for across the world. However, the search volume for movies alone among the various cultural productions of the Korean wave is much smaller (150,000) than the search volume for Korean dramas (330,000) and K-pop (760,000), for example.

The Trend of the World Content Industry

Prospects for World Content Market

In particular, the information and animation sectors are expected to grow at a CAGR of over 7%, and the gaming and advertising industries are expected to grow at a stable rate of 5% on the strength of the proliferation of mobile platforms.[1]

<Table 1> Prospects for the World Content Market (2010~2019)[2]

1 billion USD

Sectors	2010	2011	2012	2013	2014	2015	2016	2017	2018	2019	2014~19 CAGR (%)[4]
Publication	372	371	367	365	365	365	366	368	370	373	0.4
Cartoon	7	8	8	7	7	7	7	7	6	6	-1.7
Music	46	46	46	46	46	46	46	46	47	48	0.8
Game	54	58	60	65	71	75	80	84	89	93	5.7
Movie*	84	84	84	84	85	88	91	95	99	105	4.1
Animation	11	10	11	12	11	13	14	15	16	17	8.2
Broad-cast**	382	400	417	431	453	468	487	503	521	536	3.4
Advertise-ment***	418	436	451	467	492	514	542	568	596	620	4.7
Character	147	151	153	156	161	167	173	180	186	193	3.0
Knowledge Information	457	501	546	596	643	694	745	799	856	919	7.4
Arithmetic Total[2]	1,976	2,064	2,144	2,229	2,335	2,437	2,552	2,664	2,787	2,909	4.5
Total[3]	1,572	1,653	1,725	1,807	1,904	1,998	2,100	2,203	2,314	2,426	5.0

- Sources: PwC (2015), ICv2 (2014,2015), MDRI (2014), Box Office Mojo (2015), Digital Vector (2014), EPM (2013, 2014), Survey on the Trend of Overseas Content Market in 2015 (Korea Creative Content Agency).
- Arithmetic total: The sum of arithmetical total, including overlapping values of all the categories.
- Total: The sum of arithmetical total excluding overlapping values of all the categories.
- The compound annual growth rate (CAGR) is a useful measure of growth over multiple time periods.

* Animated films are included in the movie market.

** The overlapping market of satellite radio advertisement is excluded in the radio market.

*** Advertisements inserted in each media such as newspaper/magazine advertisement in publication, game advertisement within games, and theatre advertisements in cinema are included in advertisement market.

Top 15 Content Markets by Country

One-third of the world content market is occupied by the United States, followed by Japan and China. The US, the world's top content market, is

1 *2015 Hallyu White Paper*, KOFICE, 2015, 531.

2 *Ibid.*

expected to grow at a CAGR of 4.8% through 2019, leading the global content market. In addition, emerging economies such as Indonesia, Vietnam, China, India, and Brazil are expected to maintain a high annual growth rate of over 10% [yearly?]. Japan, the world's second largest content market, is expected to be overtaken by China in 2016 due to the overall economic downturn in Japan. China's content market is expected to grow at an average annual rate of more than 10% as the demand for mobile devices, the Internet, and content increases explosively.[3] (P.533 ~ 534)

<Table 2> Top 15 Content Markets by Country (2010~2019)

1 billion USD

Rank	Nation	2010	2011	2012	2013	2014	2015	2016	2017	2018	2019	2014~19 CAGR (%)[4]
1	USA	555	581	606	629	660	690	725	758	797	836	4.8
2	Japan	151	154	158	162	168	170	172	172	173	175	0.8
3	China	89	104	116	133	149	167	186	206	227	248	10.6
4	Germany	96	99	102	104	105	107	109	111	113	115	1.8
5	UK	91	93	95	98	101	104	107	111	114	117	3.1
6	France	73	75	76	78	80	82	85	87	90	93	3.0
7	Canada	46	48	49	51	53	56	59	61	64	67	4.8
8	Korea	38	42	46	49	52	55	58	60	62	64	4.2
9	Brazil	29	33	36	40	45	49	55	60	66	72	10.0
10	Italy	44	45	43	43	43	44	46	48	49	51	3.5
11	Australia	33	33	33	35	36	37	39	40	42	44	4.1
12	Spain	30	30	29	28	29	30	31	32	33	34	2.9
13	Mexico	18	20	22	24	26	28	30	32	34	36	6.5
14	India	16	18	20	22	25	28	32	35	38	42	10.5
15	Russia	17	19	21	23	25	26	28	30	33	34	6.3

* Sources: PwC (2015), ICv2 (2014,2015), MDRI (2014), Box Office Mojo (2015), Digital Vector (2014), EPM (2013, 2014), Survey on the Trend of Overseas Content Market in 2015 (Korea Creative Content Agency)

Prospects for the Regional Content Markets (2010~2019)

We can divide the global content into four major regions: the Americas, Europe, Asia, and the Middle East / Africa. All four major regions are expected to grow steadily from 2014 to 2019. The overall market across all regions is projected to grow at an average annual rate of 5%, reaching [a net worth of?] $ 2.4 trillion by 2019. The region with the highest [predicted?] growth rate is the Middle East and Africa. It is expected to grow at an annual average rate of 8.9% starting in 2014, attaining a market worth of approximately $ 74 billion

3 *2015 Hallyu White Paper*, KOFICE, 2015, 533-534.

by 2019. The Asian market is expected to grow at a CAGR of 5.7% on the back of economic growth in its emerging economies. The European market, on the other hand, is expected to mature and grow slowly.[4](P.535)

<Table 3> Prospects for the Regional Content Markets (2010~2019) 1 Billion USD

Region	2010	2011	2012	2013	2014	2015	2016	2017	2018	2019	2014~19 CAGR (%)
America	664	701	735	770	813	855	903	949	1,001	1,054	5.3
Europe	502	514	522	533	548	563	581	599	619	638	3.1
Asia	380	409	436	468	503	535	568	601	635	670	5.7
Middle East ·Africa	25	28	32	44	48	53	58	63	68	74	8.9
Total	1,572	1,653	1,725	1,807	1,904	1,998	2,100	2,203	2,314	2,426	5

* Sources: PwC(2015), ICv2(2014,2015), MDRI(2014), Box Office Mojo(2015), Digital Vector(2014), EPM(2013, 2014), Survey on the Trend of Overseas Content Market in 2015 (Korea Creative Content Agency)

The Trend of Korean Content Industry

Annual Sales for Korea's Content Industry (2010~2015)

The information and knowledge industry in Korea grew 12% year-on-year to 12.7 trillion won, demonstrating the highest growth rate among content industries, largely due to the development of information technology and the growth of virtual-reality related industries. In 2015, the content industry overall is expected to show annual sales growth in all industries except publishing. Although the publishing industry is in decline, it should be noted that it is currently the largest content industry, accounting for about 20% of the domestic content industry. In contrast, the movie industry, the character industry and the content solutions industry are expected to record high growth rates going forward. Other industries comprising high proportion of the total content industry such as the broadcasting, advertising, and knowledge and information industries have maintained relatively high growth rates.[5]

4 *2015 Hallyu White Paper*, KOFICE, 2015, 535.

5 *2015 Hallyu White Paper*, KOFICE, 2015, 544-545.

<Table 4> Annual Sales for Korea's Content Industry (2010~2015) 100 million KRW, %

Business Sector		2010	2011	2012	2013	2014	2015	% of sectors for 2015
Publication	Sales	2,124	2,124	2,110	2,080	2,059	2,030	20.4%
	Variation rate (%)	-	0.0%	-0.7%	-1.4%	-1.0%	-1.4%	
Cartoon	Sales	74	75	76	80	85	87	0.9%
	Variation rate (%)	-	1.4%	1.3%	5.3%	6.3%	2.8%	
Music	Sales	296	382	399	428	461	479	4.8%
	Variation rate (%)	-	29.1%	4.5%	7.3%	7.7%	3.9%	
Game	Sales	743	880	975	972	997	1,060	10.6%
	Variation rate (%)	-	18.4%	10.8%	-0.3%	2.6%	6.3%	
Movie	Sales	343	377	440	466	457	496	5.0%
	Variation rate (%)	-	9.9%	16.7%	5.9%	-1.9%	8.5%	
Animation	Sales	51	53	52	52	56	58	0.6%
	Variation rate (%)	-	3.9%	-1.9%	0.0%	7.7%	3.6%	
Broadcast	Sales	1,118	1,275	418	1,494	1,577	1,660	16.7%
	Variation rate (%)	-	14.0%	-67.2%	257.4%	5.6%	5.3%	
Advertisement	Sales	1,032	1,217	1,248	1,336	1,374	1,415	14.2%
	Variation rate (%)	-	17.9%	2.5%	7.1%	2.8%	3.0%	
Character	Sales	590	721	752	831	905	984	9.9%
	Variation rate (%)	-	22.2%	4.3%	10.5%	8.9%	8.7%	
Knowledge Information	Sales	724	905	953	1,039	1,134	1,270	12.8%
	Variation rate (%)	-	25.0%	5.3%	9.0%	9.1%	12.0%	
Contents Solution	Sales	236	287	303	344	389	420	4.2%
	Variation rate (%)	-	21.6%	5.6%	13.5%	13.1%	8.0%	
Total	Sales	7,332	8,297	8,727	9,121	9,495	9,960	100.0%
	Variation rate (%)	9.30%	13.2%	5.2%	4.5%	4.1%	4.9%	

Export Trends of Korean Content Industry (2010~2015)

In 2015, Korea's content industry exports are expected to grow at an average annual rate of 8.1%, to about $ 5.7 billion. The explosive popularity of Korean media in the Chinese market has led to an increase in the export of Korean video content, and the exports of the competitive knowledge and information industry has further contributed to the export growth of the content industry as a whole.[6]

6 KOFICE, *2015 Hallyu White Paper*, 546.

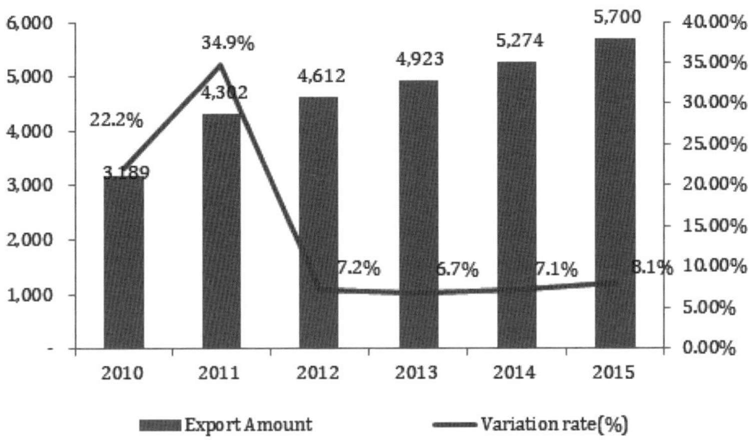

<Picture 1> Export Trends of Korean Content Industry (2010~2015) Million dollars, %

Exports of Korea's Content Industry (2010~2015)

Exports of Korea's content industry in 2015 will show steady growth in all sectors. While content exports were boosted by individual growth in the broadcasting, movies, and music industries in the past, overall exports will increase in 2015, with growth steadily growing across all sectors except the advertising industry. The sector showing the highest export growth rate is the movie industry, which is expected to resume upward growth this year despite a decline in 2014. The character industry recorded the second highest growth rate. The game industry comprises the largest portion of total content exports at about $ 3.22 billion, accounting for 56.5% of the total. Following the game industry, the character industry (9.7%) and the knowledge and information industry (9.2%) occupy the next-highest proportion. These two industries are making significant contributions to the growth of content exports overall, not only in terms of export volume but also in annual growth rate.[7]

7 *2015 Hallyu White Paper*, KOFICE, 2015, 546-547.

<Table 5> Exports of Korean Content Industry (2010~2015) 1 million USD, %

Category		2010	2011	2012	2013	2014	2015	Portion standards 2015
Publication	Export amount	358	283	245	292	247	255	4.5%
	Variation Rate(%)	-	-20.9%	247.0%	19.2%	-15.4%	3.1%	
Cartoon	Export amount	8	17	17	21	26	27	0.5%
	Variation Rate(%)	-	112.5%	0.0%	23.5%	23.8%	5.4%	
Music	Export amount	83	196	235	277	336	361	6.3%
	Variation Rate(%)	-	136.1%	19.9%	17.9%	21.3%	7.3%	
Game	Export amount	1,606	2,378	2,639	2,715	2,974	3,220	56.5%
	Variation Rate(%)	-	48.1%	11.0%	2.9%	9.5%	8.3%	
Movie	Export amount	14	16	20	37	26	29	0.5%
	Variation Rate(%)	-	14.3%	25.0%	85.0%	-29.7%	13.1%	
Animation	Export amount	97	116	113	110	116	124	2.2%
	Variation Rate(%)	-	19.6%	-2.6%	-2.7%	5.5%	6.9%	
Broadcast-ing	Export amount	185	222	234	309	336	367	6.4%
	Variation Rate(%)	-	20.0%	5.4%	32.1%	8.7%	9.2%	
Advertise-ment	Export amount	76	102	97	103	76	75	1.3%
	Variation Rate(%)	-	34.2%	-4.9%	1371.4%	-26.2%	-0.9%	
Character	Export amount	276	392	416	446	489	551	9.7%
	Variation Rate(%)	-	42.0%	6.1%	7.2%	9.6%	12.7%	
Knowledge & Informa-tion	Export amount	368	432	445	457	480	527	9.2%
	Variation Rate(%)	-	17.4%	3.0%	2.7%	5.0%	9.8%	
Contents Solution	Export amount	119	146	150	155	168	168	2.9%
	Variation Rate(%)	-	22.7%	2.7%	3.3%	8.4%	0.0%	
Total	Export amount	3,189	4,302	4,612	4,923	5,274	5,700	100.0%
	Variation Rate(%)	22.20%	34.9%	7.2%	6.7%	7.1%	8.1%	

Export Trends of Korean Content Industry

Korea's Content Exports to China (2011~2014)

It is no exaggeration to say that China is the most important market for Korea's content industry, and the export growth of Korea's content overall is largely determined by its exports to China. Exports of broadcasting contents to China in 2014 were up 213% year-on-year. As the distribution environment for media content has improved in China, the popularity of Korean broadcasting contents has spread rapidly through social media and online communities, leading to increased content demand and consumption. Korean music-related exports also increased by 418.3% to US $ 52.8 million. Major performances of Korean singers gave over 30 successful performances in China in 2014, and broadcasts of popular Korean music television programs are being exported to

China as well. Film exports also grew 176.4% year-on-year to about $ 10.96 million, with similar growth expected in 2015.[8]

<Table 6> Korea's Content Exports to China (2011~2014) 1,000 USD

	2011	2012	2013	2014	Year-on-year rate (%)
Publication	33,693	37,508	45,430	38,541	-15.2
Movie	1,628	2,008	3,966	10,961	176.4
Broadcasting	21,269	13,162	35,025	109,692	213
Music	6,836	8,806	10,186	52,798	418.3
Game	907,296	1,018,676	1,048,144	957,331	-8.7
Cartoon	662	829	986	1,241	25.9
Animation	1,659	1,712	1,603	1,848	15.3
Character	89,257	86,347	96,587	102,233	5.8
Knowledge & Information	36,287	39,586	41,534	42,356	2

Source: Korea Creative Content Agency. The Census of Content Industry in 2015

<Table 7> Korea's Content Exports to Japan (2011~2014) 1,000 USD

	2011	2012	2013	2014	Year-on-year rate (%)
Publication	62,790	61,289	74,560	60,584	-18.7
Movie	3,663	9,679	8,085	4,474	-44.7
Broadcast	102,058	112,088	138,687	79,017	-43.0
Music	157,938	189,512	221,739	235,481	6.2
Game	652,556	703,368	725,012	910,064	25.5
Cartoon	6,639	5,507	6,755	7,015	3.7
Animation	21,688	21,421	19,969	20,169	1.0
Character	20,256	22,868	25,200	30,233	20.0
Knowledge & Information	176,925	178,686	189,563	199,543	5.3

Source: Korea Creative Content Agency. The Census of Content Industry in 2015

Korea's Content Exports to Japan (2011~2014)

Japan, which accounts for the largest portion of Korea's content exports, recorded the highest volume of exports in 2014. As of 2014, exports to Japan account for 31.2% of Korea's total content exports. In particular, 70% of music and 30% of broadcasting were exported to Japan. The decline in Korean exports of films and broadcasting content to Japan in 2014 may be due to the fact that the domestic content market in Japan has stagnated and there have

8 *2015 Hallyu White Paper*, KOFICE, 2015, 554.

been no works aimed at the taste of Japanese consumers. In addition, a weak yen, diplomatic disputes between Korea and Japan, and the according rise of anti-Korean sentiment seem to have a bad influence. Perhaps surprisingly, however, exports from the Korean game and character industries grew by more than 20% in the same year.[9]

Korea's Content Exports to Southeast Asia (2011~2014)

Demand for Korean content in the Southeast Asian market continued to grow through 2014. The game industry, which accounts for the largest portion of exports to the Southeast Asian market, grew by 6% year-on-year, while the character industry and the knowledge and information industry also showed relatively high growth. The cartoon industry also recorded a high growth of 31.9% over the previous year. With a population of 600 million with increasing purchasing power due to development and rising income levels, Southeast Asia is expected to become a significant engine of new growth for the Korean Wave's content exports. In addition, the embrace of multiculturalism in the Southeast Asian market, relative to the Japanese and Chinese contexts, creates favorable conditions for the reception of Korean content .[10]

<Table 8> Korea's Content Exports to Southeast Asia (2011~2014) 1,000 USD

	2011	2012	2013	2014	Year-on-year rate(%)
Publication	29,810	29,418	35,314	29,457	-16.6
Movie	3,721	2,753	5,110	5,432	6.3
Broadcast	38,811	36,158	51,208	53,707	4.9
Music	25,691	31,146	38,166	39,548	3.6
Game	427,277	496,325	510,495	540,665	5.9
Cartoon	2,643	3,134	3,694	4,871	31.9
Animation	1,183	1,235	1,185	125	-89.5
Character	45,255	45,147	49,784	52,158	10.7
Knowledge Information	198,372	203,709	208,431	219,874	5.5

Source: Korea Creative Content Agency. The Census of Content Industry in 2015

Korea's Content Exports to North America (2011~2014)

Korean cultural productions do not enjoy widespread popularity in North America. American consumers and enthusiasts of the Korean Wave organize mainly around clubs and communities that exchange and share Korean media

9 *2015 Hallyu White Paper*, KOFICE, 2015, 555.
10 *2015 Hallyu White Paper*, KOFICE, 2015, 556.

content within a closed network. In 2014, Korea's content exports to North America dropped slightly from the previous year. The main cause of this is that the export of game industry decreased by 2.2%. However, exports of the cartoon industry increased 39.7%, and those of the animation industry increased by 3.5%.[11]

<Table 9> Korea's Content Exports to North America (2011~2014) 1,000 USD

	2011	2012	2013	2014	Year-on-year rate(%)
Publication	90,127	66,192	76,933	66,189	-14.0
Movie	1,673	2,873	3,040	3,097	1.8
Broadcast	3,563	12,565	9,366	9,232	-1.4
Music	587	857	1,024	1,058	3.3
Game	1,812,255	202,337	209,086	204,468	-2.2
Cartoon	1,766	2,353	2,826	3,947	39.7
Animation	59,397	59,167	60,355	62,490	3.5
Character	102,565	117,034	128,876	131,592	2.1
Knowledge & Information	8,802	9,727	9,660	9,801	1.6

Source: Korea Creative Content Agency. The Census of Content Industry in 2015

Korea's Content Exports to Europe (2011~2014)

Europe is the smallest market for Korean content exports, accounting for only 6% of the total, but this also indicates that the prospects for the European content market are high. In order for the export of Hallyu contents to continue to grow, a strategic approach to the unexplored European market will be needed.[12]

<Table 10> Korea's Content Exports to Europe (2011~2014) 1,000 USD

	2011	2012	2013	2014	Year-on-year rate(%)
Publication	21,557	16,180	19,520	13,956	-28.5
Movie	3,522	2,456	6,992	1,760	-74.8
Broadcast	1,480	2,201	1,850	1,685	-8.9
Music	4,632	4,231	4,827	4,778	-1.0
Game	152,369	159,258	162,924	120,340	-26.1
Cartoon	5,457	5,202	6,434	8,054	25.2
Animation	28,556	24,433	25,144	26,541	5.6
Character	82,358	88,465	93,923	105,214	12.0
Knowledge Information	3,528	3,887	4,036	4,102	1.6

Source: Korea Creative Content Agency. The Census of Content Industry in 2015

11 *2015 Hallyu White Paper*, KOFICE, 2015, 557.
12 *2015 Hallyu White Paper*, KOFICE, 2015, 558.

Export Trends of Korean Content Industry by Product

Exports of South Korean Films (2010 ~ 2015)

The total exports of the film industry have steadily increased from 2010 to 2014, but they decreased slightly in 2015 due to declining exports in the service sector. However, exports of films have been steadily growing since 2010.[13]

<Table 11> Exports of South Korean Films (2010 ~ 2015) 1 USD

Category	2010	2011	2012	2013	2014	2015
Exports of Films	13,582,850	15,828,662	20,174,950	37,071,445	26,380,475	29,374,098
Exports of Services	28,637,506	19,041,163	17,649,854	22,388,411	36,703,952	26,126,402
Total Exports	42,220,356	34,869,825	37,824,804	59,459,856	63,084,427	55,500,500

Source: Korea Creative Content Agency. The Census of Content Industry in 2015.
Korean Film Council (KOFIS). Annual Report of Korean Film Industry in 2015.
http://www.kofic.or.kr/kofic/business/board/selectBoardList.do?boardNumber=2

Exports of South Korean Films by Region (2012-2015)

Exports of Korean films to Asian countries make up most of Korea's total film exports, followed by North America. However, in North America, unlike in Asia, there is no steady and consistent fanbase, and the preferred works are relatively few, so the North American market performs inconsistently year to year. Film exports to Europe are declining.[14]

<Table 12> Exports of South Korean Films by Region (2012-2015) 1 USD

Region	2012		2013		2014		2015		Year-on-year rate(%)
	Export Amount	Portion (%)	Export Amount	Portion (%)	Export Amount	Portion (%)	Export Amount	Portion (%)	
Asia	14,439,757	71.6	17,161,096	46.3	20,867,717	79.1	22,958,571	78.2	10.0
North America	2,872,752	14.2	6,931,734	18.7	3,097,044	11.7	4,448,168	15.1	43.6
Europe	2,455,745	12.2	3,193,230	8.6	1,760,129	6.7	1,237,665	4.2	-29.7
Central South America	233,500	1.2	1,864,863	5.0	306,223	1.2	309,200	1.1	1.0
Oceania	134,196	0.7	144,822	0.4	122,630	0.5	262,785	0.9	114.3

13 *2015 Hallyu White Paper*, KOFICE, 2015, 562.
14 *2015 Hallyu White Paper*, KOFICE, 2015, 564.

Middle East	39,000	0.2	200,700	0.5	81,100	0.3	54,000	0.2	-33.4
Others	-	0.0	7,575,000	20.4	145,632	0.6	103,709	0.4	-28.8
Total	20,174,950	100.0	37,071,445	100.0	26,380,475	100.0	29,374,098	100	11.3

Source: Korea Creative Content Agency. The Census of Content Industry in 2015.
Korean Film Council (KOFIS). Annual Report of Korean Film Industry in 2015.
http://www.kofic.or.kr/kofic/business/board/selectBoardList.do?boardNumber=2

Exports of South Korean Films by Country (2012-2015)

Korea has exported the most films to China since 2014. In 2015, exports to China grew 12.8% year-on-year. The Chinese market accounted for 31.5% of total exports of Korean film, double the size of those to Japan, which comprises the second largest export market. It is noteworthy that Thailand and Vietnam have recently moved into the top 10 export markets for Korean film.[15]

<Table 13> Exports of South Korean Films by Country (2012-2015) 1 USD

Country	2012		2013		2014		2015		Year-on-year rate(%)
	Export Amount	Portion (%)	Export Amount	Portion (%)	Export Amount	Portion (%)	Export Amount	Portion (%)	
China	730,809	3.6	1,757,100	6.7	8,206,702	31.1	9,254,539	31.5	12.8
Japan	9,679,008	48.0	8,085,102	30.7	4,474,824	17.0	4,956,355	16.9	10.8
USA	2,341,685	11.6	3,040,243	11.5	2,900,625	11.0	4,428,168	15.1	52.7
HongKong	832,700	4.1	2,208,540	8.4	2,755,624	10.4	1,967,937	6.7	-28.6
Taiwan	581,908	2.9	1,123,000	4.3	1,772,500	6.7	1,725,779	5.9	-2.6
Singapore	500,000	2.5	915,145	3.5	937,650	3.6	965,104	3.3	143.4
Germany	407,794	2.0	879,700	3.3	442,836	1.7	851,600	2.9	180.7
France	1,175,300	5.8	2,452,632	9.3	409,665	1.6	515,700	1.8	-45.0
Vietnam	0	0.0	391,506	1.5	396,455	1.5	477,500	1.6	35.0
Thailand	331,892	1.7	663,000	2.5	353,796	1.3	289,000	1.0	126.3
Others	3,593,854	17.8	15,555,477	59.0	3,729,798	14.1	3,942,416	13.4	-5.0
Total	20,174,950	100.0	37,071,445	100.0	26,380,475	100.0	29,374,098	100.0	11.3

Source: Korea Creative Content Agency. The Census of Content Industry in 2015.
Korean Film Council (KOFIS). Annual Report of Korean Film Industry in 2015.
http://www.kofic.or.kr/kofic/business/board/selectBoardList.do?boardNumber=2

Exports and Imports of South Korean Broadcasting Industry (2011-2014)

Broadcast content exports are growing at a CAGR of 19.9% from 2011 to 2014. After 2012, the export and import balance of broadcasting industry

15 *2015 Hallyu White Paper*, KOFICE, 2015, 565.

showed a surplus, and the amount of surplus is also rapidly increasing every year.

<Table 14> Exports and Imports of South Korean Broadcasting Industry (2011-2014) 1,000 USD

Category	2011	2012	2013	2014	Year-on-Year Growth Rate (%)	CAGR (%)
Export Amount	222,372	233,821	309,399	336,019	8.6	19.9
Import Amount	233,872	136,071	122,697	64,508	-47.4	-30.0
The balance of trade	-11,500	97,750	186,702	271,511	45.4	63.0

Source: Korea Creative Content Agency. The Census of Content Industry in 2015.

Korea's Content Exports to Japan (2011~2014)

Japan, which accounts for the largest portion of Korea's content exports, recorded the highest volume of exports in 2014. As of 2014, exports to Japan account for 31.2% of Korea's total content exports. In particular, 70% of music and 30% of broadcasting were exported to Japan. The decline in Korean exports of films and broadcasting content to Japan in 2014 may be due to the fact that the domestic content market in Japan has stagnated and there have been no works aimed at the taste of Japanese consumers. In addition, a weak yen, diplomatic disputes between Korea and Japan, and the according rise of anti-Korean sentiment seem to have a bad influence. Perhaps surprisingly, however, exports from the Korean game and character industries grew by more than 20% in the same year.[16]

Exports of Korean Broadcasting Industry by Region and Country (2011-2014)

Japan imported the largest amount of Korean broadcasting content in 2014, followed by China. However, if broadcasting content exports to China and Hong Kong are combined, their share of the total is 42.8%, far exceeding 30.8% of Japan's share. This can be seen as a result of the explosive expansion of the Chinese market and the decline of Korean broadcasting exports to the Japanese market.

16 *2015 Hallyu White Paper*, KOFICE, 2015, 555.

<Table 15> Exports of Korean Broadcasting Industry by Region and Country (2011-2014)

1,000 USD

Region and Country		2011	2012	2013	2014	Portion (%)	Year-on-Year Growth Rate (%)	CAGR (%)
Asia	Japan	102,058	112,088	138,687	79,017	30.8	-43.0	-16.0
	China	17,241	11,000	26,139	56,035	22.2	117.8	127.5
	Hong Kong	4,028	2,162	8,886	52,694	20.6	493.0	393.7
	Singapore	3,260	3,189	1,935	3,884	1.5	100.7	10.4
	Taiwan	21,051	14,588	21,778	15,643	6.1	-28.2	3.6
	Vietnam	2,769	3,231	7,341	9,042	3.5	23.2	67.3
	Malaysia	1,815	5,577	1,703	1,328	0.5	-22.0	-51.2
	Indonesia	1,246	879	1,276	1,316	0.5	3.1	22.4
	Thailand	2,785	4,129	8,379	14,693	5.7	75.4	88.6
	Philippines	3,549	2,081	4,637	3,461	1.4	-25.4	29.0
	Myanmar	1,412	1,714	2,261	1,840	0.7	-18.6	3.6
	Cambodia	517	503	943	1,693	0.7	79.5	83.5
	Kazakhstan	390	252	145	246	0.1	69.7	-1.2
	Mongolia	59	83	208	273	0.1	31.3	81.4
	Middle East	569	2,998	836	619	0.2	-26.0	-54.6
	Others in Asia	380	15	602	288	0.1	-52.2	338.2
North and South America	USA	3,523	12,565	9,351	9,232	3.6	-1.3	-14.3
	Canada	40	0	15	0	0.0	-100.0	-
	South America	127	247	343	338	0.1	-1.5	17.0
Europe	France	212	66	304	643	0.3	111.5	212.1
	UK	0	143	95	148	0.1	55.8	1.7
	Italy	215	91	155	75	0.0	-51.6	-9.2
	Spain	25	119	29	24	0.0	-17.2	-55.1
	Hungary	78	0	0	0	0.0	-	-
	Russia	48	55	94	25	0.0	-73.4	-32.6
	Netherlands	1	1	0	0	0.0	-	-
	Romania	505	300	375	309	0.1	-17.6	1.5
	Others in Europe	396	1,426	798	461	0.2	-42.2	-43.1
	Oceania	20	5	222	78	0.0	-64.9	295.0
	Africa	45	15	66	34	0.0	-48.5	50.6
Others	Others	550	197	1,870	1,939	0.8	3.7	213.7
Total		168,941	179,719	239,473	256,276	100.0	7.0	19.4

Source: Korea Creative Content Agency. The Census of Content Industry in 2015.

Exports of Korean Broadcasting Industry by Genre (2011-2014)

Looking at exports of broadcast content by genre, Korean television drama programming accounts for 73.8% of total broadcasting exports. Exports of other Korean entertainment and culture programs have also increased. Culture-related programs in particular rose sharply to about $ 42.25 million in 2014.

<Table 16> Exports of Korean Broadcasting Industry by Genre (2011-2014) 1,000 USD

Genre	2011	2012	2013	2014	Portion (%)	Year-on-Year Growth Rate (%)	CAGR (%)
Drama	154,616	161,501	211,540	189,135	73.8	-10.6	8.2
Documentary	1,450	8,144	2,940	1,706	0.7	-42	-54.2
Animation	117	44	128	80	0.0	-37.5	34.8
Entertain-ment	10,400	7,731	14,433	19,881	7.8	37.7	60.4
Music	890	1,260	846	273	0.1	-67.7	-53.5
Culture	594	134	499	42,455	16.6	8,408.0	1,680.0
Education	10	141	19	26	0.0	36.8	-57.1
News	0	590	400	245	0.1	-38.8	-35.6
Sports	44	21	28	13	0.0	-53.6	-21.3
Others	820	152	8,640	2,462	1.0	-71.5	302.5
Total	168,941	179,719	239,473	256,276	100.0	7.0	19.4

Source: Korea Creative Content Agency. The Census of Content Industry in 2015.

Exports of Korean Music by Region (2011-2014)

Looking at the exports of Korean music industry by region, the growth of the Chinese market is remarkable. Although currently, about 70% of all music content exports are made to Japan, Chinese market is expected to soon surpass Japan and drive exports based on its size and rapidly growing purchasing power. Exports to other countries, such as the Middle East and Latin America, have continued to increase since 2013, though the relative proportion of these exports remains small.

<Table 17> Exports of Korean Music by Region (2011-2014) 1 USD

Region/Year	2011	2012	2013	2014	Portion (%)	Year-on-Year Growth Rate (%)	Average Annual Variation Rate (%)
China	6,836	8,806	10,186	52,796	15.7	418.3	144.9
Japan	157,938	189,512	221,739	235,481	70.2	6.2	11.5
Southeast Asia	25,691	31,146	38,166	39,548	11.8	3.6	12.7
North Amer-ica	587	857	1,024	1,058	0.3	3.3	11.1
Europe	4,632	4,231	4,827	4,778	1.4	-1.0	6.3
Others	429	545	1,386	1,987	0.6	43.4	90.0
Total	196,113	235,097	277,328	335,650	100.0	21.0	19.5

Source: Korea Creative Content Agency. The Census of Content Industry in 2015.

Exports of Korean Game Industry (2008-2015)

According to the Games White Paper in 2015, exports in 2014 surpassed the previous year's growth rate of 2.9% , achieving a high growth rate of 9.5% and bringing total [game?] exports close to about $ 3 billion. Currently, approximately 60% of game content exports are online games and 30% are mobile games, but mobile games are expected to eventually lead the export of games.

Exports of Knowledge and Information Industry by Region (2011 – 2014)

The sales of the knowledge and information industry has shown the most growth of any sector of the content industry. Its exports are expected to surge to $ 500 million by 2015. Smart learning market platforms are being exported with a focus on the Chinese market, and mobile-oriented businesses are driving overseas expansion. Southeast Asia accounted for 45.8% of total knowledge and Information industry exports, the largest share of exports. Based largely on the strength of applications such as NAVER Line and KakaoTalk messenger, the growth of the knowledge and information industry is expected to continue in 2015.

<Table 18> Exports of Knowledge and Information Industry by Region (2011 – 2014) 1,000 USD

Region/Year	2011	2012	2013	2014	Portion (%)	Year-on-Year Growth Rate (%)	Average Annual Variation Rate (%)
China	36,287	39,586	41,534	42,356	8.8	2.0	3.4
Japan	176,925	178,686	189,563	199,543	41.6	5.3	5.7
Southeast Asia	198,372	203,709	208,431	219,874	45.8	5.5	3.9
North America	8,802	9,727	9,660	9,801	2.0	1.5	0.4
Europe	3,528	3,887	4,036	4,102	0.9	1.6	2.7
Others	8,342	9,242	3,687	3,977	0.8	7.9	-34.4
Total	432,256	444,837	456,911	479,653	100.0	5.0	3.8

Source: Korea Creative Content Agency. The Census of Content Industry in 2015.

Consumer Trends of the Korean Wave (Hallyu)

Top 10 Most Loved Korean Dramas Overseas

The United States (14.8%) had the highest number of web searches for 60 dramas that showed high ratings between 2010 and 2014, followed by the Philippines, Malaysia, and Indonesia, each with similar search volumes between 13 to 15 percent. The top four countries accounted for more than half of the total worldwide search volume. In 2015, that total has surged, and the top countries have changed ranking positions, with Indonesia in the lead, followed by Malaysia, the United States and the Philippines.

<Table 19> Top 5 Countries searching for Korean Dramas (2014-2015)

Search Ranking	2014		2015	
1	USA	14.8% (36,934)	Indonesia	15.6% (50,726)
2	Philippines	14.3% (35,672)	Malaysia	14.7% (47,953)
3	Malaysia	14.3% (35,634)	USA	14.4% (46,952)
4	Indonesia	13.3% (33,264)	Philippines	8.6% (27,953)
5	India	4.6% (11,519)	India	6.9% (22,626)
Others	Other Nations	38.6% (96,147)	Other Nations	39.8% (129,940)
Total	100% (249,170)		100% (326,150)	

<Table 20> Top 10 Rating Korean Drama (2010-2015)

Year	English Titles of Top 10 Rating Korean Dramas
2010	The Slave Hunters, Big Thing, Athena: Goddess of War, Secret Garden, Cinderella's Sister, Pasta, Personal Taste, Sungkyunkwan Scandal, Dr. Champ, Mary Stayed Out All Night
2011	Tree With Deep Roots, The Princess' Man, Sign, Scent of a Woman, A Thousand Days' Promise, My Princess, The Greatest Love, City Hunter, Dream High, Protect the Boss
2012	Moon Embracing the Sun, A Gentleman's Dignity, Bridal Mask, The Innocent Man, History of a Salary man, Brain, The Chaser, Golden Time, Arang and the Magistrate, Dr. Jin
2013	My Love from the Star, I Can Hear Your Voice, Good Doctor, Master's Sun, The Heirs, King of Ambition, Incarnation of Money, Secret Love, Queen of the Office, That Winter, the Wind Blows
2014	Mama, You're All Surrounded, Three days, Doctor Stranger, The Night Watchman's Journal, Mr. Back, Gunman in Joseon, Pinocchio, Punch, Pride and Prejudice
2015	Yong Pal, She Was Pretty, Mrs. Cop, Unkind Ladies, Shine or Go Crazy, Mask, Heard It Through the Grapevine, Kill Me, Heal Me, High Society, Oh My Venus

The top 10 Korean dramas were selected based on critical ratings. The top 10 Korean movies were selected based on the box office performance, and the top 10 music [artists? Songs? Albums? Performances?] is selected according to The Melon, a generally representative music source distribution site. We used the Keyword Planner from Google AdWords to calculate web search volume numbers.

Top 10 Most Loved K-Pop Songs Overseas

In 2015, search volumes for K-Pop jumped 40% year-on-year, with the largest search volume occurring in the US, which accounted for 25% of the total. In 2015, search volume increased significantly in the Philippines in 2014, while search volume in the UK and Vietnam decreased slightly.

<Table 21> Top 5 Countries searching for K-pop (2014-2015)

Ranking	2014		2015	
1	USA	26.2% (142,365)	USA	24.6% (187,318)
2	Philippines	9.3% (50,448)	Philippines	15.3% (116,162)
3	India	7.6% (41,429)	India	7.2% (54,972)
4	UK	7.0% (38,280)	UK	4.8% (36,358)
5	Vietnam	4.7% (25,780)	Vietnam	2.9% (22,212)
Others	Other Nations	45.1% (245,408)	Other Nations	45.1% (343,228)
Total	100% (543,710)		100% (760,250)	

<Table 22> Top 10 Ranking K-Pop (2014 – 2015)

Year	Music Ranking Top 10 (English Title used in searching)
2010	Bad Girl Good Girl, Nagging It, Hurts Like Dying, Can't Do Even If I Die, I Can't Let You Go, Oh!, 2 Different Tears, I Go Crazy Because of You, I Was Able To Eat Well, Go Away
2011	Roly-Poly, I Cheated / Having An Affair, I am the best, On Rainy Days, I turned off the TV, So Cool, Ugly, Good day, To Live at least once, Don't say Goodbye
2012	Gangnam Style, Alone, Cherry Blossom Ending, Loving U, Fantastic Baby, If you really love me, All for you, Heaven, Every End of the Day, First Love
2013	Johnny, Tears, No No No, Shower of tears, Question mark, Give it to me, What's your name?, Monodrama, My love, Gone Not Around Any Longer
2014	Some, Wild flower, Eyes, nose, lips, See you on Friday, Friday, A midsummer night's sweetness, Not spring, love, or cherry blossoms, Mr. Chu, Meaning of you, Something, 200%
2015	Bang Bang Bang, You from the same time, Eat, Shouldn't have, Wi ing Wi ing, I'm not the only one, Loser, Bae Bae, Just, YangHwa Bridge

Top 10 Most Loved Korean Movies Overseas

In the United States, which produces the largest volume of web searches for Korean movies, the volume of searches increased from 25% in 2014 to 30% in 2015. In 2015, the proportions of web searches by other countries has also increased, indicating that Korean movies are being searched increasingly across the world. On the other hand, when compared in terms of the absolute value, the search volume numbers for movies among all Korean wave contents is much smaller (150,000) than the search volume for Korean dramas (330,000) and for the K-pop song(760,000).

<Table 23> Comparing Top 5 Nations searching for Korean Movie in 2014 and 2015

Ranking	**2014**		**2015**	
1	USA	25.7% (36,258)	USA	29.3% (44,624)
2	Philippines	19.8% (27,937)	Indonesia	8.1% (12,401)
3	Indonesia	6.7% (9,423)	Philippines	7.6% (11,572)
4	Malaysia	6.3% (8,851)	India	7.3% (11,135)
5	India	4.6% (6,453)	Malaysia	7.3% (11,087)
Others	Other Nations	36.9% (52,078)	Other Nations	40.4% (61,551)
Total	100% (141,000)		100% (152,370)	

<Table 24> Searching Computation about Popular Korean Movie in 2014 and 2015

Year	Box Office Top 10 (English Title used in searching)
2010	The Man from Nowhere, Secret Reunion, Jeon Woo-Chi, The Taoist Wizard, Moss, 71: Into the Fire, Harmony, The Servant, The Unjust, Cyrano Agency, The Housemaid
2011	War of the Arrows, Sunny, Punch; Wan-deuk-I, Detective K, Do-ga-ni, The Crucible Cast, Quick, Go-ji-jeon, The Front Line, Spellbound, Meet the in-laws, The Client
2012	Dodookdeul, The Thieves, Gwanghae, Masquerade, A Werewolf boy, The Grand Heist, Nameless Gangster: Rules of the Time, All About My Wife, Deranged, Architecture 101, Dancing Queen, Unbowed
2013	Miracle in Cell No. 7, Snowpiercer, The Face Reader, The Berlin File, Secretly, Greatly, The Attorney, Hide and Seek, The Terror Live, Cold Eyes, New World
2014	The Admiral: Roaring Currents, The Pirates, Miss Granny, The Attorney, Ode to My Father, Kundo: Age of the Rampant, Tazza: The Hidden Card, The Fatal Encounter, My Love, Don't Cross That River, The Divine Move
2015	Veteran, Assassination, Ode to my father, The Throne, Inside Men, The Throne, Northern Limit Line, The Priests, Himalaya, Detective K: Secret of the Lost Island, Twenty

Economic Effects of the Korean Wave

The Korean wave (Hallyu) popularity index by Country (2013-2014)

The Korean Wave (Hallyu) popularity Index is the value indicating the degree of popularity of the Korean Wave in any given country. For the 8 genres of Korean Wave products, the level of popularity in the country is measured on a scale of 5 points.[17] Countries can be divided into three stages according to Hallyu popularity index: the popularization stage (3.5 or more), the diffusion stage (2.5 ~ 3.49), and the minor interest stage (2.49 or less). The overall average of Hallyu popularity index was 3.02, followed by Singapore (4.00),

17 "There are few people to use (1 point)"; "It is popular in a mania market (2 points)"; "Not only a few maniacs but also a lot of ordinary people know (3 points)"; "It is widely known to the general public and the product is sold (4 points)"; "It is widely popular among the general public and the sales of related products are active" (5 points)".

Philippines (3.96), Myanmar (3.73), China (3.64), Thailand (3.58), Indonesia (3.50) and Vietnam (3.50). Hallyu popularity index was recorded to be lower in the countries of Mexico (2.07), Poland (2.18), Germany (2.31), Iran (2.38) and Brazil (2.48).

<Table 25> The Korean Wave (Hallyu) Popularity Index by Country (2013-2014)

Country		**Popularity index of Korean wave (2015, c)**	**Popularity index of Korean wave (2014, d)**	**Change of popularity index (c-d)**	**Note**
Popularization stage of the Korean wave (3.5>)	Singapore	4.00	3.87	0.14	
	Philippines	3.96	3.81	0.15	
	Myanmar	3.73	3.98	-0.25	
	China	3.64	3.58	0.06	
	Thailand	3.58	3.52	0.06	
	Indonesia	3.50	3.47	0.03	
	Vietnam	3.50	3.87	-0.37	
Diffusion stage of the Korean wave (2.5~3.49)	Malaysia	3.47	3.51	-0.04	
	Uzbekistan	3.44	3.76	-0.32	
	Kazakhstan	3.41	3.11	0.30	
	Taiwan	3.36	3.50	-0.15	
	Canada	3.28	2.79	0.49	
	UAE	3.22	2.87	0.35	
	USA	2.95	3.09	-0.14	
	Argentina	2.93	2.70	0.23	
	South Africa	2.86	2.84	0.03	
	Turkey	2.81	2.92	-0.11	
	Australia	2.69	2.82	-0.13	
	Ukraine	2.63	3.14	-0.51	
	Japan	2.61	2.62	-0.01	
	France	2.57	2.64	-0.07	
	India	2.55	1.86	0.69	
	UK	2.55	2.78	-0.23	
	Russia	2.50	2.41	0.09	
Minor interest stage of the Korean wave (>2.49)	Brazil	2.48	2.45	0.02	
	Iran	2.38	2.27	0.10	
	Germany	2.31	2.61	-0.30	
	Poland	2.18	2.31	0.14	
	Mexico	2.07	2.46	0.39	

Source: Korea Creative Content Agency & Korea Trade-Investment Promotion Agency. A Study on the Economic Effects of the Korean Wave in 2015. 2016

The Korean Wave Consumer Survey Index (KWCSI)

The Korean Wave Consumer Survey Index (KWCSI) is a value that describes how much of the Korean Wave is consumed in various countries, thereby indicating the growth rate of the Korean Wave. The KWCSI is measured by applying survey methods to calculate 'Consumer Survey Index' at the Bank of Korea. Based on the KWCSI, countries were divided into three groups:

'decline' (less than 100 points), moderate-growth (101 points to 130 points), and high-growth (more than 131 points). The average value of the KWCSI across 29 countries responding to the survey was recorded at 117.56, a slight decline from the previous year (122.25). In other words, the popularity of the Korean Wave is still growing, but its growth rate has decreased relative to 2014. In particular, in the UAE and India, the KWCSI increased by more than 10% compared to 2014, while the same indicator in countries such as Uzbekistan, Myanmar, South Africa and Mexico decreased by more than 10%. Japan and Iran also joined the decline group in 2014 and 2015.

<Table 26> Korean Wave Consumer Survey Index (KWCSI)

Category		Present KWCSI	Outlook KWCSI	KWCSI (2015, a)	KWCSI (2014, b)	Change of KWCSI (a-b)	Note
High-Growth Group	Kazakhstan	138.17	141.00	139.58	128.64	10.94	
	Indonesia	139.13	139.04	139.08	136.40	2.69	
	Malaysia	135.58	136.42	136.00	140.90	-4.90	
	Thailand	130.46	132.46	131.46	124.33	7.12	
	Argentina	128.73	133.49	131.11	142.24	-11.13	
	USA	130.73	130.87	130.80	130.77	0.03	
Moderate-Growth Group	Philippines	128.18	130.29	128.80	123.71	5.09	
	China	127.56	127.81	127.68	126.48	1.20	
	Vietnam	119.00	135.50	127.25	138.86	-11.61	
	UAE	125.67	128.08	126.88	102.04	24.83	High growth
	Singapore	124.40	123.36	123.88	120.70	3.18	
	Ukraine	120.67	124.83	122.75	120.16	2.59	
	India	119.52	125.50	122.51	92.89	29.61	High growth
	UK	116.75	118.50	117.63	121.25	-3.63	
	Canada	116.67	118.18	117.21	109.65	7.57	
	Turkey	112.01	119.63	115.82	112.05	3.77	
	Russia	114.25	117.08	115.67	113.79	1.87	
	Uzbekistan	111.11	117.33	115.14	151.52	-36.37	High growth
	Germany	113.66	114.85	114.32	119.04	-4.72	
	France	113.08	115.04	114.06	112.33	1.73	
	Poland	110.39	115.90	113.33	107.96	5.37	
	Myanmar	111.67	114.67	113.17	162.42	-49.25	High growth
	Australia	112.75	113.08	112.92	121.56	-8.65	
	Brazil	110.13	113.50	111.81	111.17	0.65	
	South Africa	108.17	109.13	108.65	125.25	-16.60	High growth
	Taiwan	104.72	101.28	103.00	104.75	-1.75	
Decline Group	Mexico	95.83	102.00	98.92	129.83	-30.92	Decline
	Iran	86.19	85.95	86.63	82.83	3.80	
	Japan	76.50	78.69	77.60	71.54	6.06	

Source: Korea Creative Content Agency & Korea Trade-Investment Promotion Agency. A Study on the Economic Effects of the Korean Wave in 2015. 2016

Production Inducement Effect[18]

The production inducement effect of the Korean Wave is 15.6 trillion won in 2015, up 9.2% from the previous year. Among the various sectors, the production inducement effect of the gaming industry was the highest at 2,718.9 billion won, followed by the automotive industry at 2,267.4 billion won and tourism at 2,181 billion won. In terms of growth rate, movies showed the highest growth rate at 245.9%. Broadcasting and music grew 40.5% and 40.4%, respectively, while cosmetics in the consumer goods sector recorded a high growth rate of 70.5%. Cellular phones decreased by 9.8% and tourism decreased by 9.7%.

<Table 27> Korean Wave's Production Inducement Effect — 100 million KRW

Sectors		2012	2013	2014	2015	Growth Rate of 2015 (%)
Culture Contents	Broadcast	4,494	5,778	5,940	8,343	40.5
	Music	4,052	4,645	4,785	6,721	40.4
	Movie	343	612	503	1,740	245.9
	Animation /Character	4,955	5,061	5,481	6,227	13.6
	Game	22,915	22,913	23,852	27,189	14.0
	Publication	1,546	1,965	1,566	1,478	-5.6
Consumer goods and Tourism	Grocery	18,777	18,094	18,980	20,878	10.0
	Cosmetic	3,947	5,464	8,424	14,362	70.5
	Clothing	6,338	6,806	6,897	6,982	1.2
	Accessories	1,552	1,176	1,191	1,185	-0.5
	Appliance	11,297	12,556	12,062	11,248	-6.8
	Mobile Phone	7,934	8,379	7,666	6,917	-9.8
	Automobile	23,400	23,872	23,209	22,674	-2.3
	Tourism	19,051	20,993	22,359	20,181	-9.7
Total of culture contents		38,304	40,975	42,127	51,697	22.7
Total of Consumer goods and Tourism		92,298	97,340	100,788	104,427	3.6
Total		130,602	138,315	142,915	156,124	9.2

Source: Korea Creative Content Agency & Korea Trade-Investment Promotion Agency. A Study on the Economic Effects of the Korean Wave in 2015. 2016

18 The production activity of each industry is mostly done to meet the final demand for consumption, investment, and export. When the final demand for a good or service occurs, its ripple effect is not limited to the production of the goods or services It will go into production of all industrial products and the size of the total output will also be determined. In this way, the level of total output in the production process of each industry by final demand is called production inducement effect.

Korean wave's Added Value Inducement Effect

In 2015, the Korean Wave generated 5.7 trillion won of added value, showing a 10.7% increase from the previous year. By item, games were the highest at KRW 1.5237 trillion, followed by tourism, food & beverage, automobiles, and cosmetics.

<Table 28> Korean wave's Added Value Inducement Effect 100 million KRW

Sectors		2012	2013	2014	2015	Growth Rate of 2015(%)
Culture Contents	Broadcast	1,986	2,554	2,625	3,688	40.5
	Music	1,977	2,266	2,334	3,278	40.4
	Movie	132	235	194	669	245.9
	Animation /Character	1,906	1,947	2,108	2,395	13.6
	Game	12,842	12,841	13,367	15,237	14.0
	Publication	555	706	562	531	-5.6
Consumer goods and Tourism	Grocery	5,427	5,230	5,486	6,035	10.0
	Cosmetic	1,206	1,669	2,574	4,388	70.5
	Clothing	1,855	1,992	2,019	2,043	1.2
	Accessories	636	482	488	485	-0.5
	Appliance	2,737	3,042	2,922	2,725	-6.8
	Mobile Phone	2,017	2,130	1,949	1,759	-9.8
	Automobile	6,008	6,129	5,959	5,821	-2.3
	Tourism	8,061	8,883	9,461	8,539	-9.7
Total of culture contents		24,825	20,549	21,191	25,798	21.7
Total of Consumer goods and Tourism		27,947	29,556	30,856	31,795	3.0
Total		52,772	50,105	52,047	57,593	10.7

Source: Korea Creative Content Agency & Korea Trade-Investment Promotion Agency. A Study on the Economic Effects of the Korean Wave in 2015. 2016

Employment Inducement Effect

The employment inducement effect by Korean wave is 111,705 people in 2015, 8.1% increase from the previous year. By product, the employment inducement effect of the game industry recorded the highest number of people with 27,450 people, followed by tourism with 20,927 people, and food and beverage with 16,731 people. (P.607)

<Table 29> Korean Wave's Employment Inducement Effect

100 million KRW

Category		2012	2013	2014	2015	Growth Rate of 2015(%)
Culture Contents	Broadcast	2,724	3,489	3,505	4,775	36.2
	Music	5,447	6,219	6,262	8,530	36.2
	Movie	325	578	464	1,557	235.5
	Animation /Character	4,696	4,778	5,058	5,573	10.2
	Game	24,504	24,405	24,830	27,450	10.6
	Publication	1,311	1,660	1,293	1,183	-8.5
Consumer goods and Tourism	Grocery	15,635	14,824	15,317	16,731	9.2
	Cosmetic	1,862	2,536	3,820	6,526	70.8
	Clothing	4,003	4,252	4,235	4,309	1.7
	Accesso-ries	1,110	828	822	806	-1.9
	Appliance	4,277	4,757	4,498	4,181	-7.0
	Mobile Phone	2,741	3,060	2,874	2,806	-2.4
	Automo-bile	7,928	8,052	7,585	7,290	-3.9
	Tourism	20,875	22,637	23,673	20,987	-11.3
Total of culture contents		39,006	41,129	41,412	49,068	18.5
Total of Consumer goods and Tourism		58,430	60,947	62,825	63,638	1.3
Total		97,437	102,076	104,237	112,705	8.1

Source: Korea Creative Content Agency & Korea Trade-Investment Promotion Agency. A Study on the Economic Effects of the Korean Wave in 2015. 2016

Tourist Arrivals in South Korea by Country (2013-2015)

Foreign tourists who came to Korea in 2015 came primarily from Asian countries and totaled 11.59 million visitors, a figure which decreased 4.2% from the previous year. In 2015, the number of Chinese visitors to South Korea decreased slightly by 1.2% year-on-year to about 5.98 million due to MERS epidemic-related fears, but nonetheless, Chinese visitors accounted for about half of all foreign tourists to Korea. Tourism from Japan has continued to decline for the past three years, dropping 10.2% year-on-year to about 1.84 million visitors. Visitors from Asian countries including China and Japan account for 88% of the total number of foreign visitors to Korea. These countries are geographically close to Korea and increasingly familiar with the Korean Wave.

<Table 30> Tourist Arrivals in South Korea by Country (2013-2015) People, %

Region	Nation	2013	2014	2015	Portion (%)	Year-on -year rate(%)
Asia	Japan	2,747,750	2,280,434	1,837,782	15.9	-10.2
	China	4,326,869	6,126,865	5,984,170	51.6	-1.2
	Singapore	174,567	201,105	160,153	1.4	-10.8
	Taiwan	544,662	643,683	518,190	4.5	-10.3
	Vietnam	117,070	141,504	162,765	1.4	7.2
	Malaysia	207,727	244,520	223,350	1.9	-4.4
	Indonesia	189,189	208,329	193,590	1.7	-3.6
	Thailand	372,878	466,783	371,769	3.2	-10.8
	Philippines	400,686	434,951	403,622	3.5	-3.7
	Myanmar	63,470	59,797	58,936	0.5	-0.7
	Kazakhstan	13,158	21,075	29,188	0.3	17.7
	Uzbekistan	44,164	49,214	56,986	0.5	7.6
	India	123,235	147,736	153,602	1.3	2.0
	Total	9,325,875	11,025,996	10,154,103	87.6	-4.0
Americas	USA	722,315	770,305	767,613	6.6	-0.2
	Canada	133,640	146,429	145,547	1.3	-0.3
	Mexico	10,953	13,042	14,049	0.1	3.8
	Brazil	15,739	15,651	15,569	0.1	-0.3
	Argentina	3,296	3,388	3,894	0.0	7.2
	Total	885,943	948,815	946,672	8.2	-0.1
Europe	France	75,947	80,518	83,832	0.7	2.0
	UK	120,874	131,080	123,274	1.1	-3.0
	Poland	13,300	14,895	13,867	0.1	-3.5
	Russia	175,360	214,366	188,106	1.6	-6.3
	Ukraine	24,299	25,788	25,117	0.2	-1.3
	Total	409,780	466,647	434,196	3.7	-3.5
Middle East	Arab Emirates	6,098	10,501	9,490	0.1	-4.9
	Turkey	19,698	22,382	23,156	0.2	1.7
	Iran	5,342	6,512	5,706	0.0	-6.4
	Total	31,138	39,395	38,362	0.3	-1.3
Oceania	Austrailia	123,560	141,208	9,756	0.1	-73.7
Africa	South Africa	10,560	11,020	10,189	0.1	-3.8
Total		10,786,856	12,633,081	11,593,258	100.0	-4.2

Source: Data from Korea Tourism Organization

Soft Power Effects of the Korean Wave

Hallyu Fans and Fan Clubs

Growth in the numbers of Hallyu fan clubs abroad and their memberships overseas can be viewed as a measure of the influence of the Korean Wave. In 2015, overseas Korean Wave-related clubs increased by 21.5% to 1,493 clubs, and their membership increased by 63.1% to include 35,590,000 people. By region, the number of fan clubs in Americas totaled 804, accounting for about half of all Korean Wave clubs worldwide, followed by 310 fan clubs in Asia and Oceania, 306 clubs in Europe, and 73 clubs in Middle East Asia and Africa. The number of clubs in the Americas increased by 183.2% (about 4.9 million people) from the previous year. In Europe, the number of Korean wave clubs increased by 68.1% (124), indicating that the Korean Wave is expanding into Europe as well.

<Table 31> the Number of Hallyu Fans and Fan Clubs Overseas (2014~2015) People, %

Region	Hallyu Fan Clubs Overseas			Hallyu Fans Overseas		
	2014	2015	Year-on-Year Growth Rate	2014	2015	Year-on-Year Growth Rate
Asia & Oceania	267	310	16.1	17,674,090	26,213,832	48.3
Americas	715	804	12.4	2,676,962	7,581,117	183.2
Europe	182	306	68.1	1,363,037	1,625,271	19.2
Africa & Middle East Asia	65	73	12.3	108,313	170,341	57.3
Total	1,229	1,493	21.5	21,822,402	35,590,561	63.1

*Source: Korea Foundation, the Current Status of the Korean Wave in a Global Village, 2015. https://www.kf.or.kr/?menuno=3255&type=view&evnt_no=2092&pageIndex=1&searchevnt=

<Picture 3> The Number of Hallyu Fan Clubs Overseas (2013~2015)

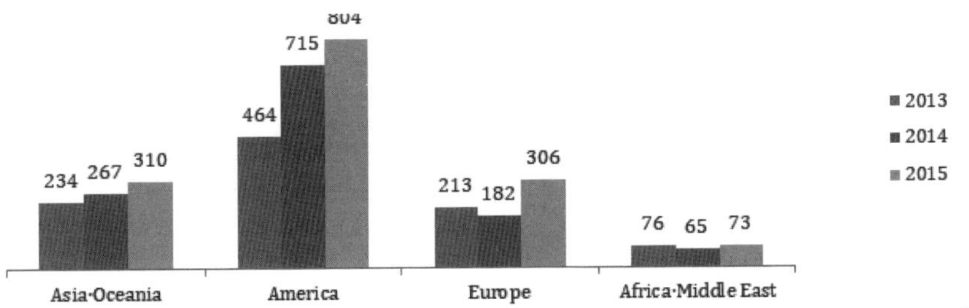

*Source: Korea Foundation, the Current Status of the Korean Wave in a Global Village, 2015. https://www.kf.or.kr/?menuno=3255&type=view&evnt_no=2092&pageIndex=1&searchevnt=

<Table 32> Hallyu Fan Clubs by Country in 2015

Fan Club Number

Asia · Oceania		Americas		Europe		Africa ·Middle East Asia	
China	63	Peru	114	Hungary	112	Egypt	23
Japan	56	Panama	98	France	30	Arab Emirate	13
Thailand	55	Venezuela	85	Russia	17	Morocco	7
Vietnam	30	Chile	79	Turkey	17	Algeria	7
Indonesia	17	Mexico	78	Germany	14	Israel	6
Australia	16	Equador	48	Romania	13	Tunisia	5
India	14	El Salvador	44	Belarus	13	South Africa	3
Philippines	11	Guatemala	43	Ukraine	10	Kenya	2
Brunei	9	Brazil	37	Spain	9	Nigeria	1
Mongol	8	USA	34	UK	9	Libya	1
Singapore	7	Costa Rica	25	Uzbekistan	7	Saudi Arabia	1
Cambodia	7	Argentina	24	Portugal	6	Ethiopia	1
Malaysia	6	Canada	21	Netherland	5	Jordan	1
Taiwan	5	Colombia	20	Italy	5	Iraq	1
Bangladesh	2	Bolivia	16	Bulgaria	4	Kuwait	1
Nepal	1	Dominica	9	Sweden	4		
Newzealand	1	Uruguay	8	Slovakia	4		
Myanmar	1	Nicaragua	6	Ireland	4		
Sri Lanka	1	Paraguay	6	Norway	3		
		Honduras	5	Belgium	3		
		Jamaica	3	Serbia	3		
		Trinidad and Tobago	1	Poland	3		
				Austria	2		
				Czecho	2		
				Kazakhstan	2		
				Greece	1		
				Switzerland	1		
				Azerbaijan	1		
				Croatia	1		
				Finland	1		
Total	310	Total	804	Total	306	Total	73

*Source: Korea Foundation, the Current Status of the Korean Wave in a Global Village, 2015. https://www.kf.or.kr/?menuno=3255&type=view&evnt_no=2092&pageIndex=1&searchevnt=

The Number of TOPIK Applicants (2010 -2014)

The number of applicants for the Test of Proficiency in Korean (TOPIK), which evaluates the Korean language ability of foreigners and overseas Koreans, is increasing every year due to the spread of the Korean Wave. The number of applicants for the TOPIK in 2014 was 179,000, an increase of 12.1% from the previous year, and the number of applicants who performed successfully on the test also exceeded 100,000 for the first time this year, showing a high increase of 18.2% from the previous year.

<Picture 4> the Number of TOPIK Applicants (2010 -2014)

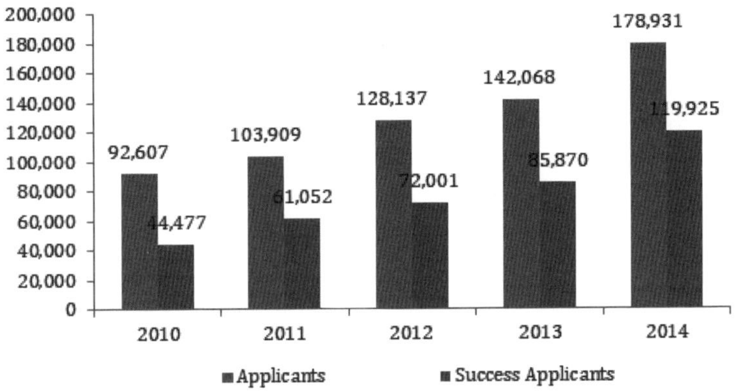

Source: Ministry of Education (2015). The Current Status of Applicants, Candidates, and Successful Candidates for the Test of Proficiency in Korean (TOPIK)
http://www.moe.go.kr/boardCnts/view.do?boardID=348&boardSeq=58745&lev=0&searchType=null&statusYN=W&page=8&s=moe&m=040103&opType=N

Korean Language Class by Country (2012 -2014)

The Korean Wave has also effected an increase of Korean language classes in elementary, middle and high schools overseas. The number of schools offering Korean language classes has grown by an annual average of 10% over the past three years, reaching over 1000 in 2013. Outside of Korea, Japan offers the largest number of Korean language classes. By 2014, there were 511 schools offering Korean language instruction and 17,718 in Japan. In Thailand, however, though the number of schools offering Korean language classes is just 75, the number of enrolled students was more than 24,000, indicating high enthusiasm among Thai people for Korean language education. The number of Korean language classes is continuously increasing worldwide as shown by the increasing number of applicants for the TOPIK every year. It is worth noting that global interest in the Korean Wave seems to induce popular interest in Korean language learning.

<Table 33> The Number of Elementary and Middle Schools establishing Korean Language Class by Country (2012 -2014)

Region	**Nation**	**2012**		**2013**		**2014**	
		Number of School	Number of Student	Number of School	Number of Student	Number of School	Number of Student
Asia	Thailand	**74**	23,093	69	22,153	75	24,065
	Japan	309	11,970	479	15,774	511	17,718
	Uzbekistan	22	7,320	20	7,102	19	7,102
	Kyrgyzstan	28	2,210	28	2,597	34	3,000
	Taiwan	48	2,214	62	3,264	56	2,607
	Indonesia	31	3,320	31	3,316	27	1,507
	Tajikistan	1	192	2	469	2	974
	Kazakhstan	20	690	18	677	19	579
	China	4	203	6	270	6	395
	Vietnam	-	-	-	-	3	65
	Mongol	-	-	-	-	-	-
	Philippines	-	-	-	-	-	-
North America	USA	109	9,421	122	10,588	126	12,428
	Canada	39	2,543	38	2,505	36	2,440
Middle Southern America	Paraguay	11	1,673	14	1,674	15	1,809
	Argentina	2	235	4	315	3	217
	Brazil	3	70	4	143	5	347
	Mexico	-	-	-	-	-	-
Europe	Russia	32	3,856	38	4,188	37	4,621
	France	19	1,817	24	2,790	28	2,378
	Ukraine	4	441	4	441	4	520
	Germany	8	96	12	207	13	248
	Bulgaria	1	46	2	99	1	155
	UK	3	80	6	88	7	97
	Netherland	-	-	-	-	3	54
	Norway	1	32	1	35	1	34
	Belarus	2	19	2	26	2	32
	Irkutsk	1	427	-	-	-	-
	Czecho	-	-	-	-	-	-
Oceania	Australia	47	5,084	57	6,992	61	8,468
	Newzealand	8	660	10	702	17	1,284
Afria	Kenya	-	-	-	-	-	-
	Cameroon	-	-	-	-	-	-
Total		827	77,712	1,053	86,415	1,111	93,144
	25 countries			24 countries		26 countries	
	23			23		25	

Source: Ministry of Education (2015). The Current Status of Applicants, Candidates, and Successful Candidates for the Test of Proficiency in Korean (TOPIK)

http://www.moe.go.kr/boardCnts/view.do?boardID=348&boardSeq=58745&lev=0&searchType=null&statusYN=W&page=8&s=moe&m=040103&opType=N

Conclusion

The Korean Wave has had a ripple effect on the Korean economy overall, leading to the increase of exports of Korean goods and services and the increase of production in related industries. Through the circulatory process by which the increase of Korean Wave related content exports leads to the increase of domestic production, which in turn leads to increased consumption of production factors. the Korean Wave will have significant direct and indirect effects on the natinal economy. We examined the national economic ripple effect of the Korean Wave in relation to its production inducement effect, added value inducement effect, and employment inducement effect.

The Korean government is strengthening its efforts to channel the Korean Wave toward economic revitalization and to the enhancement of Korea's "soft power" enhancement of Korea. Many government departments such as the Ministry of Culture, Ministry of Foreign Affairs, Ministry of Science, ICT((Information & Communication Technology) and Future Planning, Ministry of Trade, Industry and Energy, the Korea Communications Commission, and the Ministry of Agriculture, Food and Rural hold regular meetings to share information related to the Korean Wave and to cooperate with each other in promoting domestic and overseas projects on its momentum.

Through public diplomacy and cultural diplomacy projects, the Ministry of Foreign Affairs is striving to support the advancement of Hallyu contents overseas and to enhance the [global?] image of the receptive countries. The Ministry of Science, ICT and Future Planning promotes the fusion of culture and ICT; the Ministry of Trade, Industry and Energy is strengthening its national branding by combining the Korean Wave and Corporate Social Responsibility in the overseas market.

Economic Effects of the Korean Wave

The production inducement effect of the Korean Wave was 15.6 trillion won in 2015, up 9.2% from the previous year. The production inducement effect of the game industry was the highest at 2,718.9 billion won, followed by the autmotive industry at 2,267.4 billion won and then tourism at 2,181 billion won. In terms of growth rate, movies showed the highest growth rate at 245.9% over the previous year[???]. The next-fastest growing content sectors were broadcasting and music, which grew 40.5% and 40.4%, respectively, while cosmetics in the consumer goods sector recorded a high growth rate of 70.5%. On the other hand, cellular phones decreased by -9.8% and tourism decreased by -9.7%. In 2015, the Korean Wave generated 5.7 trillion won of added value, showing a 10.7% increase from the previous year. By item, games were the highest at KRW 1.5237 trillion, followed by tourism, food & beverage, automobiles, and cosmetics. The employment inducement effect by Korean wave is 111,705 people in 2015, 8.1% increase from the previous year. By product, the employment inducement effect of the game industry recorded the highest number of people with 27,450 people, followed by tourism with 20,927 people, and food and beverage with 16,731 people. (P.607)

Soft Power Effects of the Korean Wave (Hallyu)

Changes in the numbers of Hallyu fan clubs and their members overseas can be considered a key measure of the influence of the Korean Wave. In 2015, overseas Korean Wave-related clubs increased by 21.5% to 1,493 clubs worldwide, and their membership increased by 63.1% to 35,590,000 people. Additionally, the number of the Test of Proficiency in Korean (TOPIK) applicants, which evaluates the Korean language ability of foreigners and overseas Koreans, is increasing every year due to the spread of the Korean Wave. The Korean Wave craze has also effected a worldwide increase in Korean language classes in elementary, middle and high schools overseas. Schools with Korean language classes have grown by an annual average of 10% over the past three years, breaking the 1000 schools in 2013. The number of Korean language classes is continuously increasing with more applicants for the TOPIK every year, and the region of interest is spreading beyond Asia to North America, Latin America, Europe and Oceania. It is worth noting that global interest in the Korean Wave seems to induce popular interest in Korean language learning.

Index

1988 Seoul Olympics 49

A
advertising exposure 100
affective connections 46
Aging Society 24
anime 145, 156
anti-Japanese sentiment 121
anti-Korean sentiment 124
anti-Korean wave 118
apology fatigue 123
Asian financial crisis 37
Asian national identities 146
Axis Powers Hetalia 146

B
Bae Yong Joon 121
Big Bang 92
bilingualism 51
birthrate 25
brand equity 90, 91

C
Chemi Kyopo 52
China 22
Choseonjok 52
CIS Koreans 49, 56
citizen diplomacy 133
Cold War geopolitics 48
colonization 148
comfort women 123
Commonwealth of Independent States (CIS 48
Confucianism 22
Confucius Institutes 22
convergence culture 25
Cool Japan 156
Cosmopolitanisms 79
Country image 96
country image measurement 100
country-of-origin 96
country-of-origin (COO) effect 97
cram schools 23
cultural competition 127
Cultural conflicts 117
cultural consumption 57
cultural globalization 117
cultural imperialism 117
cultural-nationalist perspective 62
cultural originality 124
cultural proximity 120

D
Dae Jang Geum 32, 92
Dae Jang Geum (Jewel in the Palace) 121
democratization 131
de-territorialization 126
diaspora 45
Diaspora identities 65
diasporic nationalism 70
digital industry 135
digital technology 92
direct experience 100

division of Korea 48
Dokdo 122

E
Education 23
education fever 23
education system 23
ethnic identity 46
ethnographic interviews 47

F
Fansubs 75
fantasyscapes 146
figures 72
free elections 131
freeter 157

G
G10 163
Gangnam style 92
GDP 23
Girls' Generation 27
globalization 126, 131
Gross National Cool 156

H
hagwon 21, 23
Haja School 21
hallyu 69
Hallyu 21, 25
Hallyu 1.0 25
Hallyu 2.0 25
halo effect 98, 133
Hangul 38
hard power 38, 131, 132
heritage-language retention rate 51
heterogeneity 65
Holocaust 148
hybridity 65, 117

I
identity 46
Identity Clash 126
indirect cooperation 136
indirect experience 100
information age 132
intraethnic othering 71, 78

J
Jewel in Palace 92

K
kenkan (Hating the Korean Wave) 124
Kickstarter 145
kimchi 124
King Sejong Institute 106, 130
King Sejong the Great 38
KOFICE (Korea Foundation for International Culture Exchange) 98
KOFICE (the Korea Foundation for International Culture Exchange) 120
Korea-Japan Joint Declaration 121
Korean Americans 50, 58
Korean Chinese 54
Korean Creative Content Agency 93
Korean Diaspora 45
Korean Government 34
Korean martial art 38
Korean Peninsula 34
Korean popular culture 46
Korean War 48
Korean wave 69
Korean Wave 25, 32, 89
Korean Wave 1.0 91
Korean Wave 2.0 91
Koryo saram 52
KOTRA 93
KOTRA (Korea Trade Investment Promotion Agency) 120
K-Pop 22, 25, 26

L
Lee Myung-bak 122
literate 23

long-distance nationalism 46

M
manga 145, 156
mass candlelight vigils 131
media nationalism 126
Miracle of Han River 36
MOFAT(Ministry of Foreign Affairs and Trade) 130
multilingualism 81
multiplicity 65

N
national identity 148
National Identity 145
Nationalism 126
nationalistic identity 127
nation brand equity 92
nation brand hexagon 95
nation branding 90, 94
nation branding index 100
Nation Brands Index (NBI) 95
NATO 163
NEET 162
neoliberalism 157
neoliberal position views 62
Next Evolution Exceed Type 162
nonregular workers 157

O
OECD 23, 25
OECD DAC 138
online debates 146

P
Pacific War 146
Park Geun-hye 123
particularization of universalism 117
place branding 92
positive racism 152
Precariat 164
product category-specific 98
product-specific associations 100
product-specific country-of-origin effect 100
product-specific referents 96
pro-nationalist sentiment 118
public diplomacy 40
Public Diplomacy Act 40

R
regular workers 157
re-territorialization 126
Revolutionary Girl Utena 145
ripple effect 118
Roh Moo-hyun 122

S
Saemaeul undong 37
SEALDs (Students Emergency Action for Liberal Democracy) 162
Sejong Academy 40
semiotic objectifications 72
Sino-Japanese Wars 148
SM Entertainment 22
social adhesive 70
social boundary 70
social media 92
Social media 135
soft power 22, 26, 34, 38, 91, 118, 131, 156
Soft power 131
Soft Power 32
South Korea 21, 26
supplementary education 23

T
the former Soviet bloc) 48
TOPIK • Test of Proficiency in Korean 106
transnationalism 72
Transnationalism 145

U
unemployment rate 23
unintended equity 90

universalization of particularism 117

W
Winter Sonata 121

Y
Yanbian Autonomous Prefecture 48
Yon-sama 121
Youth Activism 162